Globalization and the Environment

The book is dedicated to my family and above all to my wife Lucila, daughter Ana and son Camilo for their constant love, support and perspective on what is important in life and without whom the fight for a globalization that is worthy of the labels 'sustainable' and 'just' would be a lot harder to maintain.

Globalization and the Environment

Capitalism, Ecology & Power

PETER NEWELL

polity

First published in 2012 by Polity Press

Polity Press
65 Bridge Street
Cambridge CB2 1UR, UK

Polity Press
350 Main Street
Malden, MA 02148, USA

ISBN-13: 978-0-7456-4722-7
ISBN-13: 978-0-7456-4723-4(pb)

A catalogue record for this book is available from the British Library.

Typeset in 11.25 / 13 pt Dante
by Servis Filmsetting Ltd, Stockport, Cheshire
Printed and bound in Great Britain by MPG Books Group Limited, Bodmin, Cornwall

The publisher has used its best endeavours to ensure that the URLs for external websites referred to in this book are correct and active at the time of going to press. However, the publisher has no responsibility for the websites and can make no guarantee that a site will remain live or that the content is or will remain appropriate.

Every effort has been made to trace all copyright holders, but if any have been inadvertently overlooked the publisher will be pleased to include any necessary credits in any subsequent reprint or edition.

For further information on Polity, visit our website: www.politybooks.com

Contents

Preface

Globalization and the Environment critically explores the actors, politics and processes that govern the relationship between globalization and the environment. Taking key aspects of globalization in turn – trade, production and finance – the book highlights the relations of power at work that determine whether globalization is managed in a sustainable way and on whose behalf.

Each chapter looks in turn at the *political ecology* of these aspects of globalization, reviewing evidence of their impact on diverse ecologies and societies; their *governance* – the political structures, institutions and policy making processes in place to manage this relationship; and finally efforts to *contest* and challenge these prevailing approaches.

The book makes sense of the relationship between globalization and the environment using a range of theoretical tools from different disciplines. This helps to place the debate about the compatibility between globalization and sustainability in an explicitly political and historical context in which it is possible to appreciate both the 'nature' of interests and power relations that privilege some ways of responding to environmental problems over others in a context of globalization.

This book has been around fifteen years in the making. Constantly disrupted and sidelined by other personal commitments and academic and political obligations, it has been slow-cooked rather than flash-fried, but should 'taste' all the better for the fusion of insights from different research projects and theoretical explorations that this has allowed and which saturate the current book.

It builds upon an on-going interest as an academic, activist and concerned citizen in the relationship between globalization and sustainable development. Much of the empirical material and fieldwork and many of the insights that feature in the book, however, derive from eighteen years of research and engagement with environmental politics in a broad range of settings, on a diversity of issues, in a large number of countries. The content of the book reflects an evolving research agenda concerned with different aspects of globalization and sustainable development: from projects on global climate politics and carbon markets to research on agricultural biotechnology, and from work on issues of corporate accountability and responsibility to projects on global and regional trade negotiations and the governance of energy finance. It also reflects insights from work in countries as diverse as Argentina and India, Ethiopia and Mexico, China and South Africa, and Kenya, Bolivia and Costa Rica. I have benefitted hugely from working in and for environmental and development non-governmental organizations (NGOs), conducting consultancy for international organizations, many of which feature in the book, providing policy advice to and working with a number of governments and from conducting training for, and being granted research access to, many corporations around the world. This has allowed me insights into the day-to-day functioning of these organizations and the dilemmas they face, an exposure which enables a richer and more personal understanding of the people and organizations that, as researchers, we sometimes tend to analyse in more abstract terms.

The book will be of interest to students of International Relations, Environmental Studies and Development Studies, Geography and Sociology.

Acknowledgements

This book has been a very long time in the making. The idea for it was first conceived in 1997 at a time when debates about globalization and its potential to transform the theory and practice of world politics were at their height, but when attention to the environmental dimensions of this was often ignored. My first attempt to get a handle on some of the issues at stake resulted in a special issue of the *IDS Bulletin* on the theme of *Globalization and the Governance of the Environment*, published in 1999.

Since that time much has changed. My interest in the 'nature' of the relationship between globalization and sustainable development came to be pursued through projects on business regulation and corporate account-ability, on social movements and trade politics in Latin America, and on the global governance of biotechnology, as well as through theoretical interests in different strands of critical political economy and historical materialism. Much of the contents of this book reflect that journey, the research undertaken along the way through a multitude of projects in different parts of the world for diverse audiences, and the intellectual evolution and learning that accompanied it.

I am grateful for research support from the Department for International Development, including through the Development Research Centres they supported of which I was a part, the Economic and Social Research Council in the UK and many other governments, donors and NGOs that have funded particular studies and pieces of consultancy work that inform the book. I would also like to extend my appreciation to those publishers that have waived permission to draw upon and update elements of work previously published by them. The basis of the material in chapter 3 was first published in the *Review of International Studies* (volume 34, 2008) and some of chapter 2 has been published in Peter Dauvergne's *Handbook of Global Environmental Politics* (2012, Edward Elgar). Chapters 4 and 5 contain substantially revised and updated material previously published in the *Journal of International Development* (volume 13, 2001) and in my chapter in the book *The Politics of International Trade in the 21st Century* (2005, Palgrave).

The personal journey has also incorporated several changes of job – from Sussex (Institute of Development Studies) to FLACSO Argentina to Warwick University, and from Oxford University to the University of East Anglia and finally back to Sussex at the Department of International Relations. Working in Departments of Development Studies and in Schools of Environment and Geography has served, I hope, to enrich my awareness of the variety of ways of approaching the central questions which frame this book beyond my core discipline of International Relations, even if exposure to such eclecticism has certainly made the path towards completion of the book longer than it needed to be.

Needless to say, the torturous route to completion has implied the accumulation of a number of personal debts. I am grateful, in particular, for the support of Jan Aart Scholte at Warwick, and Diana Liverman at Oxford for creating the space to make progress, albeit fitful and painstakingly slow, on this book. Nicola McIvor and Jon Phillips also provided valuable and much appreciated research assistance at critical moments. I would also like to thank Emma Hutchinson and David Winters at Polity for gentle guidance in steering the book to completion and for their understanding of delays along the way.

Peter Newell
Brighton
2012

Abbreviations

AIDA	The Interamerican Association for Environmental Defense
ALCA	Área de Libre Comercio de las Américas
ATCA	Alien Tort Claims Act
BRIC	Brazil, Russia, India, China
CAFTA-DR	Central America–Dominican Republic Free Trade Agreement
CAS	country assistance strategy
CBD	Convention on Biodiversity
CDM	clean development mechanism
CDR	community-driven regulation
CEO	Chief Executive Officer
CERES	Coalition for Environmentally Responsible Economies
CFCs	chlorofluorocarbons
CIF	Climate Investment Fund
CITES	Convention on the International Trade in Endangered Species
CO_2	carbon dioxide
CSD	Commission on Sustainable Development
CSO	civil society organization
CSR	corporate social responsibility
CTE	Committee on Trade and Environment
CTF	Clean Technology Fund
EC	European Commission
ECA	export credit agency
ECGD	Export Credit Guarantee Department
EDF	Environmental Defense Fund
EU	European Union
FAO	Food and Agriculture Organization
FDI	foreign direct investment
FSC	Forest Stewardship Council

FTA	free trade agreement
FTAA	Free Trade Area of the Americas
G8	Group Eight Countries
G20	Group of Twenty
GABB	BioBio Action Group
GATS	General Agreement on Trade in Services
GATT	General Agreement on Tariffs and Trade
GDP	gross domestic product
GEF	Global Environment Facility
GHG	greenhouse gas
GM	genetically modified
GMO	genetically modified organism
HIPC	highly indebted poor countries
HSBC	Hong Kong and Shanghai Banking Corporation
ICC	International Chamber of Commerce
ICCR	Interfaith Centre for Corporate Responsibility
ICSID	International Centre for Settlement of Investment Disputes
IEA	International Energy Agency
IFC	International Finance Corporation
ILO	International Labour Organization
IMF	International Monetary Fund
IPE	International Political Economy
IPR	intellectual property rights
IR	International Relations
ISO	International Organization for Standardization
IT	information technology
IUCN	International Union for the Conservation of Nature
LETS	local exchange trading schemes
MAI	multilateral agreement on investment
MDB	multilateral development bank
MDRI	Multilateral Debt Reduction Initiative
MEA	multilateral environmental agreement
MIGA	Multilateral Investment Guarantee Agency
MNC	multinational corporation
MNE	multinational enterprise
MST	Movement of the Landless (*Movimento dos trabalhadores sem terra*)
NAFTA	North American Free Trade Agreement
NEPA	National Environmental Policy Act

NGO	non-governmental organization
NIEO	New International Economic Order
ODA	Overseas Development Assistance
ODS	ozone-depleting substances
OECD	Organization for Economic Co-operation and Development
OPEC	Organization of Petroleum Exporting Countries
PPM	process and production methods
PRSP	Poverty Reduction Strategy Paper
REDD	Reducing Emissions from Deforestation and forest Degradation
SAL	Structural Adjustment Loan
SAP	Structural Adjustment Programme
SCF	Strategic Climate Fund
SEC	Securities and Exchange Commission
SME	small and medium-sized enterprise
SPS	sanitary and phytosanitary
SRI	socially responsible investment
TBT	technical barriers to trade
TCC	transnational capitalist class
TINA	There Is No Alternative
TNC	transnational corporation
TREMs	trade-related environment measures
TRIPS	Trade-Related Aspects of Intellectual Property Rights
UK	United Kingdom
UN	United Nations
UNCED	United Nations Conference on Environment and Development
UNCTC	United Nations Centre for Transnational Corporations
UNDP	United Nations Development Programme
UNEP	United Nations Environment Programme
UNFCCC	United Nations Framework Convention on Climate Change
US	United States
USA	United States of America
USAID	United States Agency for International Development
WIPO	World Intellectual Property Organization
WRI	World Resources Institute
WTO	World Trade Organization
WWF	World Wide Fund for Nature

Tables and Boxes

Chapter 1

Globalization and the Environment: Capitalism, Ecology and Power

2012 marks twenty years since the Earth Summit on Environment and Development was held in Rio in 1992 and the fortieth anniversary of the Stockholm Conference on the Human Environment. Discussed at the time as the summit to save the earth, it is remarkable that twenty years on from Rio, many of the issues and debates look and sound familiar, as frustration at the lack of tangible progress in responding to environmental threats grows and intensifies. The principal challenges of delivering sustainable development appear as elusive as when the term entered mainstream policy discourse in 1987, with Brundtland's celebrated report *Our Common Future* (WCED 1987).

Despite nearly four decades of intense institutional activity aimed at containing and ultimately reversing an array of environmental threats and claims by a range of actors to have greened their activities, many environmental problems, despite some successes, show evidence of getting worse. The tragic roll-call is summarized in box 1.1.

Many of these problems result from decades, or in some cases even a century or more, of human activity including population growth and rapid industrialization. But none of the key indicators or trends shows signs of significant improvement or reversal, despite global endeavours to do so. Why then, despite rapid advances in human development, economic progress and the application of modern technology, paralleled by a large body of international environmental law and a great many global environmental institutions, do things appear to be getting worse? It is this basic anomaly that needs to be explained if we are to advance sustainable development in a context of globalization.

As the *Global Environmental Outlook* report noted over 10 years ago:

> The global human ecosystem is threatened by grave imbalances in productivity and in the distribution of goods and services. A significant proportion of humanity still lives in dire poverty, and projected trends are for an increasing divergence between those that benefit from economic and technological development, and those that do not. This

Box 1.1   The state of our planet

- Half of the world's tropical and temperate forests are now gone. The rate of deforestation in the tropics continues at about an acre a second.

- 75 per cent of marine fisheries are now overfished or fished to capacity.

- About half the wetlands and a third of the mangroves are gone.

- There are more than 200 dead zones in the ocean due to over-fertilization.

- Freshwater withdrawals doubled globally between 1960 and 2000.

- Species are disappearing at rates about a thousand times faster than normal.

- Over half of the agricultural land in drier regions suffers from some degree of deterioration and desertification.

- 20 per cent of the corals are gone and another 20 per cent severely threatened.

- Human activities have pushed atmospheric carbon dioxide up by more than a third.

- Persistent toxic chemicals can now be found by the dozen in nearly every one of us.

Source: Speth (2008: 1–2)

unsustainable progression of extremes of wealth and poverty threatens the stability of the whole human system, and with it the global environment . . . Environmental gains from new technology and policies are being overtaken by the pace and scale of population growth and economic development. *The processes of globalization that are so strongly influencing social evolution need to be directed towards resolving rather than aggravating the serious imbalances that divide the world today* (UNEP 1999: xx; emphasis added).

The extent to which this predicament is intensified and exacerbated by an increasingly integrated global economy lies at the heart of one of the most contentious debates of our time. Is the current organization of the global economy compatible with the pursuit of sustainable development? Are we capable of securing the planet's future with the economic and political institutions we currently have at our disposal? What forms of governance and collective action are possible in a context of globalization? Can the undoubted wealth which globalization generates (for some) be steered towards more equitable and sustainable forms of development (for all), or is the very idea of sustainable development in a context of globalization an oxymoron?

A globalizing capitalist political economy provides the context in which the challenges of sustainability have to be met given the imperative of near-term action. The fate of the economy and the planet are intimately interwoven. Just as the history and evolution of globalization has had a profound influence on the nature of environmental politics, so too ecological problems bring about changes in the 'nature of globalization': what forms of resource extraction are possible by whom, at what cost and under what constraints, as well as of course constituting a manifestation of globalization in their own right. Environmental change, therefore, produces new forms of globalization just as surely as globalization creates new patterns of environmental change and accelerates existing ones.

For good or for bad then, the fate of the planet's ecology is increasingly bound up with the fate of contemporary capitalism, or what we are referring to here as globalization. This means the contradictions that are intrinsic to capitalism become ever more apparent in the ecological and social systems with which the global economy interacts, upon which it is based and which 'sustain' it. As Marx noted in *Capital*, 'the original sources of all wealth' are ultimately 'the soil and the labourer' (1974: 475). We are faced with the juxtapositions of unprecedented levels of material comfort and human development for some parts of the world while millions of the world's inhabitants live in poverty. We have witnessed spectacular and unprecedented forms of technological advance and diffusion at the very time that the environmental and social costs of some such innovations have become increasingly apparent. Calls for vast increases in finance for environmental initiatives, most notably to address climate change ($100 billion a year by 2030), will be achieved through an intensification of the very processes of production and consumption which have created human-induced climate change. As the quotation above from the *Global Environmental Outlook* suggests, important progress has been achieved, gains have been made, but the drive to accumulate, produce and consume on an ever expanding scale currently directly undermines and cancels out the effect of these measures. In order to address the question of whether the global economy, as currently constituted, is capable of addressing the challenges of sustainable development, it is critical to understand *how* and *for whom* globalization works in order to understand the prospects for effective action to promote sustainable development.

Power: The Politics of Globalization

Underlying the questions posed above is an unpopular assumption that globalization can be managed or steered or that it is, in some general sense, organized. Contrary to many popular accounts of globalization, which construct the notion of a world out of control, in which volatile capital and footloose transnational corporations move rapidly around the world without control or direction, this book shows that globalization has always been, and continues to be, driven by deliberate actions and non-actions on the part of states, international organizations and the private actors that they often serve. This is as true of global finance, where governments have removed controls on capital and provided bailouts for banks with vast sums of public money, as it is for trade, where governments have subjected themselves to the decision-making authority of the World Trade Organization, or production, where they have sought to develop legal accords to promote and protect the investment rights of transnational companies. Debates about the desirability of constructing a new financial architecture or creating a 'green new deal' also suggest that most governments, when they choose to exercise such powers, can direct market activities towards collective goals such as protection of the environment or financial stability. The problem is that most of the time they choose not to do so.

It is key to understand, then, that the relationship between globalization and the environment is mediated by policies, institutions and processes from the local to the global level and in the public and private sector and not, for the most part, anonymous and uncontrollable economic forces as befits the popular caricature. This makes globalization first and foremost a political process: it results from deliberate actions and non-actions by political actors wielding political power. Differential distributional impacts often derive from the process by which decisions are made: who is represented, who participates, who makes policy, how and for whom.

Which Globalization?

The history of the relationship between a globalizing economy and the environment can be said to stretch back at least several hundred years. Indeed, some scholars have attempted to trace the rise and fall of civilizations to environmental factors, providing us with a 'green history of the world' (Ponting 2007). Yet the globalization that is the subject of this book is that which is relevant to contemporary patterns of environmental governance and change. Both the latest stage in the historical development of capitalism and the rise of material, institutional and discursive responses to the ecological crisis can, for the most part, be dated back to the 1970s when unprecedented levels of integration were brought about through policies such as the removal of capital controls and the conclusion of trade agreements which, when combined with developments in technology and communications, enabled businesses to internationalize their operations. This period of globalization in the global economy also coincides with the era of multilateral environmental agreements and the globalization of the environmental regulations of leading states from the time of the Stockholm Conference on the Human Environment in 1972 onwards. The fact that the globalization of economic activity and the intensification of environmental degradation that prompted environmental summitry coincide is not of course coincidental, in so far as the former exacerbates the latter. The emergence of contemporary forms of global environmental governance in a liberal economic order has also significantly shaped the norms and principles which guide and underpin international environmental diplomacy, however. Steven Bernstein refers to this as the 'compromise of liberal environmentalism', which predicates environmental protection on the promotion and maintenance of a liberal economic order (Bernstein 2001).

But before proceeding further, what do we mean by globalization? There are, of course, numerous definitions of globalization (box 1.2). The range of definitions reflects attempts to capture the complex and dense interdependencies that increasingly exist across all levels of interaction between economic, political, social and cultural spheres, though clearly in some spheres, some parts of the world and for some people more than others. Many definitions are broad and all-encompassing. Mittelmann (2000: 5), citing Berresford, notes that:

> the term globalization reflects a more comprehensive level of interaction than has occurred in the past, suggesting something different from the word 'international'. It implies a diminishing importance of national borders and the strengthening of identities that stretch beyond those rooted in a particular country or region.

Often emphasis is placed on the increasing speed and intensity of exchanges (by implication in finance and communications). Giddens (1990: 64), for

Box 1.2   Definitions of globalization

'. . . the growing interconnectedness and interrelatedness of all aspects of society' (Jones 2006: 2)

'globalization refers to the widening and deepening of the international flows of trade, capital, technology and information within a single integrated global market' (Petras and Veltmeyer 2001: 11)

'globalization is a transformation of social geography marked by the growth of supra-territorial spaces' (Scholte 2000: 8)

'globalization is what we in the Third World have for several centuries called colonization' (Khor 1995)

'a process (or set of processes) which embodies a transformation in the spatial organization of social relations and transactions – assessed in terms of their extensity, intensity, velocity and impact – generating transcontinental or interregional flows and networks of activity, inter-action and the exercise of power' (Held et al. 1999: 16)

example, suggests that 'Globalization can thus be defined as the intensifica-tion of worldwide social relations which link distant localities in such a way that local happenings are shaped by events occurring many miles away and vice versa'.

It is this construction of time-space compression that has given rise to popular notions of 'one-worldism', and has nurtured fears about the poten-tial of globalization to homogenize economic and cultural life, captured in references to the 'McDonaldization of society' (Ritzer 1993). It is also this notion of intricate patterns of interdependency that is said to connect the fate of nations in an unprecedented way. We have long had debates about the organization of world systems and the existence of dependency between the global North and global South, or the 'core' and 'periphery' as it is sometimes referred to (Wallerstein 1979), to capture the uneven nature of this development. We have also had experience of the way in which crisis spreads from one pole of the economy to another, whether in the form of the Great Depression in the 1930s, which promoted the saying that 'when the US catches a cold, the rest of the world sneezes', or more recently in the 2008 financial crisis which started as a sub-prime crisis in the US housing market and rapidly went global. Crises are contagious and, as David Harvey reminds us, are not solved by capitalism but merely moved around (Harvey 2010). Perhaps what is notable about this latest stage in global capitalism is the enhanced potential for 'boomerang effects', where actions and decisions taken in one part of the world can have rapid, if not immediate, impacts elsewhere because of the level of integration of economic systems. The East Asian financial crisis in 1997 underscored this new reality in alarming terms, as did forest fires in the region some years later. Global environmental change does so even more profoundly through the spread of nuclear contamination or, more slowly but equally devastating, climate change.

Globalization/Global Ecology

Those aspects of globalization which interface with global ecology are of course numerous, including environmental change as both a manifestation and a cause of much globalizing activity. But the focus here will be the key drivers of contemporary globalization: trade, production and finance. There are, of course, cultural dimensions and manifestations of globalization that relate to the environment, including the role of media and advertising and the cultures of consumption and materialism that they propagate (Dauvergne 2008). They relate strongly in this sense to structures of production and a broader economic system, in which continual expansion of capital and the creation of new markets and desires is imperative to growth. The importance of this aspect of the globalization of material desire through global advertising and media is reflected in the growth of activism aimed at questioning wasteful consumption and raising awareness about the social and environmental costs of the ever increasing use of resources (Newell 2004). Other drivers of environmental change clearly also include migration, population and transport, to name but a few. Their governance and non-governance by national and international institutions is profoundly important for patterns of natural resource use. Such drivers, in turn, are a product of deeper economic and social forces that encourage population growth as a survival strategy in conditions of abject poverty; movement, internally and across borders, in search of work or freedom from oppression and war, following capital to zones of affluence and opportunity, or in the case of transport, the construction of infrastructures to encourage and facilitate investment.

However, it is patterns of production, trade and flows of finance, and their governance and un-governance by a growing range of actors that are most central to the interface between globalization and ecology, as the structures that literally create environmental change and shape the context in which it can be responded to. This is because those charged with tackling environmental problems and promoting sustainable development are the same actors that create the conditions for the expansion of trade, production and finance which generates environmental harm in the first place. It is imperative to be clear about the contradictions and strategic dilemmas that flow from this situation if we are to meaningfully advance a project of socially just sustainable development in a context of globalization.

For this reason, while focusing on these economic dimensions of globalization as the key structures that have to be 'greened' and realigned with ecological imperatives if the multiple challenges of sustainability are to be achieved, I argue that globalization can best be thought of as a political project. It should be understood in the context of the historical setting in which it is evolving and at the same time helping to define. In this sense it has to be viewed at once as an ideological and material project with a corresponding institutional infrastructure, rather than an objective description of global reality. Locating the process as the product of a particular historical and political moment helps us to understand for whom the discursive, institutional and material project of globalization works, and how. It also draws our attention to the social forces that promote and benefit from the existing organization of globalization and from patterns of unsustainable development, and serves to delineate opportunities for reform and possibilities of transformation. We return to these themes in chapters 2 and 3.

Ecology is also deeply political. Each of the main chapters of the book on trade, production and finance include a section on political ecology. This refers to a large literature by this name which seeks to provide a framework for understanding human-society or 'socio-natural' relations (Paulson et al. 2003; Robbins 2004). Specifically, it examines the interrelations of politics and power, structures and discourses with the environment. Political ecology is a broad label, therefore, for an eclectic set of theoretical approaches that take as their point of departure the fact that all ecology is political and all politics are ecological (Bryant and Bailey 1997; Stott and Sullivan 2000; Forsyth 2003; Peet and Watts 2004; Robbins 2004). This framing, as opposed to merely talking about environmental impacts, draws attention to the social relations which shape questions of access to resources, exposure to harm and responsibility for action, differentiated as they are by dimensions of class, gender and race (Newell 2005b). This also allows us to understand the source of grievance and the nature of the demands around which groups mobilize, which are discussed at the end of each chapter, which highlight issues of justice and inequities in processes of decision making, as well as the distribution of benefits and harm associated with different patterns of global resource use. The benefits of employing a political ecology lens are further discussed in the next chapter.

States of Caricature

One of the central debates in the literature on globalization is about the role of the state and in particular whether states have lost or conceded power to global economic actors and institutions. Perhaps nowhere is the importance of ideology in these debates better revealed than in the construction of narratives around state power and incapacity. Globalization may have certain corrosive effects on the sovereignty and territoriality of states, but this does not render them politically impotent in the way many accounts suggest (Ohmae 2004). The economic changes associated with globalization in many, but not all, cases have been produced and continue to be produced by state actions and non-actions, albeit by some states much more than others. Reaffirming state agency through reference to historical precedents (Hirst et al. 2009) and comparative experience (Weiss 1998) is important for situating contemporary globalization and for engaging in debates about the future positive potential of state action for sustainable development in a context of globalization. Challenging narratives that 'There Is No Alternative' (TINA) is important normatively and can be done with reference to ample empirical evidence which highlights the multiple forms that capitalism takes, depending on the social and political context in which it is embedded, the critical role that the state performs through acts of intervention or strategic abstention (Evans 1995; Weiss 1998), as well as the alternatives to a model of neo-liberal globalization which some states, regions and communities around the world are constructing.

We also need to go a step further, however, by looking inside the state. It is important to appreciate how some parts of the state have internationalized or globalized more than others and are more subject to the disciplines of global markets than others (Görg and Brand 2006). Through connections to global institutions with mandates in the policy areas for which they are responsible, as well as interactions with networks of financiers and foreign capital, state bureaucrats can play a key role in 'domesticating' external pressures for reform aimed at creating a favourable climate for business (Newell 2008b). While this has been the case for some time with regard to ministries of trade and commerce for example, new challenges are created where the state's ability to protect its citizens' rights to health or work or to guarantee access to critical natural resources such as water is compromised by global accords such as the General Agreement on Trade in Services (GATS) which subject them to market disciplines (World Development Movement 2002). The 'developmental space' or policy autonomy of governments to prioritize domestic poverty alleviation objectives over those of enabling foreign investment is sharply constrained by such developments (Wade 2003; Gallagher 2005), negotiated under pressure and often without leverage, or by state elites with little regard for the potential consequences for the citizens they notionally represent. As we will see later in the book, the same concern arises with respect to the scope governments have to adopt environmental measures and policies which conflict with international trade and investment rules. The question is 'whose rules rule' and how can we account for this politically? Emphasizing constraints on state policy, often self-imposed by other more powerful elements of the state or by international economic institutions, does not provide support for generic claims of state impotence. Rather, it reflects the ways in which some political programmes are supported while others are challenged or reversed by transnational policy elites.

Naturalizing Globalization

Much of the literature on globalization seeks to present it as apolitical, natural and inevitable; natural in that it is just a continuation of earlier periods of expansionist capitalism which have shown a trend towards internationalization over the last century as new sources of accumulation are sought around the globe (Harvey 2010). Marxist political economists, in particular, propose that globalization is best understood as the latest chapter in the evolving history of capitalism and does not, as such, constitute a break with previous eras (Lewis 1996; Rosenburg 2000). Indeed, there is evidence in the *Communist Manifesto* that Marx and Engels foresaw the coming of globalization as an inevitable by-product of capital's hunger to conquer new markets and territories and to find new consumers for their products. They note:

> The bourgeoisie has through its exploitation of the world market given a cosmopolitan character to production and consumption in every country . . . In the place of old wants, satisfied by the productions of the country, we find new wants, requiring for their satisfaction the products of distant lands and climes (Marx and Engels 1998 [1848]).

There is also a tendency in other strands of the globalization literature to argue that, since globalization is inevitable, states have no choice but to adapt to the new reality. Globalization is represented as a driverless machine that no actor can control. The question becomes one of accommodation and adaptation to that which cannot be controlled. At a popular level and in policy discourse, terms such as TINA bear testimony to this ideology of impotence. Similarly, economists often frame the question in terms of how, and not whether, to engage, as if there is no choice, no agency, no alternative (Kaplinsky 2001).

The effect of removing questions of power and agency from the study of globalization is to present the phenomenon as apolitical and benign: guided by anonymous private actors and technological forces beyond the realm of state politics. This makes it very difficult to determine the causes of change and the appropriate sites for reform. It also serves to obscure the intimate links between state managers charged with addressing problems of environmental degradation and poverty, and the capital they depend upon for political and economic survival. Emphasizing the inevitability and linearity of processes of globalization serves to entrench the view that states have to adapt to, rather than direct, the changes taking place in the global economy. Hence, it performs an important ideological function: the de-legitimization of some policy options on the grounds that they are no longer tenable, and the promotion of others as inevitable and desirable. Discourses of inevitability absolve governments of blame for the consequences of reckless investment and irresponsible speculation, who can deflect the responsibility onto unaccountable market actors over whom, they allege, they have no control. Former President Fernando Henrique Cardoso claimed that he does not rule Brazil, because globalization is swallowing up less powerful states. He claimed both that the 'increase in inequality and exclusion that globalization fuels is intricate and difficult to counter' and that 'globalization is inevitable, as are its consequences, its disasters, exclusion and social regression' (quoted in Mittelmann 2000: 240). For Mittelmann (2000: 240) his comments reveal 'that globalization can be appropriated by political actors and used as an excuse for the lack of a project for political reform, a mark of the failure of the holders of state power to contest evolving global structures and to craft a political solution'.

Similarly, restricting public expenditure and resisting calls for higher social and environmental standards can be justified on the grounds that responding to these demands will lead to capital flight and loss of investment: a fear that those business actors opposed to more stringent forms of environmental regulation frequently invoke. Governments, as well as business and civil society actors, benefit from constructing globalization in a particular way. Differentiating between the constraints that globalization *actually* imposes upon governments, as opposed to those they choose to emphasize for strategic reasons is, of course, a difficult task. But it remains important to de-mystify 'the market' and reveal the power relations behind this abstraction.

One way of doing this, drawing on the work of political economists such as Karl Polanyi, is to show, firstly, how markets are always created by and embedded within institutions and social relations and, secondly, how the nature of that relationship has, historically speaking, been subject to dramatic change. Polanyi, for example, invokes the notion of a 'double-movement' to describe attempts to re-embed market activities that followed nineteenth-century experiments with laissez-faire economics. Polanyi helped to explode the myth of the self-regulating market by showing how state actions are crucial to the creation and maintenance of market activities. In *The Great Transformation* (Polanyi 1980 [1944]), with a clear resonance to contemporary trends in globalization, he showed how unprecedented market expansion and social dislocation were followed by demands on the state to counteract the deleterious effects of the market. This helps us to get beyond the temptation to view contemporary globalization as the inevitable model of the future and to expect moves and counter-moves in the battle to define the direction of the global economy as ideologies of economic governance evolve, and thinking about the appropriate role of the state in economic (and environmental) management is constantly re-appraised. The shifting attempt to manufacture a consensus around the state's role in development demonstrates this process at work. The evolution of thinking can be discerned from a reading of the World Development Reports of the World Bank over the course of the late 1980s and into the 1990s, where by 1997 the report *The State in a Changing World* (World Bank 1997a) reaffirms the centrality of the state for delivering development; a belated recognition of the key role of so-called 'developmental states' in Asia (Leftwich 1994), where state-led industrialization yielded such success, and a notable departure from the anti-state neo-liberal rhetoric that preceded it.

Rather than presenting globalization as an endpoint in the economic evolution of society, as discourses around the end of history tend to (Fukuyama 1993), it is important to understand how the alleged consensus on the desirability of market-led development has been achieved. It is important to recall, for example, the way in which many states have been 'adjusted' to the realities of the global market. Structural Adjustment Programmes (SAPs), conditionalities, tied aid and the threat of retaliatory actions through global institutions such as the World Trade Organization (WTO) have been some of the mechanisms by which the policy elites in the global North have been able to use their leverage to promote their preferred form of globalization in the postcolonial world (Hoogvelt 1997; Payne 2005). This underscores, once again, the importance of understanding state power, both in terms of capacity and resilience, to shape globalization and safeguard policy autonomy from global market actors and institutions.

The Approach of this Book

What can this book add to debates about globalization and the environment? There is now an extensive literature, much of it engaged with throughout this book, which deals with different aspects of the relationship between globalization and the environment, whether it be the relationship between trade and the environment, business and the environment or finance and the environment. Each of these dimensions of globalization has received extensive policy and academic treatment. Fewer books try to capture the big picture of this relationship, however, focusing on the globalization of environmental crises (Oosthoek and Gills 2008); specific case studies) as with Gabriela Kütting's (2005) book on *Globalization and the Environment*, which focuses on West African cotton in the global political economy; or specific themes such as environmental reform initiatives: like Arthur Mol's (2003) book on *Globalization and Environmental Reform*. General surveys of competing perspectives on globalization and the environment such as Clapp and Dauvergne's (2005, 2011) book *Paths to a Green World*, or Speth's (2003) edited collection *Worlds Apart: Globalization and Environment* and monograph *The Bridge at the Edge of the World* (Speth 2008) meanwhile provide an invaluable base for understanding the themes and issues raised in this book. Other collections, while useful, are either now very out of date (Newell 1999) or in the case of Elmar Altvater's (1996) book, inaccessible to those readers with little or no German.

What is arguably missing, and which this book seeks to provide, is a contemporary, coherent, critical analysis of the way in which the relationship between globalization and the environment is being governed: by whom, for whom, and with what social and ecological implications. It does not provide a narrow description of institutional responses to environmental threats in a context of globalization however, since there are numerous books that do that already. Rather, it looks at how (global) ecologies and economies interrelate, how that relationship is mediated by politics, including institutions, but more importantly at the broader relations of power of which they are a part and in which they are embedded. Going beyond presenting a static picture, or one in which globalization is an all-powerful hegemonic project, it also explores the politics of contention and contestation about who wins and who loses from how resources are exploited in conditions of globalization, looking at patterns of resistance and mobilization for reform aimed at showing that another world, a more sustainable one, is possible. In assessing and seeking to explain these trends it draws from an eclectic range of literatures from a range of disciplines including Politics and International Relations, Development Studies, Environmental Studies and Geography. This is important to capturing the sorts of social and ecological relations and patterns of governance and politics that characterize the environment in a context of globalization that cannot be adequately understood from the perspective of any one discipline.

Why is this necessary? I have tried to illustrate above that power, politics, institutions and policy processes are key to understanding the relationship between diverse trends commonly attributed to globalization and their impact upon, and interrelationship with, the environment. The seemingly obvious statement that it is politics and power that mediate and indeed define globalization and its relationship to global environmental change is at odds with many orthodox accounts and representations of these relationships by key development actors and academics. Contrary to assumptions that markets alone determine outcomes in environmental as in other spheres of social life, this book shows that all market activity is inherently political. It reflects choices, embodies biases and ideologies and reproduces the social relations of which it is a part.

Since institutions and political processes in the public and private sphere are the source of decisions about which areas of the economy to globalize, how fast and under what conditions, it should be clear that all globalization is, first and foremost, a political project. Institutions can serve to promote, mediate and offset the impacts of particular patterns of trade, production or finance on the environment. Their ability to do so, of course, differs hugely between firms and states, depending, amongst other things, on their capacity, resources and global market position. Many states in parts of the world on the periphery of the global economy, including areas of sub-Saharan Africa, for example, are less centrally involved in mediating financial and trade flows critical to sustainable development, resulting from their lack of capacity to perform those roles or the lack of overall interest by foreign investors in investing in countries with poor infrastructures and weak institutional capacity. Institutions, either by their presence or absence, exercise a strong overall effect on who has access to which resources and on what terms. The nature of this relationship needs to be desegregated by type of globalization, and further still by sector and region and type of environmental problem. The importance of this will become clear in the chapters that follow, organized around the globalization of trade, production and finance in turn.

The focus on governance in this book goes beyond a focus on the institution of the state or global governance bodies. It directs our attention towards the processes of governing, managing, steering and organizing that account for patterns of global resource use, but which emanate not only from the centres of political authority we are accustomed to analysing (the state and international institutions) but from market and civil society actors engaged in the production of a variety of mechanisms of social regulation and governance. This is a broader notion of governance, therefore, in which authority in a formal sense is more dispersed, less concentrated only in traditional loci of power such as the state, where decision making on matters of routine importance to how resources are used implies a wide range of political and social actors whose interventions need to be understood and engaged with.

There is a broad set of theoretical and conceptual resources that can be used and refined to address the challenge of adequately explaining the relationship between globalization and the environment which are explored in chapters 2 and 3. There the case is made that a political economy approach to the relationship between globalization, governance and ecology is best placed to adequately capture these diverse trends and assess their significance. The challenge is two-fold: firstly, to understand and account for the ways in which different aspects of globalization impact upon, reconfigure and alter existing patterns of resource use and environmental governance in the broadest sense. Secondly, at the same time, to understand the extent to which they may be giving rise to new forms and patterns of environmental governance, albeit ones which are often overlooked by contemporary accounts of governance and environmental governance in particular.

Such an approach is justified and required by a series of key changes in global politics and in patterns of environmental governance within which they are embedded. It is argued in chapter 3 that changes in the locus of political authority, combined with structural changes in the organization of the global economy, require us to adopt new combinations of theoretical and conceptual approaches to understanding environmental governance in contemporary world politics. Many theoretical resources already exist that help us in such an endeavour, from historical materialist analysis of globalization to political ecology work on the interrelationship between social relations and nature as explored in chapter 2. Approaches which are overly state-centric, focused on the public sphere and formal institutional decision-making processes, or which adopt a narrow view of power and who exercises it, are increasingly redundant to an adequate understanding of global environmental politics in a context of globalization. By historicizing and politicizing environmental governance, it becomes easier to understand its origins and potential for change. Rather than viewing the 'nature' of governance as a result of an abstract rational techno-bureaucratic response to environmental crisis, the point here is to trace the contemporary dimensions of environmental governance to the political and historical conditions that shape their inception and evolution.

Structure of the Book

The next chapter articulates a political ecology of globalization which brings together work on globalization and political ecology respectively in order to understand the social relations of environmental change which characterize the link between the global political economy and specific ecologies. Chapter 3 then lays out the theoretical foundations of a global political economy account of environmental governance which provides answers to the questions who governs, what is to be governed (and what is not), how it is to be governed and on whose behalf? Taken together these chapters enable an understanding of the three key dimensions of the relationship between globalization and the environment that are examined in the subsequent chapters. Chapters 4, 5 and 6 explore the relationship between the environment and trade, production and finance, respectively. Each chapter assesses in turn (i) the *political ecology* of trade, production and finance (ii) the *governance* of these relationships and (iii) *contestations* around the ways in which they are currently governed. Finally, chapter 7 draws together key overarching conclusions from the book.

Chapter 2

The Political Ecology of Globalization

This chapter lays out some conceptual tools to help us make sense of the relationship between globalization and the environment as described in chapter 1. These enable us to go beyond mapping the interaction of economic and ecological flows to look at questions of politics and power that are decisive in terms of how the benefits of resource extraction and the burdens of human-induced environmental change are globally distributed. The governance dimensions of this are then explored further in chapter 3 on the political economy of global environmental governance.

In particular, the chapter seeks to show how the social forces which are central to contemporary capitalist globalization are also decisive shapers of environmental outcomes. The primacy of intensifying accumulation on a global scale creates critical ecological and political challenges, notably whether viable accumulation strategies can be identified which are less resource intensive or may even profit from reduced resource use, or whether environmental problems such as climate change create a crisis of capitalism because of its inability to respect ecological limits to growth (Kovel 2002; Magdoff and Bellamy Foster 2010; Newell and Paterson 2010). This context is critical for understanding the 'nature' and conduct of global environmental politics and the effectiveness of existing structures of global environmental governance. More specifically, it affects our understanding of whether such structures are capable of re-shaping the global economy and steering it onto a more sustainable footing, or whether their role is more likely to advance and deepen existing forms of capitalist globalization.

In such a rendition, global environmental governance, understood conventionally as what international environmental institutions (or 'regimes' as they are referred to in International Relations – see chapter 3) do, is dislodged from a position of primacy in the analysis in favour of an account which attempts to 'read' ecologically and socially the organization of the global political economy: the relations of power which create and sustain it and the ecological and social consequences of this way of ordering things. While such an account has implications for the orthodox study of global environmental governance since it problematizes liberal understandings of the state and the role of (international) law, its main focus is the relationship between capitalism and ecology: a relationship which international institutions and powerful states within them mediate in important ways, but which requires an analytical focus that goes beyond that (Newell 2011a). This emphasis is maintained in the chapters that follow, which explore the political ecology of each dimension of globalization covered in this book: the governance of trade, production and finance respectively and contestations of existing arrangements that go beyond and seek to challenge the nature of current responses to global environmental change.

This chapter argues, firstly, that since many aspects of (global) environmental change are produced by economic and social forces associated with contemporary capitalism, we need to develop an understanding of global environmental politics in which attempts to construct forms of global environmental governance are placed within the historical context in which they develop and the social and economic forces which shape the context within which cooperation and change is (or is not) possible. This is crucial to understanding the sources of environmental change and the possibilities of containing or reversing it, given the prevailing organization of power and distribution of resources in the global system.

Secondly, the claim is made that such an understanding can be enriched and enhanced by combining insights from critical (international) political economy with an extensive body of work on political ecology. This work explicitly seeks to explain environmental politics, often understood as struggles over access to (natural) resources, as a function of the social relations such as class, race or gender that structure issues of access, property, entitlement and justice. Work in the political ecology tradition is hugely eclectic, including feminist political ecology, cultural political ecology and post-structuralist accounts alongside work within a political economy tradition (Blaikie 1985; Rocheleau et al. 1996; Stott and Sullivan 2000; Forsyth 2003). While traditionally focused on particular sites of struggle, a (re)turn to global political ecology is increasingly apparent in the literature, which enables the sorts of cross-scalar, multi-site analysis that are critical to understanding the drivers and impacts of global environmental change as well as attempts to manage that change through institutions of global environmental governance (Carmin and Agyeman 2011; Peet et al. 2011). Here, it is argued that historical materialist lines of enquiry are particularly well placed to connect a macro understanding of social forces in global politics with micro and site-specific manifestations of these relations of power which political ecologists document with such rigour (Mann 2009). The fusion of insights from these distinct, but related, theoretical traditions offers the possibility of reading contemporary forms of globalized capitalism ecologically: capturing the nature of its material flows and their social and environmental consequences. This gives us a more wide-ranging, multi-dimensional and multi-scalar account of the everyday conduct of global environmental politics than global attempts to construct law around specific trans-border effects of production, which, as we will see in the next chapter, remains the focus of most traditional theorizing in International Relations.

Which globalization?

The historical context which this chapter describes is the current neo-liberal order that has emerged from the late 1970s onwards, but whose project of monetary discipline and global integration has deepened and intensified during the 1980s and 1990s (Cox 1994; Harvey 2005). It refers, for example, to attempts to re-scale accumulation opportunities through bilateral, regional and global trade and investment agreements, state restructuring, privatization and the use of monetary policy and enhanced capital mobility, the ecological consequences of which we will explore in subsequent chapters. Within this broad landscape, there are specific features of the organization of the existing global political economy that are of particular significance for understandings of the potential and limits of global environmental governance. These include:

(i)   the power and mobility of finance capital which has enabled the financialization of environmental services (Newell and Paterson 2010);
(ii) the critical though schizophrenic attitude towards the role of the state and regulation, particularly on the part of the US and UK, or what has been referred to as the 'Lockean heartland' after the liberal philosopher John Locke (van der Pijl 1998), which has left the plural but uneven ensemble of public and private institutions and initiatives that aim at de-regulating public, and re-regulating through private means, different sectors of the economy; and
(iii) the creation of new sites of accumulation to overcome the limits to capital by addressing crises of over-production and under-consumption (Harvey 2010). These crises occur when capital is accumulated over and above what can be reinvested profitably in

the production and exchange of commodities which means that surpluses of capital and labour are left unutilized or underutilized (see table 2.1).

This context has shaped the willingness and, to some extent, ability of states to create forms of environmental regulation threatening to powerful sections of business, or what are referred to by political economists as 'fractions of capital', amid fears of pollution flight and the relocation of industries to other parts of the world with weaker regulation. Whether a race to the bottom, top or to the middle is the appropriate term, or whether regulatory chill is a more accurate label (Vogel 1997; Neumayer 2001a, 2001b), depends very much on the country and sector in question and the degree of autonomy or 'developmental space' (Gallagher 2005) they have to assert conditions on powerful investors, as we will explore further in chapter 5. Nonetheless, the threat of capital flight is a powerful weapon in the armoury of corporations wishing to check more stringent environmental regulations and one many governments take extremely seriously and invoke themselves as a rationale for not imposing costs on their businesses which surpass those required of their competitors. It

Table 2.1 Key concepts in historical materialism

Capital	Capital is not just money, but wealth that grows through the process of circulation. In that sense, *capital* is money which is used to buy something only in order to sell it again in endless circuits of capital. Marx represented this as Money – Commodity – Money. Capital is also understood as a social relation in conflict with labour which is exploited to accumulate further capital (Marx 1981). Marxists often refer to the 'structural power of capital' (Gill and Law 1989) because of its power to shape the context in which state decision makers operate, whose primary function in capitalist society is to reproduce the conditions for capital accumulation.
Social forces	These are engendered by the production process and include capital, labour and social movements. They are not confined within the borders of states, but often have transnational dimensions. The balance of social forces at particular historical moments determines the shape of the overall political order and who benefits from it (Cox 1981, 1987).
Transnational capitalist class (TCC)	The TCC refers to a class of actors and individuals that manage the global economy, sometimes also referred to as a global managerial class. It consists of those people (policy elites within powerful states, transnational corporations and financiers) who see their own interests and/or interests of their social group as best served by identification

Table 2.1 (*continued*)

	with the interests of the global capitalist system. This class derives its material base from transnational corporations and the value-system of the culture-ideology of consumerism (Sklair 2002a, 2002b; van der Pijl 1998).
Hegemony	The concept of hegemony provides us with a way of understanding the preservation of power and order in society. Hegemony refers to the alignment of bases of power of ruling classes that maintains their privileged position in a (global) order through control, for example, over production, institutions and ideas (Cox 1981). It is preserved through coercion, accommodation and consent, and contains economic and cultural as well as military dimensions (Morton 2007). For Gramsci, hegemony was a concept used to analyse the relation of forces in a given society and a hegemonic order was one where consent, rather than coercion, primarily characterized the relations between classes and between the state and civil society (Gramsci 1971).
Historical bloc	An historical bloc refers to a historical congruence between material forces, institutions, and ideologies, or broadly to an alliance of different class forces. In this sense, historical blocs represent the dialectical link between the economic structure and the ideological superstructure. The formation of hegemony (see above) is essential to the development of an historical bloc.
Spatial and temporal fix	The spatio-temporal 'fix' refers to the way in which capitalists can avert crises through temporal deferral and geographical expansion. Creating the possibility to invest in and speculate about 'futures' or opening up new spaces (geographical areas or virtual spaces) to accumulation helps to address the chronic tendency of capital to accumulate over and above what can be reinvested profitably in the production and exchange of commodities. As a result of this tendency, surpluses of capital and labour are left unutilized or underutilized. The incorporation of new spaces and places into the system of accumulation absorbs these surpluses (Harvey 2003).
Ecologically unequal exchange	The concept of unequal exchange, often used by Marxists, has also been applied to the environmental domain to explain the unequal nature of resource flows in the global economy. In particular, it highlights how trade relations remain unfair because poorer nations export large quantities of under-priced products, whose value does not include the social and environmental costs of their extraction, processing and transportation. This helps to explain the uneven global distribution of environmental benefits and harms. It is also often closely related to the concept of 'ecological debt' that richer countries are said to owe to poorer ones for their historical over-use of the global commons to the detriment of all (Clark and Foster 2009; Roberts and Parks 2008; Martínez-Alier 2007).

features prominently, for example, in efforts to check initiatives by activists who seek new rules and regulations to govern the social and environmental behaviour of transnational corporations operating overseas (Newell 2001a), and in claims about 'carbon leakage' whereby businesses facing increased costs due to controls on carbon emissions threaten to move their operations elsewhere.

Instead of strengthened state regulation, we have seen a growth of self- and private regulation (regulation by and for business) which confers on leading business actors – principally transnational companies – the power and authority to establish their own rules of conduct and restraint in a more open (for some) global economy, a theme we return to in chapter 4 (Lipschultz and Rowe 2005). Much of the proliferation of voluntary regulation through the negotiation of codes of conduct and certification schemes can be understood as an attempt to respond to popular anxieties about the ability of corporations to exploit lower social and environmental standards in a more liberalized global economy and offers a concrete and visible way of taking action whilst not accommodating more critical demands for tougher forms of social and environmental regulation.

Beyond the question of governing globalization, what is interesting in environmental terms is the coincidence of early twenty-first-century capitalism with a growing realization that the energy base upon which modern capitalism has been built is unsustainable, whether because of scarcity induced by peak oil, concerns about climate change, or a questioning of the social costs of imperial ventures to provide energy security. Half of all emissions of carbon released into the atmosphere from the burning of fossil fuels and cement production have occurred since the mid-1970s, the period of accelerated globalization (Peet et al. 2011: 22). In this context, a set of economic strategies predicated on integrated energy markets and the movement of goods and services over ever longer distances starts to look vulnerable. Pressures to account for carbon footprints and reduce 'food miles' express anxiety about the environmental consequences of more globalized circuits of production and consumption. Then there are the unforeseen boomerang effects that reverberate around the global economy when the needs of food, energy and water compete and conspire to produce tension and crisis: For example, the drive in the US for bio-fuels as a solution to an energy crisis which pushes up the price of corn resulting in 'tortilla riots' in Mexico (Houtart 2009; Smith 2010); or the push towards land-grabs in countries such as Ethiopia and Sudan to secure future supplies of water and food for rapidly expanding economies like China, anticipating the exhaustion of their own resource bases (Borras et al. 2011).

Such strategies create new vulnerabilities at the very moment that they appear to provide a measure of resource security. Harvey's observation that capitalism does not resolve its crises, it merely moves them around, again seems extremely pertinent in this context (Harvey 2010).

These issues raise the question of capitalism's relationship to fossil fuels. Clearly much of the history of the expansion of capitalism can be told through war, conquest, colonialism and accumulation through dispossession: the enclosure and privatization of what were once considered common property resources (such as water and forests) (Harvey 2003). The pursuit of oil and coal in particular (Freese 2003; Kaldor et al. 2007) has been decisive in the making of British and American power (Rupert 1995) and in fuelling the industrial revolution. The need to secure reliable and affordable supplies of energy continues to be a significant shaper of foreign policy as any number of imperial ventures in the Middle East and elsewhere testify (Rees 2001). The question is whether in an age of 'peak oil' and climate change, a different type of capitalism can emerge to drive large-scale investments in 'clean' energy and related energy services (Newell and Paterson 2010) or whether climate change reflects a 'crisis of the capitalist mode of production' as writers such as Brunnengräber (2006: 219) claim or, as Huber (2008: 105) suggests, that 'fossil fuels represent an historically specific and internally necessary aspect of the capitalist mode of production'. In other words can there be capitalism that is not 'fossil capitalism' (Altvater 2006) and can we imagine a world beyond 'hydro-carbon civilization' (Peet et al. 2011: 10)?

Capitalism is nothing if not resilient. It has to continually adapt to changing circumstances, revolutionizing forms of production in restless waves of innovation in order to stimulate new opportunities for growth and investment. As Marx and Engels famously stated, the bourgeoisie 'cannot exist without constantly revolutionising the means of production' (1998 [1848]). While certain 'base technologies' (Storper and Walker 1989) may characterize eras of capitalism, as Buck (2006: 60) notes, it is important not to 'confuse particular manifestations of capitalism – that is, particular historical social formations – with capitalism itself, thus under-estimating the flexibility of the beast'. Even a post-oil economy, he argues, would be a capitalist one as long as there is an industrial reserve army without ownership or control of the means of production and as long as the production of commodities by commodities prevails. Hence, even peak oil can be re-worked as an opportunity for growth where fossil fuels can be replaced by a 'solar revolution' (Altvater 2006: 53). Technological dynamism is at the heart of capitalism, and as a consequence, its technological trajectories are not necessarily set in stone. Buck (2006: 63) claims that 'Capital, as value in motion, does not care about what it makes, the machinery used or the motive source. It cares only about its own self-expansion and valorization.' These are the incessant waves of creative destruction that some argue might yet be harnessed towards the goal of a low carbon economy (Derber 2010).

One area from whence this momentum may derive is finance capital's sensitivity to risk. Environmental activists have long targeted investment banks and insurance companies as powerful actors that wield significant influence over governments as well as the businesses that rely on them for capital, as we will see in chapter 6. Greenpeace sought to work with the insurance and re-insurance industry exposed to large pay-outs as a result of 'natural' disasters to encourage them to disinvest from fossil fuel investments (Paterson 2001a), while other activists have pressured leading investment banks to screen their portfolios for large fossil fuel projects which run the risk of attracting negative publicity and diminishing shareholder value (Newell 2008e). While such strategies have, on occasion, enjoyed a limited degree of success, the question remains whether finance capital can afford to be indifferent to the fate of fossil fuel industries and their dependents. It is important not to exaggerate the autonomy of financial capital from productive capital. After all, banks and insurance companies have to have something to invest in. It is also the case that many CEOs and shareholders are rewarded with stock options, tying their fate to the fortunes of the financial markets as increasing the price of stock itself becomes an objective of the corporation (Peet et al. 2011: 21). With the structures of regulation, tax and subsidies that we currently have, fossil fuels, despite clear evidence of the environmental problems they generate, continue to be systematically privileged by state managers and therefore continue to offer highly profitable returns. This explains why, despite the efforts of oil companies to re-brand themselves, as 'Beyond Petroleum' in the case of British Petroleum, or to dissociate themselves from business organizations that are openly hostile about the case for action on climate change, they continue to invest in highly destructive but highly lucrative investments like the oil tar sands in Alberta, Canada.

Over-production of course necessitates over-consumption. One of the most indelible features of the global capitalist economy over the last forty years has been the exponential increase in mass consumption that has been achieved through advertising and marketing strategies as well as the internationalization of production and transport networks, fuelled until now by cheap and abundant energy supplies. The 'shadows of consumption' that are left behind leave a trail of destruction, however. Ecological shadows, in this sense, refer to the global patterns of harm that result not just from the direct consequences of consuming, but also from the 'environmental spill-overs from the corporate, trade, and financing chains that supply and replace consumer goods' (Dauvergne 2008: xi). The changing geographies of production and consumption mirror closely the shifting profile and intensifying nature of pollution. The simultaneous de-industrialization of wealthier countries and industrialization of poorer ones, a strategy aimed at overcoming the power of unions to insist on higher wages and creating a new international division of labour, has meant that countries such as China, India, Brazil and South Africa have seen their contributions to global problems such as climate change increase significantly. China's CO_2 emissions, which amounted to 407 million tonnes in 1980, rose to 1,665 million tonnes in 2006, while India's went from 95 million tonnes in 1980 to 411 million tonnes in the same period (Peet et al. 2011: 21). The final destination for many of the goods produced during this surge of industrialization remains the rich global North. Forty per cent of China's product is exported as is twenty per cent of India's (Peet et al. 2011: 22), raising the question of 'embedded carbon' and who is responsible for the pollution embodied in the products that flow through the veins of the global economy.

The distribution of wealth and waste generated by this frenetic intensification of economic activity has been unevenly distributed, reflecting and exacerbating existing inequalities along the lines of class, race and gender as a vast literature on environmental justice has documented in detail (Pellow and Park 2002; Newell 2005b, 2006). Whether it is toxic, plastic or the sorts of e-waste (computers and the like) that end up on landfill sites in Ghana (Carmin and Agyeman 2011), global accumulation strategies enabled by trade and investment agreements create greater distance between sites of production and sites of consumption. But they also allow 'spatial fixes' (see table 2.1) (Harvey 1981) for the need to privatize gain and socialize risk and the externalities of production in sites, within and between societies, where opposition is weak and regulation either non-existent or weakly enforced. This dynamic is visible not just in relation to waste, but also through the commodification of carbon in offset markets that provide a spatial fix (and a temporal one by discounting the future) by displacing carbon reduction efforts to areas of the world where it can be achieved more cost-effectively (Bumpus and Liverman 2008). It is a function, in many ways, of the triumph of efficiency over equity as the primary organizing principle in neo-liberal environmental governance (Okereke 2010).

These, then, are just some of the ways in which capitalism's relationship to nature has evolved in a context of globalization. They suggest shifting alignments of power in the relationship between state and capital, though notably not a 'hollowing out' or 'retreat' of the state in most areas of the world, or in areas of policy of most significance to the environment, as has been claimed for other areas of policy (Strange 1996). They point rather to a reconstitution of power whereby some parts of the state have internationalized, becoming embedded within, and responding to, the preferences of a transnational capitalist class, such as ministries of trade and finance, while others have diminished in importance, such as ministries of labour grounded in social forces that have lost power and that exercise less structural influence in conditions of globalization (Sklair 2002a). They suggest a delegation of regulatory power to market actors to establish appropriate forms of labelling and certification and a strong preference for regulation *for* business rather than *of* business (Newell 2001c), one that can be traced through the history of failed and half-hearted attempts at business regulation and the simultaneous rise of trade and investment agreements that grant new powers to transnational corporations, as we will see in the chapters that follow. This is a manifestation of what Gill refers to as the 'new constitutionalism' which gives legal protection to the rights of capital over states: 'a politico-legal framework for the reconstitution of capital on a world scale' (Gill 1995b: 78–9). This occurs through the protection and privileging of investor rights in trade and investment agreements, investor arbitration panels which award compensation to corporations claiming unfair treatment, and through a widening matrix of restrictions on the scope of autonomous state action in areas that affect transnational capital. The forms of globalization described here reflect the preferences and political project of a transnational capitalist class which includes 'globalising state bureaucrats' (Breslin 2003) and powerful fractions of capital that they represent and seek to serve based in the epicentres of the world economy (van der Pijl 1998).

The landscape of power described here also reveals the ways in which strategies for responding to environmental crises have been aligned with the imperatives of capital accumulation. At the most general level this is reflected in the compromise of liberal environmentalism discussed in the last chapter (Bernstein 2001) where the norms which underpin global environmental governance come to reflect and advance those of the liberal market order of which they are part. But it goes beyond that. Whether it be the marketization of environmental governance (Newell 2008a) and the preference for market-based over so-called command and control

solutions, the rise of payments for ecosystem services approaches to conservation (whereby communities are financially compensated for their
protection of natural resources) or the commodification of water, forests
and carbon as responses to environmental problems (where attempts are
made to price their value), dominant responses serve to entrench capitalism
rather than respond to the need for structural reform in advanced capitalist economies demanded by environmental crises. Problems generated by
over-consumption of resources, such as fossil fuels, become an investment
opportunity for entrepreneurs to buy and sell 'offsets' which allow companies and individuals to purchase emissions reduction opportunities in the
developing world and claim them as part of their own emissions reductions efforts, all the while keeping existing structures of production and
consumption intact. Meanwhile, water scarcity is presented as a problem
produced by inefficient state institutions and a failure to incentivize conservation by allocating property rights; such that privatization becomes the
obvious solution (Bakker 2010). Institutions such as the World Bank play
an important role in preparing the ideological grounds for such interventions. The World Bank's 2003 World Development Report on 'Sustainable
Development in a Dynamic Economy' advances the idea that the spectacular failure to tackle poverty and environmental degradation over the
last decade is due to a failure of governance, 'poor implementation and
not poor vision'. The report (World Bank 2003) notes, 'Those [poverty
and environmental problems] that can be coordinated through markets
have typically done well; those that have not fared well include many for
which the market could be made to work as a coordinator.' The challenge
for governments is therefore to be more welcoming of private actors
through, among other things, 'a smooth evolution of property rights from
communal to private' (World Bank 2003: 3.22).

Capitalism, therefore, develops through, but also shapes, nature–society
relations. Foster (1999) and his co-writers (Foster et al. 2010) build on
Marx's adoption of the concept of metabolism in *Capital* to describe the
contradiction between nature and capitalism in terms of 'an irreparable rift
in the interdependent process of social metabolism' (Marx 1981: 949). Marx
used this concept to identify the rift brought about by agricultural and trade
practices that despoil the earth without replenishing its resources which
deny whole regions their natural conditions of production. Some studies
have applied Marx's theory of the metabolic rift to contemporary environmental problems, such as the fertilizer treadmill, ocean acidification and
climate change (Clark and York 2005; Clausen and Clark 2005; Foster and
Clark 2009). This goes beyond O'Connor's (1994, 1998) conception of the

second contradiction of capitalism which argues that the expansion of capitalism depletes natural resources, which in turn increases the production costs of capital, contributing to the creation of capitalist crises. In contrast, it focuses on capital's rupture or interruption of a natural system, considered as a socio-metabolism, rather than simply seeing the repercussions on the economy. Moore (2011a: 1) argues that the metabolic rift theory is 'an indispensable point of departure in building a unified theory of capitalist development – one that views the accumulation of capital, the pursuit of power, and the production of nature as differentiated moments within the singularity of historical capitalism'.

From this point of view 'capitalism does not develop upon global nature so much as it emerges through the messy and contingent relations of humans with the rest of nature' (Moore 2011b: 111). In Moore's terms, then, it becomes difficult to discern the boundary between capitalism, the social system and the environment. A world-ecological perspective understands seemingly discrete 'socio-ecological projects' such as 'financialization, industrialization, imperialism (old and new) and commercialization' (Moore 2011b: 114) as functioning within and relative to capital as a whole. Hence, capitalism has to continuously revolutionize its accumulation processes within the web of socio-ecological life. This builds on Harvey's (2003) ideas about accumulation through dispossession, a refinement of Marx's original 'primitive accumulation', but where logic remains the same: capital has to continuously extend its powers by searching for new territories, sectors and domains which hitherto have not been incorporated into its circulation.

So far the story of globalization and its relationship to environmental governance could be told through critical International Political Economy (IPE) accounts drawing on historical materialist analysis of (global) environmental politics (Gale and M'Gonigle 2000; Levy and Newell 2005) and broader bodies of critical scholarship on globalization and capitalism which usefully draw attention to the social forces underpinning the project of globalization, understood as the deepening, intensification and re-scaling of capitalism (Gill 2002; Sklair 2002b; Robinson 2004). What is missing from such an account, however, is more detailed evidence of the social and environmental consequences of a global economy organized in this way and premised upon these relations of power. This is where I argue that work on political ecology can make a useful contribution, balancing the macro-focus of critical IPE and grounding our analysis of the 'socio-natures' (Castree and Braun 2001) that produce and are produced by globalization.

Which Political Ecology?

What is political ecology and how does it help us to understand the relationship between globalization and the environment? At its broadest, political ecology seeks to provide a framework for understanding human-society or 'socio-natural' relations (Robbins 2004). More specifically, it examines the interrelations of politics and power, structures and discourses with the environment (see table 2.2). Here I highlight those elements which offer a bridge to critical traditions within IPE and Global Environmental Politics discussed above (and in further depth in chapter 3) (Paterson 2001b; Saurin 2001; Newell 2008c): materialist political ecologies that posit linkages between economies and the ecologies of which they are a part. For example, the global political ecology that Peet, Robbins and Watts engage in 'emphasises global political economy as a main causal theme' (Peet et al. 2011: 23). For them:

> Political ecology is predicated on an ecologically conceptualised view of politics: it is attentive to the hard edges of capitalist accumulation and global flows of labour, capital and information, but also attuned to the complex operations of power-knowledge . . . all within a system prone to political-economic crisis (Peet et al. 2011: 23).

It is a research agenda that coalesces around the impact of capitalist development on the environment, as well as its emergence through particular socio-natures. It centres both on the social and political implications of prevailing practices of environmental protection and management, and the political economy of the way 'new natures' are produced. Such lines of enquiry have been pursued through work on the practices of commodification of 'neo-liberal natures' (Castree 2003, 2008; Budds 2004; Mansfield 2004, 2007; Bakker 2005), as well as through 'classic' political ecology concerns with questions of access to material and natural resources, and issues of resistance, equity and justice in the negotiation and distribution of social and environmental benefits at multiple scales (Peluso 1992; Bryant and Bailey 1997; Paulson et al. 2003; Zimmerer and Bassett 2003).

One strand of political ecology which developed in the wake of, and by way of response to, the Rio Earth summit in 1992 is that associated with the work of Wolfgang Sachs, Nicolas Hildyard, Vandana Shiva and others, which perhaps resonates most directly with the traditional preoccupations of International Relations (IR) scholars (Sachs 1993). Critical of the contents of the Rio agenda, this work provided a powerful and timely antidote to the optimism and faith placed in the institutions of global governance

Table 2.2 A typology of political ecologies

Type of political ecology	Focus and approach	Examples
Critical political ecology	Focus on the relationship between knowledge and power in the production of knowledge and the construction of narratives about the environment and 'nature'	Fairhead and Leach 1998; Robbins 2000; Stott and Sullivan 2000; Forsyth 2003
Feminist political ecology	The links between patriarchy and ecological degradation	Rocheleau et al. 1996; Rocheleau and Edmunds 1997; Shiva 1998; Schroeder 1999
Third world/first world political ecology	The differences between environmental politics in the so-called Third and First Worlds	Bryant and Bailey 1997; Bryant 1999; Martínez-Alier 2002; McCarthy 2002
(Neo)Marxist political ecology	The relationship between class, inequality and environmental degradation	Blaikie 1985; Blaikie and Brookfield 1987; O'Connor 1998; Peet et al. 2011
Urban political ecology	The 'nature' of cities, urban environments and the social relations that produce them	Swyngedouw and Merrifield 1996; Swyngedouw 2004; Heynen et al. 2006; Swyngedouw et al. 2006

to deliver effective environmental and development outcomes. It drew attention to what went 'unsaid at UNCED' in terms of the neglect of the role of militarism, debt and consumption in driving environmental degradation, and the corporate actors that had secured for themselves a place at the negotiating table in deciding appropriate forms of global managerial action, while deflecting attention away from their own implication in accelerating ecological crisis (Chatterjee and Finger 1994; Thomas 1996). It was critical of 'the aspirations of a rising eco-cracy to manage nature and regulate people worldwide ... largely devoid of any consideration of power relations, cultural authenticity and moral choice' (Sachs 1993: xv).

But there is actually a much longer lineage of work on political ecology, which is 'global', less in the *spatial* sense of privileging global institutions as the site of enquiry and the location of politics, and more in a *causal* sense by exploring the ways in which particular ecologies and the social relations in which they are embedded are a product of broader social relations, particularly class relations. Piers Blaikie's work was particularly pioneering in this sense, combining 'the concerns of ecology and a broadly defined political economy' (Blaikie and Brookfield 1987: 17): studying, for example, how the nature of social erosion in Nepal could be usefully understood in relation to the global capitalist political economy (Blaikie and Brookfield 1987). Other work on metabolism, metabolic rifts (Clarke and York 2005; Burkett and Bellamy Foster 2006) mentioned above, and entropy (Altvater 2006), drawing on Marx, as well as ecology and ecological economics is also useful here for its attention to ecological and energy flows in a way which is not bound by ontologies that privilege the state or international institutions as 'units' of analysis. Instead, the focus is on mapping and accounting for 'ecologically unequal exchange' (Martínez-Alier 2007) (see table 2.1), the social roots of global environmental change (Roberts et al. 2003) or the points of tension between how ecological systems operate and how capitalism functions. Such work provides us with an invaluable account of the economic and social *causes* of global environmental change.

But it also affords insights into how the expansion of capitalist logics under globalization and their extension to the environmental realm has intensified conflicts over natural resources and how they are valued (Martínez-Alier 2002). Studies on resistance to extraction, commodification and privatization of resources on the part of marginalized groups reveal the specific social and site-specific ecological consequences of attempts to open up mining, forestry and water to private investors (Goldman 1998; Newell 2007a). Increasingly, attention is also being paid to the 'local' social and environmental consequences of market-based initiatives deriving from global environmental institutions, whether it is the Kyoto Protocol's Clean Development Mechanism (CDM), REDD (Reducing Emissions from Deforestation and forest Degradation) or conservation efforts centred around payments for ecosystem services (Bachram 2004; Brockington and Igoe 2006; Lohmann 2006; Adams and Hutton 2007; Newell and Bumpus 2012). This complements work on the activities of key neo-liberal economic institutions such as the World Bank as well as on environmental bodies such as the Global Environment Facility (Young 2002; Goldman 2005). Because issues of access, property rights and livelihoods are affected by and enrolled in global circuits of capital, political ecology provides useful ways of identifying and tracing the social and environmental consequences of neo-liberal forms of environmental governance. This contributes to lines of enquiry aimed at understanding who wins and who loses from particular (global) environmental governance arrangements which we discuss further in the next chapter.

Given that site- and resource-specific conflicts increasingly result from and are embedded within 'global' configurations of politics and social forces, strands of critical IPE usefully connect with 'local' political ecologies, to show how broader structures of power are reproduced and present in struggles around natural resources which often embody inequalities based on class, race or gender (Blaikie 1985; Blaikie and Brookfield 1987; Peet and Watts 2004). The globalizing reach of international regimes and their role in creating markets in, and determining access to, resources as crucial as water, energy and seeds means that critical accounts of global environmental governance have to widen their analysis beyond the 'international' level and beyond conventional theoretical foci to comprehend how the structures of power which shape and circumscribe 'global' environmental governance may also configure sites of resource governance at other scales. The dynamic also runs the other way. These sites, in turn, impact upon global regimes through the value they create or fail to produce as commodities to be exchanged on global markets (in the form of carbon credits, for example), or the symbolic value vested in them as examples of successful projects (that bring 'co-benefits' to communities beyond their value as a commodity), or because of the controversy generated through acts of resistance by affected communities and social movements (Newell and Bumpus 2012).

 Political ecology's focus on material, institutional and discursive practices of power complements in many ways framings of power in global environmental politics which draw on the Italian Marxist Antonio Gramsci's understanding of hegemony (see table 2.1) to illustrate how governance arrangements reflect and often serve to globalize particular sets of material and political interests (Levy and Newell 2002; Mann 2009). As with all hegemonic projects, however, for the sorts of solutions to problems of global environmental change promoted by global institutions to maintain their 'common sense' status, strategies of accommodation are required to bring on board critics and make concessions to other groups in the name of preserving the power of an historic bloc. Hegemony is never complete and acts of resistance serve to re-make them, producing legitimacy crises that their advocates then have to address. We see this clearly in the way in which the governance reforms taking place both within the CDM and the standards created in voluntary carbon markets aim to tackle instances of climate fraud (such as the double-counting of carbon credits) exposed by activists, so as to contain threats to the credibility of the market as a whole (Newell and Paterson 2010). Studies within political ecology also draw attention to the ways in which globalizing projects are resisted and rejected, or 'reworked' into more positive local impacts. For example, how people create opportunities within the global carbon economy by 'manoeuvring through and finding spaces at the interstices of the same political economy that in other ways simultaneously constrains and structures their agency' (Bebbington 2003: 300).

Conclusions

Contrary to much conventional analysis discussed in chapter 1, it is suggested here that globalization is most usefully understood as a political and economic project, often incoherent and unevenly applied, but one which seeks to overcome limits to capital accumulation by opening up markets through new suites of trade and investment agreements, securing property rights for investors and constructing institutions able to lock in an integrated global economy on terms set by its most powerful actors. This produces a range of environmental as well as social challenges that require theorists and practitioners to find analytical tools and resources that allow us to make sense of what is going on, on whose behalf and with what consequences. It has been suggested here that attempting to read globalization 'ecologically' through the use of a diverse and eclectic set of works that falls under the umbrella of political ecology provides a useful starting point in this endeavour that complements insights gleaned from critical traditions within IPE and global environmental politics. This is so because of political ecology's explicit attempt to link ecological concerns with political economy, because of its attention to the way in which social relations produce, as well emerge from, different 'socio-natures', and because of its lack of respect for the sort of analytical categories and distinctions which prevent us from capturing trans-scalar political, economic and ecological dynamics. This enables us to explain both the causes of global environmental change as well as the context in which they are being addressed by states, international institutions and a multitude of other actors trying to steer globalization in a more ecologically stable and socially responsible direction.

The next chapter moves from analysis of the relationship between globalization and the environment from the perspective of political economy and political ecology to the question of how best to understand and explain the governance of this relationship. It analyses the actors, institutions and politics that mediate the interface between globalization and the environment by looking at the political economy of global environmental governance.

Chapter 3

The Political Economy of Global Environmental Governance: Power(in) Globalization

We saw in the previous chapters how the relationship between globalization and the environment is first and foremost a political one. It is shaped by decisions and non-decisions, interventions and non-interventions, proactive policy and active neglect on behalf of powerful actors, social forces and classes that together shape the 'nature' of globalization. This chapter builds on that general understanding to develop a critical political economy account of global environmental governance in particular. This helps to inform the discussion of the governance of trade, production and finance in the chapters that follow, and provides us with the tools to think about the potential for, and barriers to, effective environmental reform in a context of globalization. I argue that such an approach is able to enhance our comprehension of the *practice* of environmental governance by emphasizing historical, material and political elements of its (re)constitution and evolution. It is argued that an account of this nature is better placed to address the key questions which drive our enquiry into environmental governance in a context of globalization. These are:

- What is to be governed? (and what is not?)
- Who governs and who is governed?
- How do they govern?
- On whose behalf?
- With what implications?

The first part of the chapter reflects on the insights and limitations of conventional interpretations of environmental governance. The second part articulates the need for a differently grounded approach, driven both by the analytical weaknesses of existing approaches as well as changes in the global system that require more sophisticated and critical approaches to explanation. The third part elucidates the key elements of a political economy approach, assembling diverse theoretical tools towards this end and providing examples of the insights they generate in practice that help to respond to the questions identified above. The chapter concludes with reflections on the benefits that might be derived from such an approach that will inform the rest of the book.

Global Environmental Governance: Conventional Perspectives

Despite repeated acknowledgements that patterns of globalization render the fragile systems of global environmental governance increasingly irrelevant or impotent, orthodox theorization of the challenge of managing global environmental change, especially within the discipline of International Relations (IR), continues to look to international institutions and regimes for the answers. It is not a caricature to suggest that environmental governance for many scholars of IR continues to be reduced to the study of international environmental *law* and the *institutions* that produce it and enforce it, even if there is increasing attention to the ways in which non-state actors can facilitate inter-state bargains (Newell 2000a; Betsill and Corell 2001; Arts 2005). Debate continues to centre on how to motivate *self-interested states* to act in ways which protect and enhance the global commons. This reflects the legacy of so-called 'regime' approaches which continue to enjoy a privileged status in the study of global environmental politics (see table 3.1; Haas et al. 1993; Young 1998, 2010). Applied to the problematic of managing the global commons, regime theory appears to provide a useful analytical grounding for the conceptualization of such problems (Vogler 1995).

From the point of view of understanding the ineffectiveness of international cooperation in containing, let alone reversing, the problems it has been set up to address, however, regime theory provides few clues beyond the answers that any traditional IR account would offer: the problem of managing free-riders that benefit from public goods without taking action themselves, the weakness of sanctions in the absence of global government, institutional fragility in the absence of the backing of a hegemonic state, or the need to create a 'shadow of the future' to induce cooperative behaviour (Hurrell and Kingsbury 1992; Ward 1996). There is little attention to the peculiar nature of environmental problems and the political and material relations which create them and within which they are managed. Traditional theoretical tools and assumptions about the nature of global politics are instead brought to bear on the issue of environmental change. Understanding environmental problems and politics from the point at which they enter the remit of global institutions is to neglect the

Table 3.1 Conventional and critical approaches to global environmental governance

Theory	Assumptions	Focus	Examples
Power-based regime theories	The most powerful states have a decisive influence over the formation, nature and effectiveness of a regime	How powerful states use their political, economic and strategic power to advance forms of cooperation consistent with their interests and veto those which are not (Grieco 1988)	The role of the US in precipitating the demise of the Kyoto Protocol or in driving forward the Montreal Protocol on ozone depletion
Interest-based regime theories	International institutions themselves are able to bring about cooperation through creating an expectation of future gain, exchanging information and building trust	Identifying features of institutions and actors which make them more likely to be able to induce cooperation (Young 1998, 2010)	The role of entrepreneurial leaders in the success of the ozone regime; the importance of effective systems of monitoring and compliance for forest governance
Knowledge-based regime theories	Knowledge-based expert communities, which share a common understanding of a problem and common preferences regarding solutions, exercise power in conditions of uncertainty regarding states' interests	The role of scientific and other expert-based communities (Haas 1990a)	The role of scientists in enabling effective responses to pollution in the Mediterranean sea and the threat of ozone depletion (Haas 1990b; Litfin 1995)
Critical international political economy	Centrality of the relationship between states and markets	The power of business to influence global environmental politics (Levy and Newell 2005); the effect of the broader global political economy on the nature and effectiveness of global environmental governance (Brand et al. 2008; Newell 2008c)	The power of fossil fuel industries in vetoing international measures on climate change, which threaten their interests (Newell and Paterson 1998)

prior political and material relations that account for the production of environmental harm. The question 'which social relations make environmental degradation possible?' helps to identify the interests and relations of power at play and serves to draw attention to the existing networks of environmental governance that inter-state responses need to engage and reform. As is argued below, it is highly unlikely that these operate exclusively within public domains, are managed solely by states or, in many cases, are amenable to interventions by international institutions. Conventional theoretical approaches tend to misread who the key actors are in the everyday practice of environmental governance and to overlook the multiplicity of arenas where environmental politics occur. They do this by (i) centring on bargaining between states, assumed to be cohesive rational actors with the resources, capacity and willingness to engage in environmental reform, (ii) focusing largely on international public arenas, assumed to be the key arenas in which decisions are made about the environment, and (iii) at the international level, assumed to be a sphere in which 'global' politics occur and within which 'global' environmental change has to be addressed.

The appeal of regime theory for scholars of the environment nevertheless endures (Kanie and Haas 2004; Vogler 2005; Young 2010) despite critiques from a range of quarters regarding the static nature of much regime analysis, the state-centricity of the approach, and its neglect of many of the broader political and economic forces that condition the context in which regimes emerge, evolve and the extent to which they are effective (Strange 1983; Gale 1998). Attempts to evolve regime theory in new directions and to build on critiques of mainstream approaches may yet help to articulate a pluralist account of global governance in which non-state actors play a more active part, perhaps further developing ideas about 'complex multilateralism' or re-invigorating debates about 'transnationalism' (Keohane and Nye 1972; O'Brien et al. 2000). Gale's construction of a neo-Gramscian perspective on international regimes, combined with Keeley's earlier Foucauldian reading of international regimes as 'regimes of truth' (Keeley 1990), represent perhaps the most innovative departures, opening up the possibility that 'international organizations are arenas of struggle between global actors over the normative structures that govern (or should govern) specific issue areas' (Gale 1998: 270).

Even if it can be argued that a focus upon regimes is appropriate for IR specialists wanting to account for institutional arrangements that have been constructed at the global level to protect the environment, however, this question cannot increasingly be divorced from an understanding of the nature of the contemporary global political economy and its implications for the future direction of environmental politics. This is especially so amid increasing evidence of private actors assuming public functions of regulation and stewardship with regard to natural resources (Levy and Newell 2005; Lipschultz and Rowe 2005; Pattberg 2007). As Saurin (2001: 80) notes 'international political analysis continues to be conducted as if environmental goods and bads are produced, accumulated and therefore regulated by public organisations. They are not.' Tracking shifting patterns of trade, production and finance will tell us much about the sources and drivers of environmental change. Likewise, studying the investment decisions of firms, banks and other financial actors and the political role of these actors in environmental governance will provide the basis for understanding what forms of action are possible and practicable in the contemporary neo-liberal global economy. Both in terms of their influence financially and politically as well as their ecological footprint, they dwarf the role of state environmental agencies that remain the point of reference for most IR specialists. Appreciating the critical role and influence of such actors, not formally ascribed the term 'environmental', is not to fall into the trap of thereby assuming state impotence. As we saw in chapter 1, decisions not to steer private flows, or regulate private actors and to delegate power and authority to financial and corporate actors constitute an act of power and have to be understood in terms of the relationship between state and capital and not as a zero-sum transfer of power from one to the other. As Görg and Brand argue: 'States are not generally opposed to the logic of the market but absolutely necessary for their functioning. National states and their apparatuses will remain a central terrain of social struggles. But at the same time the capacity of national states to shape social power relations is weakened and transformed from hierarchic government to new governance processes' (2006: 107).

Given the centrality of market actors to environmental governance, we should expect IPE to provide the basis of a clear articulation of a political economy of the environment. However, IPE scholars have tended to neglect environmental issues. Indeed, it is more the case that writers on the environment have sought to make use of concepts and debates in IPE to account for the global politics of the environment (Saurin 1996; Paterson 2001b; Stevis and Assetto 2001; Williams 1996; Newell 2005c; Clapp 2006; Brand 2008). Only rarely have scholars of IPE sought to understand the significance of environmental issues for mainstream theory, or used green political theory to challenge conventional thinking within International Relations (Helleiner 1996; Laferrière and Stoett 1999). Insights from IPE on these issues have yet to capture the imagination of much mainstream thinking in IR, however, which continues with a relatively state-centric reading of questions of international cooperation.

Exploring in detail the intimate relationship between global environmental change and the contemporary organization of the global economy continues to demand, therefore, a realignment of our priorities for theoretical enquiry and practical application. The appeal of existing modes of engagement is that they draw on prevailing theoretical orthodoxies and assumptions about the role of international institutions, the 'nature' of the international system and the organization of global politics. Normatively, however, if we start from a desire to understand the political nature of environmental change and a commitment to identifying the most effective types of political intervention, we assume an obligation to think outside of traditional and convenient theoretical parameters.

Aside from the shortcomings of conventional theoretical thinking regarding the contemporary practice of environmental governance, there is a strong, and related, sense in which changes in patterns of authority and decision making in the global economy have served to reconfigure patterns of environmental governance in ways which suggest the need for theoretical innovation. These changes include a widening and deepening in the *range of actors* producing environmental harm and involved in its regulation (dispersed, global, private, sometimes beyond state regulation). Changes in the governance and exploitation of environmental resources have been brought about through shifting patterns of production and investment, through changes in the nature of standard-setting and institutional authority, and through increased participation by business and civil society actors in global environmental debates. Denser, multi-sited and increasingly transnational forms of governance that have resulted from shifts in the relationship between states and markets and between public and private international bodies with authority in the environmental domain require a theoretical account able to adequately capture these dynamics.

A Political Economy Approach

Both as a result of changes in the global system described above and the limitations of conventional approaches to environmental governance noted previously, an emerging body of critical work has sought to demonstrate, often in issue-specific as well as very general ways, the merits of what might be considered a *critical political economy* approach which locates global environmental governance within broader patterns of governance designed to promote (and manage) the globalization of the economy (Paterson et al. 2003). Studies of the governance of particular technologies (Newell 2003; Loeppky 2005) or in relation to specific actors, such as the role of business in global environmental governance (Levy and Newell 2005; Falkner 2008), provide indications of the insights to be gained from such an account of environmental governance, but have yet to be articulated as a generic approach. This is in spite of attempts to explore disparate elements of an 'ecological political economy' (Gale and M'Gonigle 2000), or to analyse in general terms the interface between the global economy and global environmental politics, adopting case studies or competing perspectives to account for this relationship (Kütting 2005; Clapp and Dauvergne 2011). Critical, often Marxist-inspired, accounts meanwhile have sought to address the question of capitalism's (in)compatibility with the achievement of sustainability, without exploring in detail the governance mechanisms which seek to manage this relationship (Vlachou 1993, 2004; O'Connor 1994; Sandler 1994).

We still lack, therefore, a clear articulation of the contents and application of a coherent political economy approach to global environmental *governance*, one that has potential to provide explanations across diverse issue areas, offering a different view of 'global'(ity), what counts as 'environmental' and how we conceive of 'governance'. The approach developed here builds upon and resonates with the work of Paterson (2000, 2001b) and Saurin (1996, 2001), but rather than develop a general theory of global environmental politics, the task in this chapter is more modest: to refine and demonstrate the utility of a political economy approach in relation to contemporary patterns of environmental *governance* that will enable us to understand the patterns of governance (of trade, production and finance) described in the chapters that follow. The starting point is to explain the apparent incongruence of a worsening environmental crisis in the face of unprecedented degrees of international coordination, regulation and technical advance that opened the discussion in chapter 1. Explaining environmental degradation as a routine consequence of existing structures of power, means to 'disrupt the notion that international power structures are neutral with respect to environmental change' by demonstrating that environmental change originates not in 'interstate collective action problems, nor in a set of *ad hoc* trends, but in the internal dynamics of both systems of accumulation and exploitation and systems of domination' (Paterson 2001: 5). The approach developed here seeks an understanding and explanation of the relationship between the *economic* structures and agents responsible for the production of environmental harm and those actors, coalitions and networks engaged in the construction of environmental governance in the contemporary global political economy. The following sub-sections develop the key elements of such an account.

Placing the Relationship between States, Markets, and Civil Society Centrally

A political economy of global environmental governance has to place the dynamic relationship between states and markets centrally, reflecting the fact that global environmental governance cannot be understood separately from broader shifts in authority in global politics. It can do so, however, in a way that does not assume an artificial separation between state and market or the *a priori* autonomy of either. Rather than reify this relationship at the expense of civil society, it places their interrelationship at the heart of enquiry, exploring its configurations across global society. This is fundamental to challenging what Saurin calls a 'misidentification' of the nature of the modern environmental crisis which rests upon 'the persistence with and development of the separation of the political and economic, the public and private and the corresponding differentiation of agents, agency, structure, responsibility and liability on a global scale' (Saurin 2001: 63).

Such an approach allows us to understand how key changes in the relationship between and within states and markets produce new forms of environmental governance. Debates about the transfer of power from state to market have a long lineage, yet narratives about globalization have given them a new salience in debates about whether state power is in retreat, being reconstituted or may actually be expanding, as we saw in chapter 1 (Strange 1996; Weiss 1998). The answer to these questions depends very much on which part of the state or aspect of state power is under scrutiny. While state budgets for environmental action are often squeezed in the face of fiscal discipline imposed by international financial institutions, state authority is often also strengthened by the acquisition of new bureaucratic functions of pollution monitoring and enforcement that are associated with membership of global accords. In more critical terms, Benton (2000) also argues that states have been empowered by the ideology of globalization and by the increased mobility of capital which has enabled them to 'weaken environmental legislation and generally to align state policy more closely with the interests of dominant and transnational capital' (Benton 2000: 104). The extent to which these trends towards the erosion or reconfiguration of state power apply also depends very much on the state in question. In a context of weakened state structures, the power and privileges of business groups are enhanced such that 'At the very time statist theorists were 'bringing the state back in', the importance of private actors in formulating state policies was actually increasing in Africa and elsewhere in the developing world' (Cox 1996: 5). As with other areas of global politics, there are few conveniently simple, globally applicable narratives about state power in environmental governance.

Theories of the state need to look inside the state for an understanding of the importance of bureaucratic politics and policy networks. This is significant because businesses are better connected with some parts of the state than others, and these patterns of influence extend into the international sphere (Newell 2008c). Environmental bureaucracies in stronger states tend to be well embedded in global processes by virtue of engagement with global decision-making processes on the environment and through close ties to global epistemic (knowledge-based expert) communities (Haas 1990a). Ministries of trade and finance, however, with which they are often in competition over environmental policies where there are significant budgetary or trade policy implications, are equally well globalized, but operate in global arenas such as the WTO that are conferred greater authority than their environmental counterparts.

Power imbalances within the state are mirrored and re-produced by inequalities in the distribution of power between international institutions. Likewise, uneven distributions of power between states and firms at the national level, where the latter's mobility and ability to relocate provide enhanced bargaining leverage, are reflected in and reinforced by public inter-state legal protection of private power (Sornarajah 2006). When multilateral rules ostensibly aimed at protecting the global commons conflict with attempts to multilaterally protect private access to, and control over, those resources, the telling question is 'Whose rules rule?'[1] Multilateral environmental negotiations are increasingly conducted in the shadow of world trade rules, as we will see in the next chapter, which potentially restricts the use of trade-restrictive policy measures even when they yield positive environmental outcomes (Conca 2000a; Pritchard 2005). This prioritization of economic over environmental rule-making reflects what Gill refers to as the 'new constitutionalism' to describe the ways in which the rights of capital over states are being enshrined in international trade and investment agreements (Gill 1995a). In the environmental field, the debate

---

1 This phrase was used in a World Development Movement campaign about the impact of trade rules on the world's poor.

within the Convention on Biodiversity (CBD) over access, benefit-sharing and Intellectual Property Rights (IPRs) can be interpreted as a struggle to define corporate entitlements to the commons. Debates about bio-piracy and bio-prospecting are concerned with the boundaries of corporate access to natural resources and the compensation firms are expected to provide to the communities from which the resources have been extracted. Indeed, it was primarily concerns about how the CBD would affect the access of the US pharmaceutical industry to such resources that led President Bush Senior to refuse to sign the accord (Raustiala 1997).

Strange's model of 'triangular diplomacy' that describes the triangle of relations among states, between states and firms, and among firms provides a useful way of understanding many dimensions of global bargaining, even if it has less to say about the role of civil society actors (Strange 1994). Firms with a presence at international negotiations on the environment bargain with one another over which positions to adopt in an attempt to reflect diverse and often contradictory interests. They then adopt formal and informal strategies to register their views with government through bodies such as the Global Industry Coalition on biotechnology (Newell 2003). A political economy account goes further, however, in asking why some coalitions of interest prevail over others. In contrast to pluralist accounts (Falkner 2008), a structural approach would suggest that owners of capital exercise structural power over state managers, in that they are able to shape the context in which states make decisions. As Paterson (2001b: 46) shows 'because of the necessity of growth for capitalism to survive, those organising such growth, defined generally as capital, gain a great deal of power with respect to state decision-making'. There have been many documented examples of the leading role played by large firms in vetoing provisions of global environmental accords threatening to their interests (Newell and Paterson 1998; Andrée 2005). Some structuralist approaches go further in questioning the very division of state and capital. Vlachou (2004: 928) puts it the following way: 'state policies towards nature and the ecological changes initiated in capitalism are not "external or artificial" barriers to capital. They are the outcome of internal processes and also constitutive elements of capital as a social relation.'

That a political economy account requires a theory of the state is reinforced by recognition that the state is not a neutral actor in environmental governance. Conca (2005: 181) notes:

> The emergence of the centralizing, industrializing, national state, with its capacity to centralize decision-making, concentrate capital, strip local

> communities of their historical property rights in nature, supply coercive
> power and protect elite interests, has been a key social innovation along
> the road to global planetary peril.

Risk and hazard, access and benefit, are routinely, necessarily allocated in
ways which reflect and enhance existing social inequalities; a point amply
underscored in the political ecology literature discussed in the last chapter.
This reflects the fact, in part, that political elites have major interests in key
economic sectors which exact significant environmental damage including
commercial logging, mineral and oil exploitation and plantation cropping
(Haynes 1999). We find evidence of Marx's contention that the capitalist
state is 'based on the contradiction between public and private life, on the
contradiction between general interests and private interests' (Marx 1975:
46). Its role is to maintain market discipline and mediate between the
contradictions of general and particular interests within capital, such that
competing fractions of capital seek to present their interests as consistent
with those of capital-in-general in environmental as in other issue areas
(Newell and Paterson 1998). This produces uncertain outcomes in contests
over the form that environmental governance should adopt. Vlachou
(2004: 933) notes:

> Although the state assumes the capacity to secure the natural and other
> conditions for capitalism, the choice of particular policies, their require-
> ments as well as the incidence of benefits and costs of such policies on
> different agents . . . is not pre-determined.

Nevertheless, the state is not seen as a separate sphere with its own
logic, not 'suspended in mid-air' as Marx noted, but giving form to economic institutions and production relations. This allows us to locate the
state within those larger relations that are implied in the production of
environmental degradation.

The lack of state theory employed in conventional analysis of environmental governance has implications for how we conceive of the law and its
potential to serve as a vehicle for tackling environmental harm given the
importance attached, *a priori*, by conventional accounts, to international
law as *the* governance mechanism for managing the global commons
whilst ignoring social relations within which law is cast and which it serves
to entrench. Cutler (2002: 233) argues 'The possibility for the law to exhibit
bias or to serve unrepresentative interests or undemocratic ends is ruled
out by presumptions of the law as natural, neutral and consensual order.'
Even accepting that state laws do not intend to generate inequalities, 'State
permitting laws remain neutral or blind toward these [environmental]

inequalities; they therefore perpetuate, and indeed exacerbate, distributional inequalities' (Cole and Foster 2001: 71). In this reading, legal rules cannot be divorced from the material conditions in which they are produced and seek to preserve since they form 'a crucial constituent of property relations and privatized class power, and also form the "legal culture" of a transnational bloc advancing a globalizing neoliberal agenda under the guise of naturalized representations of property, market and capital' (Rupert and Smith 2002: 10). Environmental politics are inevitably played out on this broader canvas of material and institutional power.

Building upon these insights without over-ascribing a 'productionist' logic to all governance arrangements, insights derived from the work of Antonio Gramsci are useful here. Neo-Gramscians have developed the core ideas articulated in Gramsci's *Prison Notebooks*, produced while held as a political prisoner in Italy, regarding the notion of hegemony and historical bloc (as discussed in the last chapter; see table 2.1), which help to explain the ways in which dominant groups and classes sustain their position of power over subaltern and weaker groups. They add value to our understanding of global processes by going beyond some of the more reductionist elements of structural accounts to look at the ways in which coalitions are formed between state, capital and civil society in order to preserve the hegemony of blocs whose interests are threatened by environmental regulation. An environmental account would posit the ways in which fundamental economic interests and privileges are protected through strategies that reify those structures of property and decision making from which the transnational managerial class benefits. Alliances with conservative elements within the environmental movement have been key to this strategy of accommodation, producing, as Sklair (2002b: 276) shows, 'a global environmental elite which has been more or less incorporated into the transnational capitalist class'. The function of this sustainable development historic bloc is to distance global capitalism from the sources of environmental problems, accommodating some mild criticism of consumerism and globalization without allowing the 'fatal connection' between the capitalist mode of production and the ecological crisis to be addressed (Sklair 2002b: 57). Global ecology literatures that emerged in the wake of the United Nations Conference on Environment and Development (UNCED) of 1992, discussed in the previous chapter, suggest that this bloc has been very successful in the task of obscuring its own role in the processes it is ostensibly regulating, a process described as analogous to putting the 'foxes in charge of chickens' (Hildyard 1993; Chatterjee and Finger 1994).

Embedding Institutions within Global Economic Processes

Grounding a political economy account still further requires us to demonstrate and analyse the empirical links and theoretical implications that flow from the intimate relationship between environmental change and its governance on the one hand, and the organization of the global political economy on the other. A political economy rendition of environmental governance explores how trade, production and finance shape the possibilities and limitations of governance arrangements; analysing them as *economic structures* and through the *policy processes* they generate. This is the approach adopted in this book. A focus on the mode of production and the social relations which flow from this help us to understand this in terms of 'specific, historically and geographically variable forms of social organisation' (Benton 2000: 85). This is in contrast to orthodox IR approaches to the study of global environmental change which, as Saurin (2001: 74) notes, take as given 'the questions of what is produced, how it is produced, who controls production – in other words all the key questions pertaining to the actual transformation of nature'.

Non-environmental regimes, those governing trade, production and finance: those not thought of as environmental regimes but which have substantial environmental profiles, both in terms of the authority they exercise over resource access and use and their ecological footprint, are critical to the possibilities of effective environmental governance. Debates about the types of regulation and political action necessary to tackle many environmental problems are increasingly conducted in the shadow of, and often trumped by, parallel concerns with trade and global market integration. This narrowing of the terms of the debate to political solutions that can comfortably be accommodated within the business-as-usual model of contemporary neo-liberalism serves to marginalize and de-legitimize alternative modes of environmental governance that may be more effective.

For example, calls to tie the liberalization of trade to basic environmental standards (see chapter 4), to regulate the activities of multinational companies through a corporate accountability convention, as proposed by activists at the UN World Summit on Sustainable Development (see chapter 5), or to strengthen screens on private financial flows for their environmental impacts (see chapter 6), have so far been successfully resisted. Instead, there is growing evidence of a staggering and highly damaging degree of policy incoherence whereby there are low levels of integration of environmental goals into mainstream economic, trade and development policy such that policy in these areas systematically undermines the achievements of environmental policy. The manifestations of the way in which the potential achievements of environmental governance are routinely undermined by the initiatives promoted by global economic institutions are many. Export credit guarantees and the use of overseas aid money, provided bilaterally and through funding for multilateral organizations such as the World Bank, continue to be allocated to development projects with devastating environmental consequences, offsetting the gains made by environmental regimes, as we will see in chapter 6. Internationally, lack of policy integration between regimes means that the goals and possible net gains from agreements on climate change, for example, are reduced to nothing because the WTO, at the same time, negotiates increases in trade which will increase emissions of CO_2 well beyond the savings carefully negotiated in the climate treaties, by transporting greater volumes of trade around the world (NEF 2003). We explore this issue further in chapter 4. Similarly, while there is discussion of the need to promote higher standards of environmental protection amongst firms, regional trade accords such as the North American Free Trade Agreement (NAFTA) include provisions that allow companies to challenge national and local governments seeking to raise environmental standards in the name of non-discrimination against foreign investors and to extract compensation from them (Newell 2008d).

What appear to be, from an environmental point of view, cases of alarming incoherence in policy objectives, actually make perfect sense once we understand that discussions about the ecological footprint of market-led globalization are strictly off limits. Reform proposals that deviate from received wisdoms about the pre-eminence of individual property rights and (ostensibly) laissez-faire economics, are discredited and ridiculed. While economic orthodoxies are sacrosanct and protected from scrutiny, environmental measures are always evaluated according to their potential to negatively affect capital accumulation objectives. Describing this in terms of a realignment of power between the public and private realm, Saurin (2001: 76) shows that while the public realm is left attempting to resolve harms generated by private actors, 'the private entities – businesses and corporations – retain authority over production systems'.

The increasing popularity of market-based instruments of environmental regulation in the form of environmental taxation, labelling, voluntary (self-)regulation and permit trading, is indicative of this re-organization of power and authority between state and capital, reflecting and embodying many of the trends described above. Threats to accumulation imperatives mean that environmental measures have to be 'attuned to the incentives and growth possibilities of capitalist firms' (Vlachou 2004: 937). This marketization of environmental policy is certainly not hegemonic, however. It is an expression of the contemporary organization of the global economy and the ideologies that rationalize its operations. Not only are there deviations from it in the form of different national and regional approaches to regulation, but in everyday practice around the world, customary patterns of resource stewardship continue to survive, existing alongside market structures or subversive of them. This occurs even as private actors seek to enclose more areas of the global commons. Marketization, therefore, describes a particular historical juncture already subject to significant contestation, as we will see in the chapters that follow, but currently flexible enough to successfully accommodate challenges to its reach without confronting the relations of power which underpin it.

A Broader Notion of Governance

Drawing on critiques from political geography about the narrow understandings of governance that are often applied to environmental politics, a political economy approach moves beyond traditional thinking about hierarchies of levels, the boundedness of actors and linearities of decision making which are assumed to follow a 'cascade' model where one level of political authority flows to the next in a natural downward trend. This allows us to understand multi-cited network formations, as well as be sensitive to the different forms that governance takes (Bulkeley 2005), challenging reified categories of *national/global* as these 'may obscure and subordinate such axes of analysis as ecology, race and gender' (Adkin 2000: 70) which are important to understanding who governs and on whose behalf. We saw in the last chapter how strands of political ecology work, which take the interaction between social relations and the environment as the starting point, help to transcend territorial and spatial categories rather than focus on one 'level of analysis'.

To adequately capture the dynamics of bloc formation and more embryonic forms of coalition evolution across scales, a political economy approach has to be transnational in scale, able to explore dynamics *within* and *across* the state, within firms, across 'levels' and bridging public/private divides, such as they exist. This departs from conventional analysis of environmental governance which tends to reify 'the level of analysis problem' in IR. Transnationalist approaches, such as that developed by Risse-Kappen (1995), which look at how global political outcomes are mediated through domestic institutions and coalitions, may help to advance a theory of regimes that transcends state/non-state and domestic/international analytical divides. Adopting a political economy frame, however, allows us to account for why some coalitions and alliances of interest have a greater bearing on global policy than others. Policy responses and the governance structures that give rise to them are understood as products of a particular configuration of historical and material circumstances. A political economy of transnationalism means being open to a plurality of governance forms, without falling into liberal assumptions about equality of power among actors or the neutrality of institutions. The sort of neo-Gramscian framework described above is helpful in this regard. As Gale (1988: 277) argues, 'A neo-Gramscian approach forces us to widen our focus beyond the diplomats who are formally engaged in negotiations to include the struggles taking place among competing social forces over the principles, norms, rules and procedures of the international regime'. Politicizing and historicizing the function of institutions in this way is important to negating the idea that the impacts of institutions are socially and environmentally neutral and that the decisions they make embody general and public rather than specific private interests.

Arguing for such an approach does not amount to an endorsement of exaggerated and therefore problematic claims about the entrenchment of a 'post-sovereign' or 'neo-medieval' form of (environmental) politics; a liberal reading of global governance which conveys, explicitly or implicitly, 'a pluralistic and post-ideological conception of the world' (Duffy 2005: 309). As with some accounts of the rise of private environmental governance, there is a tendency to underplay the role of the state as the centrifugal unit in such networks. Even where they seemingly bypass the state, as with private certification bodies, they often ultimately require forms of state authority or at the very least government consent to operate in an authoritative institutional manner (Falkner 2003). Duffy (2005: 319) shows, for example, that while patterns of global environmental governance claim to 're-order' politics whereby 'complex networks of non-state actors govern, authorise and regulate, the process of implementation is still heavily reliant on national governments'.

There is an important and conceptually significant difference, therefore, between the performance of governing roles and the exercise of authority. Although it is not appropriate to reduce the question of authority to sovereignty, gaining competence in the provision of some state functions 'does not in itself elevate the non-state to an equivalent position of authority' (Conca 2005: 189). If the exercise of authority implies both the power of sanction and enforcement (of law) on the one hand, and claims to representation on the other, it excludes most non-state governance providers. If, however, acting authoritatively, even producing law (through standards, etc.), without the backing of a democratic mandate is sufficient, then non-state actors can legitimately be said to be 'authority brokers'. Recognizing multiple sources of authority and competition between governance providers in global environmental governance is not the same as claiming that each carries equal weight, authority or legitimacy, merely that in seeking to account for the changing landscape of global environmental governance, our understanding of governance has to decentre the idea that states are the exclusive providers of effective environmental governance. The 'denationalization of governance' (Koenig-Archibugi 2006) means that while some forms of environmental governance remain state-dominated (UN treaties), others reflect market dominance (environmental management systems) or predominant roles for civil society organizations (civil regulation), but more often they embody hybrid formations whose governance practices are only possible through cooperation and competition between each of the key 'governance providers'. Indeed, Arts (2005: 184) notes that 'the environmental domain has been a laboratory for new modes of governance *par excellence*'.

From a political economy perspective, de-centring spatiality with *causation* as the reference point for identifying and explaining patterns of *global* environmental governance yields important insights (Ford 2005). An emphasis on causation requires us to look for governance practices in global politics in domains traditionally considered neither political nor capable of 'governing'. This is a notion of governance where the environment is 'governed' in ways that derive from routine market transactions of huge ecological significance. Business is not just a subject of a regulatory system imposed by the state. Rather, business is an intrinsic part of the fabric of environmental governance, as rule-maker, and often rule enforcer. Businesses construct and enforce their own systems of environmental and market governance through programmes of certification, such as the FSC (Forestry Stewardship Council) for example, and processes of standard setting along the supply chain (Garcia-Johnson 2000). These in many ways exist outside of formal patterns of environmental governance, traditionally understood. Grant claims, for instance: 'International firms create the need for improved governance, but they do not and cannot provide it' (cited in Koenig-Archibugi 2006: 10). At a fundamental level, however, corporate strategies do generate 'norms, rules and decision-making procedures in a given area of International Relations', following Krasner's (1983: 2) classic definition of a regime. This is because of their command of capital and the impact on resource use that their operations imply at company, sectoral level and along the supply chain. They are, in other words, regime actors in their own right, though not in a way that would fit the narrow definitions of governance traditionally employed by scholars of IR and IPE.

Once it is accepted that market actors, in particular, are key sites of environmental governance in the global political economy, we need theoretical tools to understand *how* they practice governance; we need to get inside the firm as a governance actor. Looking 'inside' market actors enables us to understand their strategies and influence and therefore their role within systems of environmental governance. A political economy approach, while recognizing the embeddedness of regimes in broader structures, needs then to address the specific conditions under which market actors engage with particular issue arenas; to demonstrate the relationship between the macro and micro dimensions of governance. In so far as shifts in the corporate strategies of leading firms circumscribe the policy space available to environmental regulators whose actions, in turn, bring about shifts in technological choices, investment options and production processes, we need to account for these reciprocal relationships. Levy and Newell (2002) have constructed one possible framework for such an enquiry, and issue- and firm-specific work (Kneen 2002) that has sought to understand and weigh the significance of different drivers of firms' behaviour in relation to environmental policy (Prakash 2000) suggest future directions for research. Greater attention is needed, though, to the role of financial actors: the banks, stock markets and credit rating agencies that steer flows of finance in the global economy with enormous implications for cycles of environmental degradation (Helleiner 2011). We explore their role more fully in chapter 6.

Looking at market actors as governance institutions in their own right challenges us to go beyond treating corporate interests at an abstract, aggregate level; capital rather than corporations. By opening up the 'black box' of the firm to more critical scrutiny, we may be better placed to locate the linkages and connections between inter and intra-firm decision making and the activities of firms as agents of environmental governance. Amoore's (2000) notion of the 'contested firm' is useful in this regard, as it seeks to go beyond treating firms as 'actors, reactors and transmitters of global imperatives' (Amoore 2000: 183). Falkner (2008), for example, challenges the idea that business passively adapts to the 'technology-forcing' pressures of environmental regulation. Rather, he argues persuasively that the innovative capacity of firms represents a form of 'technological power', which can play a critical role in shaping the design and phasing of environmental regulations. Such approaches require us to do more than regard firms as transmission belts between national and global levels of analysis and to challenge their predominant construction in IPE as atomized, rational, unitary actors; an approach which is subject to many of the failings of conventional IR theory.

If including analysis of market actors provides answers to the question 'who governs', we can deepen our understanding of 'how they govern' by locating the everyday practices of environmental governance within the broader politics of neo-liberalism which produce them. Marketized environmental governance is a mode of neo-liberal governance. That is to say, the modalities, ideologies and forms which environmental governance assumes inevitably bear the characteristics of the neo-liberal economy of which they are a part (Castree 2000, 2003). The de-politicization of aspects of environmental governance through its conduct in private arenas, free from public scrutiny and participation, reflects attempts to settle political questions in a 'technical' manner within institutions where states have less control (such as the International Organization for Standardization). The emphasis on voluntarism embodies an anti-statist neo-liberal presumption about the inefficiency of traditional 'command-and-control' state-based approaches to regulation. The fetishization of partnership, which reached a climax at the World Summit on Sustainable Development, reflects the desire for a consensus-based 'stakeholder' form of politics, which obscures the existence of underlying social conflicts. The hegemony of discourses of eco-efficiency in pronouncements by states and influential bodies such as the World Business Council for Sustainable Development (Schmidheiny 1992) reflects the purchase that market-based concepts have as validating devices in broader political discourse. Indeed, the logic and goals of neo-liberalism infuse environmental initiatives. The ends of political interventions thus have to be justified in terms of their contributions to competitiveness and efficiency, hence the rise of the 'business case' for sustainable development, just as businesses have to be persuaded that poverty reduction presents a potential accumulation strategy in order to induce action (Prahalad 2005; Wilson and Wilson 2006). In the EU, environmental measures have to be justified in relation to their ability to help achieve the goal of full market integration (Grant et al. 2000). The use of cost-benefit analysis continues to be the preferred way of determining the economic value of environmental policy measures, despite the controversy surrounding its use and the way such assessments apportion value (Jacobs 1997).

Multi-dimensional View of Power

An enlarged and reframed understanding of what governance is, the forms it takes and the actors engaged in its practice requires a multi-dimensional view of power. Beyond reflections about the changing nature of state-based power noted above, there is clearly a need to develop further approaches which are able to capture non-state forms and expressions of power. There is already a great deal of work on global environmental politics that seeks to assess the observable political influence of different non-state actors (Arts 1998; Betsill and Corell 2001). Rarely, however, does it explore second and third dimensions of power (Lukes 1974), taking seriously less observable forms of power at work that determine which issues get addressed (and are subject to governance regimes), which are not and why. This neglect is also true of the broader forms of structural power which shape the conduct of global politics of which regimes are just one manifestation (Strange 1983). Elsewhere (Newell 2000a), I have made the case for the importance of importing into the study of global environmental politics ideas developed in debates about community power around 'anticipated reaction', and the 'Un-politics' (Crenson 1971) of issues that are screened out of debates by the 'mobilisation of bias' (Schattschneider 1960). Newell and Paterson (1998) have also developed a structural account which places the relationship between state and capital centrally as a key element in understanding the position of states vis-à-vis environmental threats from which they benefit economically and which derive from economic actors with whom they have close ties and are reluctant to regulate.

A more nuanced and persuasive account also demands attention to the *material, organizational* and *discursive* elements of power and their interrelationship which find form in the contemporary practices of environmental governance. The material element needs to take seriously Cox's (1987: 1) notion that 'production creates the material basis for all forms of social existence, and the ways in which human efforts are combined in productive processes affect all other aspects of social life, including the polity'. The arguments above about the ways in which the production of environmental harm establishes the contours of action and probable effectiveness of initiatives undertaken by the environmental polity bear this out. In turn, 'Institutions reflect the power relations prevailing at the point of origin and tend, at least initially, to encourage collective images consistent with these power relations' (Cox 1987: 219). Taking institutions seriously, however, means engaging with the possibility of autonomous institutional effects not guided exclusively by the needs of capital or derived rigidly from a particular mode of production. The conflicts described above where regimes and other forms of governance become sites of contestation over access to resources and their control is indicative of this uncertainty of political outcome. At a discursive level, the embrace of ideas about 'ecological modernisation' (Mol 2003) and 'sustainable development' indicate the way in which discourses and the institutions which adopt and diffuse them play a part in reconciling contradictions that derive from the conflict between the nature of production in the global economy and the ecological harm it generates, which public institutions are then expected to remedy, manage and control (Bailey et al. 2011). We saw in the last chapter, for example, how the World Bank, through promotion of a payments for ecosystem services agenda, advances the notion that it is the absence of private property rights and a failure to treat environmental resources as services that accounts for their lack of protection. Discursive power then reflects 'the argumentative struggle that determines which perceptions at some point start to dominate the course of affairs in environmental politics' (Hajer 1995: 19).

A meaningful analysis of power in global environmental governance has to operate across a number of sites. At a macro level we have to understand the power of transnational firms as a product of a series of structural changes in the global economy that have changed the relationship within and between states and firms. Many of these changes have been institutionalized in global accords, whereby the rights of capital are protected from state interference as we saw above. These rights are secured and advanced through the machinery of bodies such as the WTO that can discipline states not abiding by the 'laws' of the market. The internationalization of production and mobility of capital, brought about both through changes in technology and state policy in the form of removing capital controls, have enhanced the leverage of firms to set the terms of investment. This power has translated into the sorts of political roles, described above, where in their own right, as well as through practices of coalition-building, firms have been able to shape environmental agendas at national, regional and international levels. In turn, the positions that leading firms have adopted across a range of issues from climate change to biotechnology are driven by their corporate strategies and the constraints imposed by technology and production choices. At the same time, the dynamic also flows the other way, whereby global discourses and regulatory arrangements impact upon choices at firm level and, therefore, also set the parameters of corporate strategy. What we observe then is a reciprocal relationship between corporate strategy and governance, operating across a number of levels.

For hegemony to be exercised, though never complete, material, organizational and discursive elements of power need to be closely aligned (Levy and Newell 2002). Change in each form of power opens up continual opportunities to contest existing forms of environmental governance and produce new forms of governance. Since state actors are increasingly not the only sources of material, organizational or discursive power, the understanding of power central to political economy accounts has to account for the power exercised by corporate and civil society actors in their coalition-building across different sites in the global political economy, and involving engagements between a plurality of non-state and state actors.

Critical

In so far as it seeks to understand the current organization of the global political economy in order to change it, a political economy account is critical in Cox's (1981) understanding of critical theory, which distinguishes itself from problem-solving theory. In this sense it seeks to identify a moment of exploitation or degradation and attempts to understand the historical, material and political forces that brought it into being. However, unlike conventional approaches that would look to the state or international institutions for the source of the problem, assuming evidence of a governance failure or absence of coordinated inter-state action, a political economy approach casts the analytical net wider, looking at a broader range of actors and structures which create and sustain environmental degradation.

This means not viewing environmental problems as discrete issues manageable in their own terms, but as products of existing patterns of political and social power. Here again, drawing on the sorts of political ecology work reviewed in the last chapter yields immense insights into causation and the social distribution of benefit and harm. Vast bodies of work on environmental justice demonstrate vividly the way in which environmental degradation is often a signifier of social neglect and tends to be concentrated in areas of the world (North and South) where poorer people 'Work, live and play' to coin a phrase from the environmental justice movement (Bullard 2005). Questions of race, class and gender are key here in accounting for the production and distribution of environmental harm and the profits derived from it; in other words what is governed and on whose behalf (Newell 2005b). A critical approach has to engage in serious analysis of the ecological effectiveness and social impact of prevailing governance arrangements. Analysis needs to be driven by the nature of the problem rather than the requirements of pressing problems into conventional theoretical categories. As Kütting (2005: 3) argues, 'Institutions . . . are not the defining boundaries within which effectiveness is analysed; they are given by the structures, origins and remedies of the problem of environmental degradation'. Such problems, if they are to be addressed, need to take account of the fact that, as Strange (1983: 488) argues,

> Since the chain of cause and effect so often originates in technology and markets, passing through national policy decisions to emerge as negotiating postures in multilateral discussions, it follows that attention to the resultant international agreement of some sort is apt to overlook most of the determining factors on which agreement may, in brief, rest.

A political economy account is also critical in the Coxian sense of seeking to identify moments of potential transformation; emphasizing the dynamic in world politics rather than patterns of order and stability, even if it employs historical and material analysis to account for how and why particular environmental governance arrangements came to be and continue to persist. Emphasis on the multiplicity of environmental governance forms, described above, is derived from a reading of *change* in the sites of authority, and *shifts* and realignments in relations of power between state-market and civil society. Once the political and social forces that produce environmental change are placed centrally in the analysis, it becomes easier to decipher moments of change and potential sites of resistance. Because specific constellations of social forces and production produce particular types of environmental change, disruptions in the relationship between state, market and civil society actors and the historical blocs of which they are a part, give rise to new patterns of environmental governance. Competing interests, even or especially within capital, provide opportunities to construct new coalitions that may ultimately produce new patterns of environmental governance or even broader economic transformations.

This can operate at the level of near-term strategic engagements such as Greenpeace's attempts to woo the insurance industry into a coalition of actors advocating action on climate change; playing on the industry's sensitivity to large pay-outs associated with climate-related damage to client's property, aimed at fracturing the unity of the industry bloc opposed to action (Paterson 1999). The Climate Group, in their attempt to make the economic case for action on global warming, have also sought alliances with progressive local government authorities and businesses to counter the claims of powerful industry lobbies that oppose action on climate change regarding the scale of economic costs associated with tackling the problem (The Climate Group 2006). But it can also operate at the level of deeper shifts in the economy, of the type and scale required of attempts to meaningfully de-carbonize the global economy (Newell and Paterson 2010). Once the shift from a narrow focus on governance *outcomes*, thought to be the existence of a treaty or an institution, to governance *processes* takes place, we are better placed to engage in the necessary critical forms of enquiry about the contestation of processes which is ongoing and never reaches closure. Environmental governance from this perspective assumes a more dynamic quality, inevitably reflecting and embodying the broader political and economic structures and processes of which it is a part.

Finally, consistent with the duty of adopting a critical approach, a key obligation is to identify and engage with strategic dilemmas facing progressive movements for change. In the light of the analysis above, it is clear that the environmental movement cannot afford to focus its attention exclusively on those global actors and institutions that identify themselves as environmental in isolation from the global economic processes in which they are embedded. As we will see in the following chapters, environmentalists have been heavily involved in campaigns around global investment accords such as the MAI (Multilateral Agreement on Investment), in global trade negotiations hosted by the WTO and in campaigns to hold transnational companies to account for their social and environmental responsibilities wherever they operate. The strategic dilemma is where to concentrate efforts; working with those bodies developing legally binding international environmental law with all its limitations, or mobilizing to influence the activities of firms, banks and those actors whose day-to-day decisions impact more directly on patterns of natural resource use than any global institution could ever hope to.

Ultimately, we return to the state as an important, if not central, site in the struggle for sustainability. As unreliable an ally as the state can be, given the networks of power in which it is embedded and the interests it responds to and represents, it remains a key source of authority and power that can force changes that are almost impossible to imagine by other means. As Conca (2000b: 142) notes, 'governments are central to any meaningful action for global sustainability – just as they have been central to the processes of modernization, marketization and enclosure that have delivered us to our current circumstances of ecological peril'. The challenge is to work with progressive elements within the state when it makes sense to, lobby firms and investors directly when such pressure is likely to achieve more, and to form global coalitions to shift the agendas of global institutions when decisions reach beyond the sphere of either of these. In engaging in such short-term politicking, we have to keep alive a vision in which choices about which globalization we want are subject to the imperative of constructing a more sustainable global system and not the other way around.

Conclusions

This chapter has outlined the elements of a critical political economy account of global environmental governance. It is one which departs from conventional theoretical perspectives in its view of governance and power and, it has been claimed, is better able to capture the multi-sited, marketized and increasingly transnational forms of governance that characterize contemporary global environmental politics in a context of globalization. This provides us with an improved and less bounded sense of who governs and on whose behalf, how they govern and the implications of those practices of governing, in social and environmental terms. By understanding patterns of environmental governance as a product of the neo-liberal context in which they develop and at the same time reproduce, we are better placed to understand why environmental politics take the form they do and the likely barriers to attempted reforms that go beyond the 'ecological modernization' of capitalism as usual (Mol 2003).

The challenge is to connect empirically, and account for theoretically, the ways in which 'macro' social and economic forces in the global economy configure the 'micro' practices of environmental politics in particular sites without losing a sense of what makes those sites unique. In the previous chapter we explored the potential of literatures on political ecology to address this challenge. Transnational managerial elites and the role they play in key global economic institutions, public and private, undoubtedly serve to circumscribe the scope of autonomy and policy difference at national level. But the process is not a passive one, and varieties of environmental capitalism compete with one another, are diverse in nature and are contested. They are always in transition, though the end point remains uncertain. The differences in political culture, ideology of regulation and relationships to business between the European Union and the United States, which have been at the heart of global conflicts over the governance of agricultural biotechnology and climate change, for example, have had widespread repercussions for the global management of those threats (Murphy and Levidow 2006).

To feed the potential of these new forms of theoretical enquiry requires a different empirical focus, one which seeks to explore the ways in which particular environmental practices are embedded within broader relations of political and economic power, which determine the limits of the possible and the likely sites of resistance. This means understanding the intimate relationship between the economic forces that generate environmental change and the political coalitions and institutional forms which assume the responsibility for delivering environmental protection. It is not enough increasingly, if it ever was indeed, to study global actors and institutions that identify themselves as environmental in isolation from the global economic processes in which they are embedded and which ultimately they will have to regulate if they are to make a difference.

For this reason the following three chapters, structured in turn around the three key pillars of the global economy, look, firstly, at the *political ecology* of trade, production and finance, in terms of the ecological consequences of the current organization of the global economy; secondly, at the *governance* of that process in terms of the actors and institutions involved in governing the environmental consequences of globalization in a multitude of ways; and, finally, at exploring efforts to construct new forms of governance as well as *contestations* around existing patterns of governance.

Chapter 4

Global Trade and the Environment: Whose Rules Rule?

For many anti-globalization activists, world trade and who governs it has been at the centre of their opposition to a form of corporate-led globalization that they believe to be so destructive of the environment. This became abundantly clear during the so-called 'Battle of Seattle' in 1999, when protestors used the occasion of the World Trade Organization ministerial summit to express their frustration with the WTO and all it stood for. The WTO was targeted as the institutional embodiment of all that concerns people about globalization (Graham 2000; Young 2005); in particular that the imperative of accelerating trade liberalization is increasingly being allowed to take precedence over social and environmental regulations. A number of high profile and controversial legal cases that have come before the dispute settlement panel of the WTO, discussed below, have served as a testing ground for assessing whether or not trade rules can work to protect the environment. These events have conspired to place the debate about the compatibility of trade liberalization with the goals of environmental protection centre stage in debates about globalization.

This chapter takes a critical look, then, at the relationship between trade and the environment. It explores this relationship at a number of levels that will provide the structure for the chapter. The first part of the chapter explores the *political ecology of trade*: how global trade flows interact with and impact upon patterns of resource use. The second section offers an examination of the *governance of trade*: the policy processes and institutions set up to manage this relationship, reviewing in particular how the General Agreement on Tariffs and Trade (GATT) and WTO have dealt with environmental issues in their agreements, including evidence from some of the cases that have come before these institutions. The links between *process* and *distribution* are explored: issues of access, transparency and accountability in decision making; questions of power to effectively shape trade outcomes in global fora; and the influence of economic actors that benefit from trade liberalization to secure outcomes favourable to their interests. Finally, the chapter looks at forces *contesting trade policy* at the international and regional level and beyond. This includes an assessment of the evolving role of non-governmental organizations (NGOs) and social movements contesting *how* trade is governed and *for whom*.

The Political Ecology of Trade: The Nature of Trade

The question of whether trade liberalization can be supportive of, or is necessarily detrimental to, the goal of protecting the environment, and the pursuit of sustainable development more broadly, is hugely contested. Generalizations on all sides of the debate tend to cloud analysis of specific resource, regional and supply chain dynamics that shape the extent to which and the ways in which attempts to open up markets serve either to alleviate environmental pressures or to intensify them with uneven social consequences. Although there are clearly positions that can be held between these two polarities, there are broadly two conflicting perspectives that can be identified on this issue which might be characterized as (neo-)liberal, on the one hand, and ecological, derived from the *ecologism* of radical environmental perspectives and green political theory, on the other (Dobson 1990; Williams 1994).

Trading Our Way Out of Trouble

Free trade advocates argue that environmental concerns can be accommodated within the basic paradigm of free trade. This is so for a number of reasons. First, trade liberalization encourages the removal of wasteful activities damaging to the environment. Examples here include the removal of harmful subsidies, which encourage unsustainable industrial or agricultural practices or wasteful energy use. The EU's Common Agricultural Policy which in the past has generated infamous 'butter mountains' and 'wine lakes' has been a particular focus of attention (Hutter et al. 1995). In the light of increasing concern about climate change the OECD (Organization for Economic Co-operation and Development), World Bank and OPEC (Organization of Petroleum Exporting Countries) have also been leading initiatives to phase out fossil fuel subsidies. G20 countries have also committed to work towards fossil fuel subsidy reform given that, according to IEA (International Energy Agency) estimates, direct subsidies encouraging wasteful consumption totalled a staggering $312 billion in 2009 (IEA 2010).

Second, and at a more fundamental level, advocates of free trade claim that competition promoted by open markets provides incentives for firms to use resources more efficiently. In order to reduce costs and to compete in global markets, firms increasingly recognize that they have to minimize the throughput of resources and reduce waste in the production process which adds costs to the final product and in so doing reduces competitiveness (Schmidheiny 1992). This is in addition to pressures upon firms from buyers and importers to demonstrate compliance with private environmental standards such as ISO 14001 discussed below (Prakash and Potoski 2006; Angel et al. 2007).

A third line of argument assumes that trade generates the wealth and growth that funds environmental programmes. Jagdish Bhagwati (1993), for example, argues that growth enables governments to tax and raise resources for protection of the environment. His claim echoes one made by many governments in the global South. During the NAFTA debate, then-Mexican President Carlos Salinas argued that 'Only through widespread prosperity can we have the resources to channel toward the protection of land, air and water' (cited in Hogenboom 1998: 180). There are two assumptions behind this argument. One is that funding environmental programmes is a more effective way of tackling ecological degradation than tackling the causes of that degradation. This is the 'end-of-pipe' paradigm that environmentalists decry which focuses on clean up rather than prevention. The argument also makes a leap of faith in assuming that because trade creates potential resources for environmental protection that those resources will necessarily be used towards that end. Without hypothecation, there is no guarantee that this will be so.

A fourth argument posits that measures that restrict trade and go against the thrust of trade liberalization are ineffective at bringing about the desired change in environmental practices. Eco-protectionism, economists argue, is both damaging to the environment and has negative economic impacts, particularly for developing countries (Wolf 2004). Not only do barriers relating to the way a product is produced potentially conflict with international trade law, but they also discriminate against exports from developing countries, in particular, those countries where resource intensive activities are more heavily concentrated. In many cases bans on particular products, labelling regimes and restrictions on imports also fail to promote the desired change. Sáez (2000: 21), for example, shows that since 'Indonesia introduced a ban on log exports in 1985, replacing it in 1992 with very high export taxes . . . there has been an increase in domestic processing capacity, which has led to an increase in total demand for logs rather than a reduction'. As van Bergeijk (1991: 106–9) argues, 'a solution on the basis of trade impediments will waste the potential contribution that international specialization can make to global environmental efficiency . . . liberalizing trade is probably a necessary (but not sufficient) condition for sustainable development'.

More fundamentally, behind this position lies a broader concern that the gains of trade that have been built up over 50 years of negotiations 'should not be easily surrendered to new protectionism sanctioned by environmental concerns' (Whalley 1996: 6). There is caution not to set a new precedent such that special treatment for one issue will lead to claims for special treatment on a range of issues, subverting the generality of the rule regime in the trading system. This issue taps into a broader debate about the potential for countries to invoke trade-restrictive measures on environmental grounds as a cover for protectionist interventions. This has, of course, been the dilemma facing the dispute settlement panel of the WTO in determining whether barriers erected to trade on environmental grounds are being used to protect domestic industries. For example, the allegation in the dolphin tuna case (discussed below) was that the US was restricting imports of Mexican yellow-fin tuna in order to protect its own tuna industry from competition rather than for the reason publicly given: that the nets used to catch the tuna were inadvertently trapping and killing dolphins.

A further increasingly popular argument in the armoury of those advocating free trade is that environmentalist concerns about the growth of pollution havens (areas of the world where, as a result of globalization, mobile capital can more easily relocate) are at the very least over-stated, if not plain wrong. Copeland (2008: 68) claims:

> Fears that trade liberalization will cause an exodus of polluting industry to poorer countries with weak environmental policy appear to be unfounded. Although there is evidence that stringent environmental policy does reduce competitiveness in industries intensive in production-generated pollution, there is no evidence that it is the most important factor affecting trade and investment flows.

Contrary to narratives about a 'race to the bottom' in environmental standards, whereby mobile capital exploits reduced barriers to trade to relocate and invest in areas with poorer standards of environmental regulation (discussed further in chapter 5), many assert that the overall effect of trade liberalization has actually been a 'trading up' of standards. David Vogel (1997), in his book *Trading Up*, supports this claim with reference to evidence from NAFTA, the WTO and the EU. Upgrading is achieved because of the desire of traders to access the most profitable markets for their products, which, in many cases, will be the triad economies of North America, Europe and Japan where environmental standards are higher. To access these markets exporters have to conform to higher standards encouraging a global ratcheting up of standards rather than a competitive race to the bottom. It will be interesting in this sense to observe in the coming years what effect China's thirst for natural resources will have on levels of regulation in exporter countries.

Related to this is the claim that the costs of meeting environmental standards constitute a fraction of the overall costs faced by industry and certainly pale into insignificance when compared with other factors such as labour costs, the skills base of the workforce or the available infrastructure in an investment location, with costs to industry from domestic environmental regulation estimated to rarely exceed 1.5 per cent of overall production costs (Brack 1997; Williams 2001b). Whatever the actual costs of meeting standards, which of course differ hugely by sector (Leonard 1998), environmentalists contend that repeated threats of relocation in response to the proposed raising of environmental standards have the effect of creating a 'regulatory chill' effect, where there are strong incentives not to upgrade standards of protection. Chapter 5 shows that many countries continue to use their abundance of natural resources as a source of comparative advantage[1] over other countries and, more insidiously, their absence of regulation as an invitation to international firms to relocate there, and that investors continue to raise the prospect of capital flight in the face of increased costs as a result of regulation. However unenforceable or unlikely those threats may be, states in an open and competitive global economy can rarely afford to ignore them. Some economists have accepted that countries can achieve a comparative advantage through lower environmental standards and that this is not necessarily a bad thing. D'Arge and Kneese, for example, claim that relocations to pollution havens 'are desirable from a global efficiency viewpoint, since comparative advantage and differences in preferences are reflected' (cited in Williams 1994: 85).

Policy decisions to freeze or reduce environmental standards or to embark on an environmentally destructive development trajectory often reflect not just the pursuit of autonomous national development strategies by state elites, but also result from sustained pressure from the World Bank and other actors to create an attractive climate for investors (see chapter 6).

---

1 The law of comparative advantage, commonly associated with the economist David Ricardo, refers to the ability of a country to produce a particular good or service at a lower marginal and opportunity cost based on relative efficiencies (in labour or other production costs) over their competitors.

Evans et al. (2002) show how the Philippines revised its mining code downwards to make fewer demands of foreign investors in response to World Bank pressure to 'open up' its economy, with devastating environmental effects. Likewise the conflict between Argentina and Uruguay over the paper mills located on the Uruguayan side of the river the countries share came after over a decade of pressure from the World Bank to open up the region to foreign investors in this sector. Activists in Argentina mobilized around the possible contamination of the river by the chemicals used in the production process that the company Botnia is not permitted to use in its home country Finland, involving road blockades and cases brought before the International Court of Justice (Newell 2007a; Palermo and Reboratti 2007).

Beyond the issue of regulation or its absence, neo-liberals argue, in any case, that trade liberalization and the internationalization of production have created the conditions for the transfer of clean technologies and improved production processes. In its World Development Report of 1992, the World Bank claimed 'Liberalized trade fosters greater efficiency and higher productivity and may actually reduce pollution by encouraging the growth of less polluting industries and the adoption and diffusion of cleaner technologies' (World Bank 1992: 67). In many cases, investors 'export' environmental standards to new investment locations either because it is more costly to adapt a production process to a new site, or because public and consumer expectations regarding a company's social and environmental conduct mean that it is politically inadvisable to exploit the existence of lower environmental standards (Garcia-Johnson 2000). The extent to which firms' ability and willingness to transfer best available technologies and the most advanced production processes to developing countries is a function of the size of the firm and the sector in which they operate is discussed in chapter 5. Often, as Leonard (1998: 116) shows, it is more the case that increases in regulatory demands in firms' home countries drive them overseas instead of 'modernizing technology, finding substitute products or installing expensive pollution controls'.

Trading with the Future

Contending the claims above and articulating an altogether different political ecology and view of the relationship between nature and society – beyond claims of resource and eco-efficiency savings and the export and upgrading of environmental standards that trade is said to deliver – are a set of powerful environmental and Green critiques. The first thing to note is that there is not one 'environmental' view of the relationship between trade and the environment, just as there is not one, internally coherent, critique of the impact of globalization on the environment. Environmentalists have been divided on the extent to which market-based solutions to environmental problems can be effective and whether increased trade can raise, rather than lower, environmental standards. These divisions have been apparent in the global debate about the extent to which the WTO should accept minimal environmental standards for all its members, and regionally in NAFTA discussions about whether its environmental side-agreement does enough to deter mobile polluters from relocating to zones of weaker regulation, as we shall see below. Here I engage with a more radical Green view of the political ecology of trade, as opposed to a more narrowly conceived environmentalist position, which might hold that under certain conditions trade liberalization can be made compatible with the goals of sustainable development (WWF 1991), as it challenges many of the assumptions and premises that form the starting point for the (neo)-liberal position discussed above.

First, a key source of concern for ecologists is that trade externalizes environmental costs. The social and ecological impacts or costs associated with trade are not reflected in the price of goods. They are not, in the language of economists, 'internalized'. Instead they are passed on to the environment and society in the form of waste and pollution. Both the ecological costs of producing and transporting costs are rarely included in prices, hence the emphasis on ecological taxation as a means to internalize those costs. The problem for Daly (1993: 25) is that since international trade increases competition and competition reduces costs, in the absence of equivalent institutions as exist at the national level that 'bar reductions in the social and environmental standards of domestic industries . . . free international trade encourages industries to shift their production activities to the countries that have the lowest standards of cost internalization'.

More fundamentally, however, critics point to the enormous environmental impact of trade which results from the transportation of goods around the world over increasing distances. For example, it is estimated that one tenth of world oil production is consumed by just moving goods around the world (see box 4.1). Under this reading, potential efficiencies that might be produced by the liberalization of trade are offset by the net impact of increased trade on the environment. LeQuesne (1996: 73) cites the EC Task Force on the Single Market that concluded 'The favourable environmental effects of efficiency in the use of resources are likely to be outweighed by the growth in demand, with consequent increases in environmental pressures'.

Box 4.1   Trade miles

Asparagus
To import 1 kg of asparagus from California to Europe requires four litres of fuel. If grown domestically, the 'energy grab' from transport would be over 900 times less.

Kiwis
Kiwi fruit by freight carrier plane from New Zealand to Europe results in the release of 5 kg of CO_2 for every 1 kg of fruit carried.

Yogurt
Delivering glass cups of yogurt produced for the German market in the mid-1990s required journeys for the contents and finished product that added up to 8000 km.

Cotton
Energy-intensive transport of textile products is increasing with globalization. After soil erosion and the effects of chemical use in the growth of cotton, transport is, by a long way, the next highest environment cost of cotton production.

Source: NEF (2003)

Likewise, it is clear that, left unchecked, the growth in transport-related CO_2 emissions associated with new areas of trade liberalization alone, will offset in no time any reductions achieved in the carefully negotiated Kyoto Protocol and subsequent climate change agreements.

The question of assessing and quantifying the environmental impact of trade is a difficult one and not one that the WTO, or the GATT before it, were inclined to entertain, despite calls from activists for a social and environmental impact assessment of previous trade rounds before launching another one, on the basis that such effects were either negligible or unimportant. By way of an illustrative anecdote, while working in Brussels in 1995 for the Climate Network Europe, I was invited to attend an invite-only civil society 'consultation' organized by the WTO on the relationship between trade and the environment. The discussion and presentations were handled in such a way that only narrow technical discussion of the legal compatibility of specific trade and environmental measures was permissible. When I asked when we were to discuss the question of trade's impact on the environment, the bemused reply came back that the question was irrelevant since trade, by definition, promotes efficiencies in resource use! Such narrow framings around questions of the legal compatibility of trade and environmental rules tend to exclude meaningful discussion of the impact and sustainability of patterns of globalized trade. Likewise, emphasis on the effect of trade pressures on environmental regulations often diverts attention from the larger restructuring that occurs in resource sectors as a result of liberalization. Boyce (2008: 97) suggests the debate about whether NAFTA would produce a race to the top or bottom meant that people were 'oblivious to what may turn out to be NAFTA's most serious environmental impact: the erosion of Mexico's rich biodiversity in maize as Mexican campesino farmers abandon traditional agriculture in the face of competition from cheap corn imported from the USA'. The social costs of livelihoods displaced by competition are often also sidelined in the discussion, but have unsurprisingly been the focus of mobilizations by campesino and farmers' organizations claiming, for example, that 'sin maíz, no hay país' (without maize, there is no country) (Newell 2008g; Wise et al. 2003).

Underpinning this concern is a broader questioning of the logic of comparative advantage from an ecological point of view. While economic orthodoxy dictates that producing a product from components sourced from all over the world to capitalize on the lowest possible costs and comparative economic advantages of different countries makes perfect sense, the ecological costs can be very high, as box 4.1 shows. Critics suggest that the environmental impact associated with production across many sites is unacceptable. In conventional economic terms, it may be logical to transport components across hundreds of miles, using extensive packaging and utilizing vast amounts of pesticides and preservatives, in order to allow a product to endure large-scale transportation and enjoy a longer shelf-life. Ecologists insist, however, that the same product can often (though certainly not always) be produced locally at greater benefit to the community and with much lower associated social and environmental costs.

A further tenet of the theory of comparative advantage is an emphasis on specialization and export-oriented growth. Not only is this the driving ideology behind trade liberalization within the WTO, but it is a key plank of the reforms required of developing countries by the World Bank and International Monetary Fund (IMF). Alongside the concerns of social activists that this approach locks developing countries into inherently unfair and exploitative trade relations (LeQuesne 1996; Curtis 2001), Greens also raise objections to the environmental costs associated with resource-intensive export-led growth. Not only does processing goods for export require extra packaging, it also requires forms of production, in agriculture for example, which are polluting, damaging to health and use land so intensively that it often rapidly degrades (Madeley 2000). A broader critique still is the idea that export-led growth is often at the expense of meeting basic needs. Cash crops are grown in countries where people are starving because they generate more revenue, when that land could be better used to grow subsistence crops from which the poor are more likely to benefit directly. Icke (1990: 63–64) argues:

> the poorest countries in the world grow cash crops on land that could be growing food for their own people. That's why Ethiopia was still exporting food at the height of the famine . . . in Ghana half their farming land is not growing food for the malnourished, but cocoa for western chocolate bars . . . 40 per cent of the food growing land in Senegal is growing peanuts for western margarine . . . during the great drought in the Sahel the production of peanuts for export increased there while tens of thousands starved . . . in Colombia where malnutrition is common, fertile land is used to grow cut flowers for the rich in the west.

What this critique often overlooks is the impact of richer countries reducing dependency on imports from poorer countries or, in the short term at least, of poorer countries moving away from export-based development models, built as they are on an abundance of cheap and often informal (sometimes seasonal) labour. This has prompted some development organizations to promote a 'good for development' label in the wake of calls for wealthy consumers to reduce the carbon embodied in the 'food miles' required to bring food from the farm gate to the dinner plate. The concern is that 'new labels on products which have been air-freighted may unfairly jeopardise export opportunities for over a million poor farmers in the developing world' (Ellis and Warner 2007: 1).

The critique of trade is, in part, informed by a broader Green critique of prevailing development paradigms, which owes a lineage to the debates about the limits to growth derived from the Club of Rome report by that name published in the early 1970s. It also resonates, however, with more contemporary Green critiques of globalization and corresponding calls for 'localization' and a reduction in the volume of international trade (Lang and Hines 1993; Douthwaite 1996; Trainer 1996). Lang and Hines (1993) call this the 'new protectionism' which attempts to re-legitimate active interventions in markets aimed at exercising social control over them. Rather than being anti-capitalist per se, many Greens are in favour of forms of small-scale market activities and support to local business and alternative local currencies such as the LETS (Local Exchange Trading Schemes) (Glover 1999; North 2007). Self-sufficiency is seen to be important socially as well as ecologically, as it enhances peoples' control over their resources, closing the loop between the site of production and the site of consumption and reducing vulnerability to the whims and unpredictable nature of global markets; a form of disengagement from exploitative relations of exchange (Douthwaite 1996).

The Governance of Trade

Having briefly mapped out the political ecology of trade and the environmental consequences of the contemporary organization of trade liberalization in the global political economy, it is important to consider the governance of that relationship; the institutions set up to manage it and the extent to which they have been able to bring about the greening of trade.

GATT, WTO and the Environment: The Record to Date

Although we tend to think of the relationship between trade and environment rules and institutions as a new one, Charnovitz (2008: 237) reminds us that the debate has a much longer history. The *Convention for the Protection of Birds Useful to Agriculture* signed in 1902 made use of an import ban as an environmental instrument, while the trade agreement the *Convention for the Abolition of Import and Export Prohibitions and Restrictions*, signed in 1927, contained within it an exception for trade restrictions imposed for the protection of public health and the protection of animals and plants against diseases and extinction.

The word environment appears nowhere in the text of the GATT, however, although the term sustainable development is mentioned in the preamble to the agreement that brought the WTO into being. At the 2001 Ministerial meeting in Doha, members of the WTO agreed to launch a new round of multilateral trade negotiations. The relationship between WTO rules and the trade obligations set out in international environmental agreements was included in the formal negotiating agenda, and it was agreed that the Committee on Trade and Environment (CTE) will continue its work on the broader effects of environmental measures on market access (Morici 2002). This was a significant move on from the conclusion of the Uruguay Round of the GATT, where delegates failed to agree on the inclusion of the environment as a permanent feature of the trade agenda.

It should be recalled, however, that the CTE is made up of representatives of member states acting for their own governments and is rarely able to make specific recommendations that can be acted on as it operates on a consensus basis (Barkin 2008).

There are, in fact, a number of provisions in the agreements of the WTO that can be used as a basis for validating actions in defence of the environment (see box 4.2). GATT Article XX provides exceptions for measures 'necessary to protect human, animal or plant life or health' and 'relating to the conservation of exhaustible resources . . . made effective in conjunction with restrictions on domestic consumption and production'. Emphasizing the distinction between product and process-based standards, dispute settlement panels have not permitted members to invoke exceptions for measures that regulate unincorporated PPMs (Process and Production Methods) to protect the environment (or other social policy objectives) (Lee 1994). Hence as Morici (2002: 4) notes 'governments have been able to regulate how imports affect their domestic environment (e.g. emissions standards for cars) but not how imports are produced or how they may affect the environment beyond their jurisdiction'. The exceptions require that the measure be 'necessary' in so far as there is no reasonably available and WTO-consistent alternative measure that the regulating government could reasonably be expected to employ to achieve its policy objectives. In determining the availability of such measures, panel decisions have to consider the extent to which the alternative measure 'contributes to the realization of the end pursued', whether the alternative measure would achieve the same end, and whether it is less restrictive of trade (Charnovitz 2008).

The exceptions (see box 4.2) do little to quell concerns that many environmentalists have about the way in which the use of policy instruments aimed at protecting the environment is increasingly undermined on the grounds that they are incompatible with trade rules and disciplines. Expressing this concern LeQuesne (1996: 73–4) notes:

> current WTO rules provide an inadequate framework for sustainable development precisely because they do undermine governments' ability to legislate in favour of environmental sustainability . . . current trade rules discourage governments from pursuing a strategy of internalising costs precisely because they prohibit governments from protecting their domestic industry from cheaper competition from countries who have not internalised costs to the same extent.

Labelling schemes, bans, border taxes, subsidies and other trade restrictions have previously been used to explicitly discriminate between

Box 4.2   WTO rules for environmental protection

Examples of provisions in the WTO agreements dealing with environmental issues include the following:

- *Rule of Exceptions (Article XX)*, which allow exceptions for measures 'necessary to protect human, animal or plant life or health', and 'relating to the conservation of exhaustible natural resources', if such measures are made effective in conjunction with restrictions on domestic production or consumption. The word 'environment' is not expressly found in Article XX, but the text has been interpreted as general environmental protection. However, 'measures must not constitute arbitrary or unjustifiable discrimination between countries where the same conditions prevail' nor be a 'disguised restriction to international trade'.

- *Technical Barriers to Trade (TBT) Agreement*, which specifically covers environmental protection and recognizes the legitimacy of government policies to this end. Any tighter standards imposed in pursuance of this objective must be scientifically justified and necessary to achieve legitimate objectives. The Agreement provides that, in addition to the two conditions imposed by Article XX, environmental standards should not create unnecessary obstacles to trade, and countries can seek resolution of disputes that may arise.

- *The Sanitary and Phytosanitary Agreement* negotiated in the Uruguay Round specifically mentions environmental issues, in broadly the same terms as the TBT Agreement.

- *The Agreement on Subsidies and Countervailing Measures* specifies that subsidies provided for the adaptation of existing facilities to new environmental requirements cannot be countervailed by a partner country. Subsidies are allowed for up to 20 per cent of firms' costs in adapting to new environmental laws.

- *The Agreement on Agriculture* exempts payments made to farmers under government environmental or conservation programmes from the general requirement to reduce subsidies.

- *Intellectual property*: governments can refuse to issue patents that threaten human, animal or plant life or health, or risk serious damage to the environment (TRIPS Article 27).

- *GATS Article 14*: policies affecting trade in services for protecting human, animal or plant life or health are exempt from normal GATS disciplines under certain conditions.

environmentally destructive and environmentally benign activities. Most problematic for Greens is the fact that discrimination on grounds of production process is key, yet largely prohibited by trade rules, as the dolphin tuna and many subsequent cases have clearly demonstrated. This is the basis of the campaign for the incorporation of PPMs into trade rules. It is increasingly difficult to maintain a distinction between production processes and products in the light of increasing emphasis on life-cycle approaches, the popular use of eco-labelling and efforts to address the use of energy which are necessarily caused by the PPM and not the product. As LeQuesne (1996: 81) notes 'from an environmental point of view, there is no meaningful distinction to be drawn between environmental harm which is generated by a product, or the harm generated by its process and production methods'. *The Economist* (quoted in Lee 1994: 322), meanwhile, in slightly dramatic tones, adopts the opposing position that

> This distinction between products and processes may seem mere semantics; actually it is crucial if a liberal trading order is to be maintained. It is hard to see how GATT could sanction trade restrictions based on processes rather than products, without setting off a protectionist tide.

A related concern in this regard is the use of trade-restricting measures in MEAs (Multilateral Environmental Agreements). Many such agreements, in different ways, employ restrictions on the trade in substances considered to be harmful to the environment. The *Montreal Protocol on Substances that Deplete the Ozone Layer*, for example, restricts the trade in CFCs (Chlorofluorocarbons) to those that have signed up to the accord, thereby excluding non-parties from the trade in ODS (ozone-depleting substances) and therefore violating the most-favoured nation principle (Brack 1996). The rationale behind this is to create positive incentives for countries to comply with the accord and reduce the potential for free-riding by non-parties to the Protocol. The CITES (Convention on the International Trade in Endangered Species) agreement elaborates a list system which bans altogether the trade in certain endangered species of plants and animals and imposes restrictions on the trade in others, depending on the degree of perceived threat to their future. Similarly the Basel Convention on the trade in hazardous wastes outlaws certain forms of trade (Krueger 1999). The use of trade embargoes in these instruments violates WTO prohibitions against quantitative restrictions. The CTE of the WTO has identified 22 MEAs that require or cause governments to implement trade measures that may violate their WTO obligations, yet the use of TREMs (Trade-Related Environment Measures) in these MEAs has not been challenged to date. The 1996 Singapore Ministerial meeting endorsed the CTE finding that members may bring to the WTO disputes concerning MEA-related trade measures, but no conclusions have been reached on proposals to modify Article XX of the GATT to incorporate MEAs explicitly, and there remains no consensus that MEA trade restrictions are compatible with international trade rules (Barkin 2008).

What is interesting is that the use of trade measures in new environmental agreements has been subject to significant contestation in negotiations, shaped by the need to anticipate and pre-empt conflicts with trade rules. The Cartagena Protocol on Biosafety provides a case in point in this regard. The preambular language to the Protocol reflects strong differences of opinion between the EU and US over what was known as the 'savings clause' determining the extent to which the provisions contained in the Protocol should be subordinate to the trade rules of the WTO. The result is a product of political compromise embodying the concern of the EU that the instrument should not be subordinate to trade disciplines, and of the US that the Protocol should be consistent with WTO rules (Newell and MacKenzie 2000). Likewise there is increasing interaction between the climate and trade regimes aimed at ensuring 'mutual supportiveness' and avoiding conflicts between border tax measures and allowances in emissions trading schemes, for example, and international trade rules (ICTSD 2011a). Environmentalists resent, however, the way in which environmental agreements are assumed to be subservient to trade regimes. They feel that social and environmental protection should not be accorded less priority than the objective of trade liberalization. While some would like to see a general exception for environmental measures from WTO rules (Morici 2002), others endorse a more full-frontal attack on the mentality of 'the market über alles' (Hines 1997: 5).

Trade and Environment Disputes

Perhaps the most high-profile of the cases involving trade rules and environmental protection measures was that involving the US and Mexico in a dispute over restrictions on the import of Mexican tuna on the grounds that it was caught with nets that were trapping dolphins. Under pressure from domestic environmental groups, in 1990 a US district court ordered the secretary of commerce to ban the import of canned, fresh and frozen tuna from Mexico, Venezuela and the Pacific Islands of Vanuatu because their methods of catching tuna violated the Marine Mammals Protection Act. Meanwhile, as Vogel (1997: 108) notes, 'For Mexico, the American tuna embargo was symptomatic of the efforts of developed nations to protect themselves from growing competition from third world countries.' The case marked the first time a GATT dispute panel had been requested to address the extra-jurisdictional scope of a national environmental regulation.

For many, the outcome of the dolphin-tuna case confirmed the inevitable pro-trade bias of decisions taken within a trade body. The decision, made in 1991, in favour of Mexico, was that the restriction of trade for protection of the environment outside a country's border contravened GATT rules and that production process standards are considered to be non-tariff barriers. The key issue is that while governments may impose regulations on imports comparable to those imposed on domestic goods regarding their physical characteristics and performance, they are not allowed to discriminate on the basis of how a product is produced if those methods have no effect on product characteristics or performance. In determining whether the US legislation was consistent with the exemption clause of Article XX, the panel concluded that this provision only applied to activities within the jurisdiction of the country adopting the measure, and was not intended to affect production and consumption outside that jurisdiction. US environmentalist Ralph Nader described the decision as a 'breathtaking attack on progress made in the last ten years' (quoted in Vogel 1997: 114).

A second case concerned a challenge by Venezuela and Brazil in 1996 to the implementation of the US Clean Air Act of 1990 which, they argued, discriminated against foreign refineries. The Dispute Panel ruled in favour of Venezuela and Mexico and the Appellate body confirmed this ruling. The decision served to entrench the view of environmentalists that the dispute settlement procedures in the world trading system were biased against environmental interests. A third dispute arose from a challenge by India, Malaysia, Pakistan and Thailand to a US measure prohibiting the import of shrimp from countries that do not require the use of turtle exclusion devices on shrimp fishing nets in areas where sea turtles are found. Interestingly, the shrimp-turtle case established that, subject to certain conditions, a nation can take unilateral action to protect a resource in the global commons. The US was permitted to embargo shrimp caught without sea-turtle excluding devices. In this case, support for the decision was found in the fact that, through membership of CITES, all parties to the dispute have adopted the policy that sea turtles should be protected; sea turtles are highly migratory; none of the parties may claim exclusive ownership of them and the US has sought to negotiate agreements to protect sea turtles, so the evidence against an instance of disguised protectionism was stronger. The Appellate body did not endorse unilateral action, but rather opened the door to such measures when an international consensus has been achieved regarding a conservation goal, when measures applied beyond national jurisdictions are necessary to accomplish these goals and when the government taking action earnestly seeks an international agreement on these issues (Morici 2002). The WTO secretariat also continues to declare, however, that 'trade restrictions cannot be imposed on a product purely because of the way it has been produced' and, whilst in the gasoline and shrimp cases, the US was able to address the alleged violation without sacrificing its environmental policies, as Charnovitz (2008: 241) notes, 'The original panel decisions, if carried to their logical conclusion, had seemed to undermine the right of a government to carry out environmental regulation that affected trade'.

A fourth case concerns the European Commission's de facto moratorium on genetically modified (GM) products which the US contested at the WTO with the support of Canada and Argentina. Both parties to the dispute claimed victory in the case which proceeded over three years. Despite claims by the US that the case makes clear that moratoria on GM products are incompatible with WTO commitments, the European Commission (EC) and environmental activists have been quick to suggest that specific and general moratoria could still be permissible even under WTO rules. The EC claimed in regard to the regulations in question that 'Nothing in this panel report will compel us to change that framework' (Third World Network 2006). The most important issue raised by the case was the failure of the European Union (EU) to apply its own rules properly, particularly with regard to provisions for avoiding 'undue delay' with regard to twenty biotech products (CIEL 2006; Friends of the Earth International 2006; Third World Network 2006; Lieberman and Gray 2008). The process by which the decision to implement a ban is taken is the key issue. Countries wanting to apply product-specific bans must provide a risk assessment of such products that meet the requirements of the SPS (Sanitary and Phytosanitary) measures agreement and its provisions on 'sound science'.

A more recent potential trade conflict at the WTO in 2011 over the fairness of China's clean technology subsidies and domestic sourcing requirements (so-called import substitution subsidies), was narrowly avoided when China agreed to end the use of the subsidies in question (ICTSD 2011b). But proposals to adopt border tax adjustments (or Border Carbon Adjustments), as has been proposed by some in the US and EU, continue to cause unease. These take a range of forms, but essentially serve as a way of deterring carbon leakage whereby investors shift their production to areas of the world not subject to emissions reduction obligations under the Kyoto Protocol, or act as a driver for developing countries to accept emissions reductions (Cosbey 2008). The effect of their use would impose higher taxes on products which are produced in a highly energy or carbon-intensive fashion. Fears on the part of export-led developing countries that the use of such measures may signal the rise of climate protectionism will need to be addressed if such measures are to gain traction (ICTSD 2011a).

The conflicts and disputes discussed in this section in many ways reflect the parallel and independent bodies of public international law that have emerged and the absence of a global forum to mediate the competing claims that each places on governments. Where the WTO has taken on the discourse of sustainable development, it has done so for its own ends and consciously adopted a 'weak sustainability' agenda, rather than addressing many of the concerns that underpin the ecological view outlined above, with the preamble to the 1994 agreement calling for expanded production and trade in accordance with the objective of sustainable development.

The Standards Debate

Partly as a result of the ad hoc, case-by-case decision making on these issues and a preference for commonly agreed standards rather than the unilateral use of environmental measures subject to political whim and protectionist abuse, there has long been a debate about the desirability of negotiating environmental standards within the WTO. For some, such standards would provide important floors, if not ceilings, below which countries would not be expected to fall in the provision of basic standards of environmental protection, crucial for addressing concerns about a potential race to the bottom noted above. What many environmentalists are concerned to address is the situation whereby countries seeking to advance environmental protection by internalizing environmental costs suffer a competitive disadvantage. To counter this situation and incentives that may exist to accelerate a race to the bottom in environmental standards, some have called for a floor of internationally agreed minimum environmental standards to which all countries must adhere; a minimum parity level for some of the most environmentally damaging production processes. The attraction of such an approach for some environmentalists is the use of the sanctioning mechanisms of the WTO to penalize those countries failing to comply with minimal environmental obligations. This is also, of course, what concerns many developing countries that fear they would be the target of such sanctions.

It is worth noting, however, that many other environmentalists are not demanding that the WTO set environmental standards. Instead they want to restrict the WTO's right to circumscribe environmental policy at national level and in international environmental regimes. Meanwhile, those opposed to having environmental standards within the WTO question the probable effectiveness of standards set by a body whose primary goal is the liberalization of trade and raise concerns about market access and the imposition of environmental conditions on trade measures, tying trade gains to environmental protection measures. Since the arrival of the WTO, countries negotiating trade rounds have to accept all the terms of a round as part of a 'single undertaking' and not just pick and choose à la carte as they were able to do before (Jackson 1998). Therefore, in order to access trade gains that have been negotiated during a round, they may also be forced to accept environmental commitments. Many are concerned about the potential of the trade–environment debate to re-ignite North–South divisions in the international trading system (Whalley 1996). Some developing countries argue that poverty is the cause of low standards among countries desperate to attract investors on terms that are not of their choosing, and that access to Northern markets which has been denied to them is vital to raising environmental standards. At the same time, environmentalists argue, the pursuit of trade expansion without environmental safeguards will only impoverish the resource base upon which many developing countries depend for their wealth.

These issues form the background to the debate about which institutional venue is the most appropriate for mediating these conflicts. LeQuesne suggests

> The setting of environmental standards should not be undertaken by the WTO itself, since it has neither mandate nor competence in this area, but by another mechanism or body with the appropriate expertise which would be transparent, democratic and accountable; possibly a body established under the auspices of the Commission on Sustainable Development (CSD) or a new Intergovernmental Panel on Trade and Sustainable Development (1996: 77).

A combination of NGOs and developing country governments continue to oppose the idea that the WTO should set environmental standards.

Contention over which institution is best placed to adjudicate on the relationship between environmental standards and trade has meant that bodies such as the WTO have, to some extent, outsourced authority for decision making to private standard-setting bodies such as the International Organization for Standardization (ISO). The push towards the universalization and harmonization of rules relating to standard-setting in the areas of health and environment has had the effect of encouraging governments to employ standards created by international regulatory bodies such as the ISO (14001, for example) and the OECD (such as its guidelines on risk assessment of genetically modified organisms, GMOs) (Finger and Tamiotti 1999; Newell 2003). Potential problems remain, however, in the adoption or recognition by public bodies of what are essentially private standards. Krut and Gleckman (1998: 68) suggest, for example, that:

> Standards set by international bodies are now ceilings which require a country to justify if its practices are more rigorous than an existing international standard. A country that may have higher standards is unlikely to prevail against a challenge on the grounds that the international ISO standard is too weak.

In so far as particular environmental management systems – as opposed to quantitative standards – will be preferred, it should be of concern that bodies such as the ISO poorly respond to the needs of SMEs (small and medium-sized enterprises) or regulators from the developing world that are under-represented in the body (Clapp 1998, 2005). The moves described here indicate the ISO's transition from a purely technical organization to one 'at the forefront of world trade developments' (Krut and Gleckman 1998: 71).

Outsourcing regulatory problems to other arenas is one solution. Forum-shifting is another (Braithwaite and Drahos 2000). This refers to the way in which powerful actors seek to have an issue or conflict resolved in arenas that are the most sympathetic to their interests, where the mandate of an organization most aligns with the outcomes they are pursuing, and where they have the greatest degree of access. Sell (2003) shows how, in the case of agricultural biotechnology, the pharmaceutical and biotechnology companies sought to ensure the contentious issue of IPRs was resolved in the WTO rather than World Intellectual Property Organization (WIPO) or the Food and Agriculture Organization (FAO), because stronger forms of protection and sanctioning powers apply and developing countries wield less influence.

It should also be made clear that decisive political battles are not only won and lost in the corridors of the WTO, but rather in bilateral contests where strong-arm tactics can be more readily employed than in open multilateral bargaining. Hence powerful states such as the US are able to use bilateral pressures to cajole countries into removing perceived trade barriers. Sri Lanka, Croatia and Bolivia are examples of countries whose regulations on GMOs have been targeted in this way (Newell 2007b). Also, where regional efforts to secure these provisions have stalled, such as in the case of the Free Trade Area of the Americas (FTAA), the US has sought to promote new export opportunities and protect investor rights through bilateral trade agreements. One such agreement was concluded with Peru which demands IPR protection along US lines allowing for the patenting of genetic resources and traditional knowledge, and calls for the harmonization of SPS provisions, making it easier to get GMO varieties accepted in the market by reducing the scope of government leeway to raise social-economic concerns not based on 'sound science'.

Regional and bilateral trade agreements present specific governance challenges because they are either embedded within broader projects of regional economic integration or, in the case of bilateral agreements, serve to heighten power inequities where powerful states negotiate one-on-one with smaller developing countries. This has important social and ecological implications as agreements cover resources such as water, seeds and energy upon which millions of livelihoods depend. In this regard NAFTA has perhaps generated the most interest because of its environmental agreement, and it is the most high profile of the regional trade regimes because of the involvement of the US and Canada. The environmental side agreement was one of the most sensitive issues in the NAFTA negotiations, aimed at countering the fears expressed by some environmentalists that pollution-intensive industries would relocate to the Maquiladora area on the Mexican side of the border. Indeed President Clinton made support for NAFTA conditional on the conclusion of an environmental side agreement (Audley 1997).

The agreement is meant to ensure an upward harmonization of environmental standards so that a country can set the standard it considers most appropriate for achieving the level of protection it desires, even if these are stricter than those established internationally (Schatan 2000). Formally, companies are also required to return production waste back to the country of origin, but the NAFTA rule of national treatment meant companies could dispose of waste according to Mexican environmental laws where there is concern that monitoring and enforcement is weak. In one survey, more than a quarter of companies said stronger environmental provisions in the US prompted them to relocate in Mexico (French 1993) and, according to Mexico's Secretariat of Urban Planning and Ecology, more than half the Maquiladora plants produce hazardous waste and, while waste is supposed to be transferred to the US, 'compliance has been the exception rather than the rule' (LeQuesne 1996: 68).

Despite the fact that an environmental commission was established to provide periodic reporting on the state of the environment and the impact of NAFTA in particular, sanctions against persistent violators of legislation are seen as a last resort. Indeed, at the end of 1995, the US Congress threatened to reject 'fast-track' authority for the incorporation of new countries into NAFTA unless sanctions were removed from the side agreements. Where a party is not implementing its own environmental laws effectively, it can be taken to dispute settlement through a complex process whereby the complainant (which can include communities threatened by a violation of environmental law) has to prove systematic non-implementation according to weakly defined criteria, after which the country is required to pay a fine where there is evidence of a 'persistent pattern of failure to effectively enforce its environmental law' (Article 22). Alongside this, however, is a provision which determines that standards can be challenged if it is felt that they negatively impact trade and do not employ recognized risk assessment and sound science criteria. For example, in August 2000 the California-based *Metalclad* corporation used Chapter 11 provisions to sue the Mexican government for $16.7 million for rejecting its proposal to build a hazardous waste facility in an already 'highly contaminated' community (Roberts and Thannos 2003).

There is clearly some way to go in designing a workable architecture for mediating the relationship between trade liberalization and the environment, one that goes beyond the weak notions of sustainability employed by the WTO, but is sufficiently sensitive to the concerns of developing countries and smaller producers about the potential for trade restrictive environmental measures to be used discriminately and arbitrarily against them. The proliferation of private standard-setting bodies such as the ISO and the popularity amongst multinational firms in particular of certification schemes that certify responsible production practices add further to the institutional messiness that complicates the relationships between public and private bodies, international and national regulators. What is becoming clear is that future agreements on the environment and future rounds of trade liberalization will be more sensitive to potential conflicts with other institutions than has previously been the case. This does not mean that the conflicts will become any easier to solve, especially in so far as the dialogue of the deaf, between neo-liberal trade advocates on the one hand and ecologists on the other, persists.

Contesting the Politics of Trade

It has been noted already that the pursuit of a globalized economy through the vehicle of trade liberalization has provoked opposition from a range of groups and movements, including the environmental movement, concerned about (a) the ecological impact of heightened volumes of global trade and the export-oriented model of development which it rests on, and (b) the use of trade agreements to challenge or override existing environmental regulations or which create a chilling effect on the development of new regulation. There is a diversity of opinion within the environmental movement about whether, and the extent to which, trade liberalization can be compatible with the pursuit of sustainable development. This final section of the chapter looks in more detail at the ways in which groups working within existing institutions of trade governance, as well as those opposed to them, have pursued their preferred strategies of change. This involves strategies that seek to contest the impacts of trade liberalization, as well as contest the *distributional* effects of trade agreements on natural resource use. But it also includes those that advocate changes to the *process* by which decisions are made and the institutions that make them. This covers those whose aim is to improve and make use of existing governance structures, occupying and expanding those spaces of public participation that exist, as well as those that reject the authority and legitimacy of trade bodies making policy on such sensitive questions often without, in their opinion, a valid public mandate to do so (Icaza et al. 2010).

Those that have sought to engage global trade institutions with the aim of reforming them have encountered a series of barriers to meaningful participation and engagement. Although the WTO dispute settlement mechanism is more transparent than the GATT system it replaced and panel findings have been published more speedily than before (Brack 1997), it effectively remains closed to non-participants in the dispute. Although in the shrimp-turtle case, the Appellate body allowed NGOs to submit amicus briefs to panels and appellate bodies, broader forms of participation from independent experts have not thus far been permitted.[2] Moreover, panels and the appellate body continue to meet behind closed doors and submissions of parties are not automatically made available to non-participants. This became an issue once again in the recent GMO trade dispute between

---

2 In the EC-Asbestos case, the Appellate Body decided it had no need to consider any of the amicus briefs submitted in the case while still maintaining that panels and the Appellate Body have the right to take unsolicited amicus briefs into account should they choose to do so (Bartels 2004).

the EU and the US, Canada and Argentina, described above, where 'the misrepresentation of the findings of the WTO panel' has been possible because of the organization's continued 'tendency towards secrecy and a closed-door approach' that are 'endemic to dispute settlement in the trade sector' (CIEL 2006). Williams (2001a: 46) notes elsewhere that while

> the earlier closure of the WTO process to non-corporate actors has been tempered . . . the venue still privileges those who possess structural power, granting them superior instrumental access. While the WTO has progressively expanded access to non-governmental organisations, the fact that the organisation includes business groups in the NGO category reinforces the influence of the corporate sector in the policy process.

The work of Susan Sell (1999, 2003) supports the finding that business groups have played a key part in shaping and driving government positions on commercially-sensitive agreements such as the TRIPs (Trade-Related Aspects of Intellectual Property Rights) accord. She notes that, through these means, 'A small group of corporate executives of US-based multinational corporations succeed[ed] in making intellectual property policy for the rest of the world' (1999: 169).

The WTO has evolved a relationship with civil society whereby NGOs (not broader social movements), particularly those 'concerned with matters related to those of the WTO', are regarded as a 'valuable resource' that 'can contribute to the accuracy and richness of the public debate', that can 'increase the awareness of the public in respect of WTO activities'. Allowing them to fulfil this role requires members to improve transparency and communication with NGOs, making information available more rapidly and improving public access to documents through the internet. This is in addition to

> the organisation of ad hoc symposia on specific WTO-related issues, informal arrangements to receive the information NGOs may wish to make available for consultation by interested delegates and the continuation of past practice of responding to requests for general information and briefings about the WTO (WTO 1996).

As Wilkinson (2002: 203) notes, citing Marceau and Pedersen, the danger with this model is that symposia serve as 'a useful arms-length exercise in NGO-WTO relations with the secretariat serving as a "buffer" between Members and NGOs'. There remains limited scope for institutionalized forms of engagement by civil society groups. Item 5 of the Guidelines for arrangements on relations with NGOs makes clear that 'If chairpersons of

WTO councils and committees participate in discussions or meetings with NGOs it shall be in their personal capacity unless that particular council or committee decides otherwise'. More bluntly still, WTO (1996) item 6 states:

> As a result of extensive discussions, there is currently a broadly held view that it would not be possible for NGOs to be directly involved in the work of the WTO or its meetings. Closer consultation and cooperation with NGOs can also be met constructively through appropriate processes at the national level where lies primary responsibility for taking into account the different elements of public interest which are brought to bear on trade policy-making.

Not only, then, are NGOs not involved in the work of the WTO or its meetings, but there are safeguards in place to secure the essentially intergovernmental nature of WTO decision making. Where interaction does have to take place, the emphasis is clearly on organized elements of civil society with what the WTO would define as a legitimate interest in its work. As Wilkinson (2002: 204) argues, 'The emphasis is on the development of relations with NGOs, rather than with the more informal, less well organized tracts of public opinion. And, by committing itself to court only those willing to engage with the WTO, large sections of more critical public opinion are marginalized.'

Within the environmental movement, NGOs have adopted different positions on the best way of promoting environmental concerns within the WTO. For example, while Friends of the Earth have called for the closure of the CTE on the grounds that it has failed to promote sustainable development within the WTO, WWF, while critical, have called for the continuation of the Committee's work. Alongside this, the group also established their own Expert Panel on Trade and Sustainable Development to generate policy recommendations to be circulated among WTO members (Williams 2001a). This difference in approach reflects a broader split within the environmental movement between those who view trade liberalization per se as antithetical to ecological sustainability and those who take the view that under certain conditions trade liberalization can contribute to sustainability. In a discussion paper on the GATT, for example, WWF (1991: 4) claim that the agreement

> does have the potential to promote sustainable management of the world's resources and protection of its fragile environment [but] to realize this potential, the narrow trade-focused orientation of the agreement must be broadened to balance and integrate trade and environmental policy objectives.

Although many mainstream environmentalists continue to seek to secure institutional provision for the handling of environmental issues within regional and international trade bodies, there is growing momentum among a broader set of movements which questions in more fundamental ways the model of trade governance being promoted through these means, and its impact on sustainability. For example, in the Latin American context, trade accords dealing with control of natural resources (such as gas and water), agriculture and knowledge (through IPR provisions) bring the interests of regional and global capital into conflict with those of indigenous peoples and social justice oriented environmental groups (Newell 2007a). Within these coalitions, environmental groups, critical of the process and sceptical about the compatibility of trade liberalization with sustainable development, have articulated concerns which resonate with a much broader critique of neo-liberal development models. There are the familiar concerns about both the potential for mobile capital to exploit lower environmental standards as well as the environmental impact of increased volumes of trade. As *Acción Ecológica* (2004) of Ecuador argue, the FTAA (or Área de Libre Comercio de las Américas, ALCA) 'implies a direct increase in the consumption and therefore production of fossil fuels, this implies an increase in CO_2 emissions which the US does not want to control'.

An innovative array of protest strategies and tools have been used aimed both at opening up the process of trade policy making to a broader range of social interests and contesting the skewed distribution of costs and benefits resulting from existing agreements. In the context of NAFTA, for example, social movements have used solidarity tours that link communities affected by the social and environmental impacts of company relocations in the wake of the trade agreements, while plebiscites and 'trade literacy' campaigns have been used to raise awareness about FTAA negotiations. For example, in Brazil during the first week of September 2002, more than 10 million people in 3,894 municipalities from across the country voted in a popular plebiscite on the FTAA. The results of this consultation showed that 98 per cent of the people that participated were opposed to the signing of the FTAA, versus 1 per cent that supported the treaty (*Jornal do Brasil* 2002). Material for popular education was also produced and widely distributed (40,000 booklets, 5,000 videos, 15,000 books, 50,000 posters, CDs that were circulated to local radio, and 3,000,000 information leaflets on the FTAA) (Icaza et al. 2010).

The narrow form of democratizing trade policy, understood as bringing more voices and actors into a set of institutions and policy processes

whose purpose and process are already established, is a far cry from recognizing the broader and multiple social and ecological systems which
support and will be affected by the expansionist ambitions of trade policy
and setting up policy spaces and processes that can cope with the complexity that flows from this. This stands in contrast to current attempts either
to negate the relevance of the social and environmental impacts of trade
policy or to press these issues into the service of trade liberalization objectives. Side agreements without meaningful enforcement, procedures for
citizens to bring legal claims once harmed by polluting industry, such as
those included in NAFTA, or the suggested 'drop box' whereby activists
can deposit ideas about improvements to the FTAA negotiations, without
any obligation on the part of negotiators to respond to these, hardly count
as a serious effort to engage with civil society, let alone democratize trade
policy in any meaningful sense of the word. Many such mechanisms reproduce the WTO logic that only groups with a 'legitimate' interest in the
organization's work, defined as having a 'direct interest in issues of production, distribution and consumption' by the Mercosur agreement, are
entitled to a say. Groups are regarded as a 'valuable resource' in making
the case for trade liberalization in the public domain. The political function of the FTAA's Committee of Government Representatives on Civil
Society (since they are clearly unable to represent themselves) is made
clear in the draft text of the agreement: 'to build broad public understanding of and *support* for hemispheric trade liberalization' (emphasis added).

Conclusions

What does the story of trade, as one central pillar of the global economy,
tell us about the relationship between globalization and the environment?
In different ways and for different reasons countries have traded with one
another for centuries. The terms of exchange under colonialism and earlier
more blatant forms of accumulation through dispossession have given
way to the use of legal accords to define the terms of engagement between
states and, increasingly, states and corporations. The need on the part of
more globalizing fractions of capital to acquire new investment opportunities and gain access to new markets on a world scale has given rise to
demands to construct institutions which serve that need. The GATT was
no longer up to the job and the WTO was created in 1995 complete with
provisions for sanctions in the form of retaliatory action, a single undertaking to bind countries to all aspects of agreements and a dispute settlement
procedure to uphold the provisions of the organizations' agreements. This

architecture provided the institutional basis for disciplinary neo-liberalism whereby less powerful states can be locked into trading arrangements which benefit those that draft trade rules and which wield the economic and political might to overcome resistance to them. What causes such concern to citizens and the movements described above is the extension of trade, through international law and the power of global institutions, into the everyday political ecology of water use, agricultural practices, land use patterns and energy access. In this sense the contemporary constitution of trade governance provides the means to deepen, extend and manage in an orderly way attempts to bring common goods into the private sphere for accumulation by transnational capital.

Nevertheless, despite efforts and proposals to enrol many more natural resources into global trade flows, many circuits of (natural) capital lie beyond the formal public regime of the WTO and the regional and bilateral institutions and treaties discussed in this chapter. Here, important sites of environmental governance include systems of certification and private governance or more general import and export regulations – some of which are discussed more fully in the next chapter. In this sense, the trade regime constitutes a fragmented and dispersed 'regime complex' (Raustiala and Victor 2004) operating across a number of levels, but underpinned by a common project which aims at maximizing trade and minimizing barriers to it, premised on the assumption, and reinforced by a powerfully reproduced discourse, that trade is critical to growth which is a prerequisite both for poverty alleviation and sustainability.

Critical movements that have sought to challenge this dominant ideology through broad repertoires of protest have succeeded in stalling many initiatives to open up markets in new sectors and regions of the world. A potent combination of material and institutional power continues to sustain and legitimate the idea that trade liberalization is both a means and an end in itself, however. This continues to frustrate those arguing either that the merits of liberalization should be assessed on a case by case basis rather than accepted as given *a priori*, that there are limits to liberalization in that some sectors are of such vital importance that they should not be privatized (such as water), or, more profoundly, that there are ecological limits to growth which the continued expansion of trade threatens to surpass.

Chapter 5

Global Production and the Environment: Racing to the Top, Bottom or Middle?

If the WTO is the institutional embodiment of the concerns that many environmentalists have about globalization, transnational corporations (TNCs) are the actors whose power, reach and control over natural resources inspire both awe and alarm in those working towards sustainable development. With inflows of foreign direct investment (FDI) expected to reach $1.6–2 trillion in 2012 (UNCTAD 2010), the rising economic and political importance of transnational corporations[1] is both a driver and a symbol of globalization. Exporting best practice and bringing about great improvements in technology for some, TNCs are key actors in delivering sustainable development, feted for their efforts to green their activities (Schmidheiny 1992) and 'walk the talk' (Holliday et al. 2002). For others, the mobility of capital and the internationalization of production that make international investment possible, give companies unprecedented freedoms to access and exploit natural resources where it is most profitable to do so, often at the expense of communities and their environment (Karliner 1997; Madeley 2000).

As vast consumers as well as producers of natural resources, TNCs inevitably feature centrally in any analysis of globalization. To take one example, from the Business Council for Sustainable Development: 'Industry accounts for more than one third of energy consumed worldwide and uses more energy than any other end user in industrialised and newly industrialising economies' (Schmidheiny 1992: 43). Reflecting the central role of industry to any global efforts to tackle global environmental problems such as climate change, the International Chamber of Commerce (ICC 1995) also notes:

---

1 I use the term transnational corporations here to denote the fact that control and decision making is often concentrated within the western branches of these companies. Given that power, resources and authority are not diffused throughout the organizations, the term 'multi' exaggerates the global scope of the company (see Gill and Law 1988). Throughout the chapter, I use the terms MNC, TNC and MNE since different terms are used by the different international organizations described here.

Industry's involvement is a critical factor in the policy deliberations relating to climate change. It is industry that will meet the growing demands of consumers for goods and services. It is industry that develops and disseminates most of the world's technology. It is industry and the private financial community that marshal most of the financial resources that fund the world's economic growth. It is industry that develops, finances and manages most of the investments that enhance and protect the environment. It is industry, therefore, that will be called upon to implement and finance a substantial part of governments' climate change policies.

The enormous power that flows from this control of finance, trade, production and technology translates into high levels of political influence, as we will see in the following section. It means that state actors, notionally charged with the responsibility of responding to environmental threats, have to negotiate with corporate actors that are often able to exercise a veto over policy responses they consider threatening to their interests. As Levy (1997: 56) puts it, 'if an agreement cannot be crafted that gains the consent of major affected industries, there will likely be no agreement at all'. But what of the everyday consequences of corporate decision making for the pursuit of sustainable development as opposed to the sporadic, uneven and drawn out nature of multilateral public environmental negotiations?

The Political Ecology of Production: The Nature of Production

Despite the abundance of general claims about the environmental benefits that flow from foreign direct investment (World Bank 2000) and counter-claims about corporate plunder of the planet (Cromwell 2001), it is important to distinguish, amongst other things, between the size, sector and location of companies, both geographically and in terms of their place within the supply chain in order to understand the nature and scale of the environmental and social impacts of their activities. Significant and important differences determine the environmental performance of transnational corporations as opposed to SMEs (small and medium-sized enterprises), the sectors in which companies operate, as well as where a company is located in the global economy, geographically and in the supply chain (Newell and Frynas 2007). This is because of the scale of the impacts (of TNCs as opposed to SMEs; dispersed or localized), the nature of their business (whether in primary extraction, processing or the service sector) and the country and region in which they are both hosted and based, which will profoundly affect the regulatory context in which they operate and the sorts of social expectations that shape their day-to-day business conduct. TNCs cast a longer ecological shadow because of their size and the reach of their operations. Precisely because of their visibility and presence in so many sites in the global economy, however, they are also often subject to more intense social pressure and activism than state-owned companies that are often protected by their government owners (Newell 2005a).

In terms of sector, TNCs in the oil, mining and energy sectors often attract the most attention in debates about globalization and the environment because of the visibility and extent of the pollution and social displacement that their activities can often generate. Their tendency to work in remote areas, often inhabited by indigenous and tribal peoples, produces a particular political ecology where social divisions and relations of race, class and gender are brought to bear upon and magnify the nature of resource conflict (Collinson 1996; Newell 2007a). But the ecological shadow of other 'lighter' sectors such as electronics or information technology (IT) industries is also significant, though less visible and, therefore, often overlooked. Pellow and Park (2002), for example, explore the darker side of the IT 'silicon valley of dreams' where migrant labourers are involved in the outsourcing of circuit cleaning and assembly using an array of toxic chemicals in their own homes and in the vicinity of children. Carmin and Agyeman (2011) also draw attention to the e-waste from computers that ends up in waste dumps in the global South, in Ghana, for example, where a scavenger economy operates in disassembling the goods for onward sale. The manufacture of 'green' commodities – solar photovoltaic modules or compact fluorescent lights – may also reproduce the unequal occupational health and environmental pollution burdens found in analogous industries. There is a tendency to treat all clean energy technologies as homogeneously 'green'. Yet, solar photovoltaic technologies rely on semiconductor technologies built out of hazardous industrial chemicals (Newell et al. 2011). The legacy of environmental injustice in the wake of the semiconductor manufacturing in the 1970s and 80s – toxic waste sites and occupational health problems, largely in immigrant women workers – reminds us that all commodities come at unequal costs as emphasized by the literature on ecologically unequal exchange discussed in chapter 2 (Clark and Foster 2009; Martínez-Alier 2007; Roberts and Parks 2008). An ecological reading of commodity chains is useful, then, for highlighting the impacts generated throughout the social life of the products we consume (Dauvergne and Lister 2010), but needs also to incorporate an appreciation of how socio-environmental costs are borne unevenly by different social groups along the chain of accumulation (Selwyn 2012).

For some, such examples point both to the mismatch between the scale and scope of national regulation and the global reach of TNCs, as well as the under-development and inadequacy of international law regarding the social and environmental responsibilities of corporations. Evidence about the relationship between FDI and environmental regulation is mixed, however, and can be used to sustain competing claims of an upgrading effect and a downgrading effect depending on the sector, region and the type of standard under investigation. It is possible to find examples both of a 'race to the bottom', of FDI having an upgrading effect and of a 'race to the middle' (Vogel 1997; World Bank 2000). For instance, the lack of environmental regulation in many developing countries, desperate to attract investment on any terms, has been used as a comparative advantage to attract the processing of environmentally hazardous substances such as toxic wastes and the production of asbestos that have been banned in the global North (Clapp 2001; Waldman 2011). It is also the case that many countries, particularly developing ones, have abundant natural resources which make them key locations for extractive industries whose activities, by definition, bring a heavy environmental cost. According to the World Bank (2011), close to one third of the wealth of low-income countries comes from their 'natural capital' which includes forests, protected areas, agricultural lands, energy and minerals. For years activists have berated the mining industry for its poor track record on environmental pollution, human rights violations and displacement of indigenous peoples (Evans et al. 2002). The oil industry too has been accused of double standards when it operates in developing countries (Okanta and Douglas 2001). The activities of firms such as Shell in the Niger Delta, Nigeria and Texaco in Ecuador have attracted global attention as a result of activist exposure and high profile legal actions against those companies (Frynas 2000; Newell 2001a; Garvey and Newell 2005). Zarsky (2006: 395) meanwhile finds that:

> While there is little evidence that MNCs select investment sites on the basis of lower environmental standards, it seems safe to conclude that many perform below standards of global best practice once they get there. They do not, in other words, actively seek out a 'pollution haven' but, if the local environmental regulation is weak, create one through their operations.

Others have found that, more significant than the lowering of standards, may be the stalling of the introduction of new environmental regulations

(WWF 1999). Many have observed a 'chilling' or even a 'deepfreeze' effect on countries' environmental regulations whereby reforms are not undertaken, or new policies either not introduced or not implemented for fear of deterring investors (Zarsky 2006). For example, in response to pressure from the US government on behalf of its soybean exporters, the Chinese government delayed plans to introduce a series of more restrictive biosafety measures (Newell 2008b). Evidence of positive upgrading is less reliant on state regulation which tends to set minimum requirements of companies, but can rather be found when globally networked firms adopt progressive environmental stances or sign up to standards and codes, discussed below, which they then insist global suppliers comply with. The global retailer Walmart, for example, as part of its commitment to reduce greenhouse gases by 20 per cent by 2012 at its existing stores, clubs and distribution centres around the world, is seeking to eliminate 20 million metric tons of greenhouse gas emissions from its global supply chain by the end of 2015. When a company as powerful as Walmart decides on such a course of action, the knock-on effects on other retailers and suppliers can be enormous. As the company itself claims, 'As we make progress, we plan to share our innovations throughout the supply chain, which we believe will create a ripple effect and magnify these solutions on a global scale' (Walmart 2011).

It is also important, however, to differentiate between countries regarding the extent to which the 'greening of business' has taken place (Utting 2002). It is now commonplace for larger companies based in the global North to claim that they adopt the principles of sustainable development in their investment decision making. Among globally connected industry associations in the developing world (such as the Makati Business Club in the Philippines or the Confederation of Indian Industry), and among businesses seeking contracts with more environmentally conscious buyers, the discourse and practice of corporate environmentalism is being diffused, picked up and used in marketing and export strategies. However, it remains the case that many of the drivers of CSR (corporate social responsibility), including government incentives, civil society watchdogs and consumer and investor pressure, are currently under-developed in many parts of the world (Newell and Frynas 2007). Consistent with the 'trading up' argument described in chapter 4, it appears to be the case that firms within countries with strong trading ties to overseas markets, where compliance with tougher environmental regulations is expected, will have higher standards than firms in parts of sub-Saharan Africa, for example, that are more isolated from such global pressures.

The Governance of Production

It is clear from the preceding discussion that investment by TNCs can bring social and environmental benefits as well as be hugely exploitative, depending on who and where we are talking about. What determines which outcome ensues is, arguably, regulation and governance: the existence, or not, of clear and enforced standards of conduct and mechanisms for ensuring and overseeing the distribution of benefits from investment. In the absence of this, we find evidence of export processing zones, enclave economies (Gallagher and Zarsky 2007), sites of production exempt from the regulations that apply to other economic actors (such as special economic zones), or instances of short-term socially disruptive and environmentally destructive forms of investment aimed at extracting the largest amount of resources in the shortest time frame possible. The power to create regulation and negotiate terms with powerful corporate actors is, of course, highly unevenly distributed. So who governs global production and how?

Building on what was said in chapters 1–3, answering this question accurately means keeping an open mind about what governance is and who the relevant governance actors are. Here, I look firstly at attempts to regulate the environmental responsibilities of TNCs at the national and international level by states and international organizations in the face of globalizing forms of production. I then look at forms of private and self-regulation that producers themselves have created in the form of codes of conduct, certification and labelling schemes and voluntary commitments to reduce environmental pollution. The final section then looks at attempts by a diverse range of environmental NGOs and movements to contest the limits of existing modes of governance and to construct alternatives.

Contemporary interest in regulation is born of concerns about the continued lack of effective regulation of TNCs at the international level (see box 5.1). Critics point to the fact that there is little recognition in international environmental agreements of the role of TNCs in causing social and environmental problems (Chatterjee and Finger 1994). The issue of TNC regulation was dropped from the UNCED agenda and, while Agenda 21 includes recommendations that affect TNCs, it does not take the form of a code of conduct. An international code of conduct to regulate the activities of TNCs has been on the international agenda since the 1970s, however. The UN Centre for TNCs (UNCTC) was set up in 1973, largely at the request of developing country governments amid concern about the power of TNCs, but was unable to conclude negotiations on a code of conduct.

Box 5.1   International business regulation in brief

- 1970s: New International Economic Order (NIEO): Calls for tighter regulation of TNCs
- 1973: UNCTC set up
- Early 1970s: UN Draft Code of Conduct for TNCs
- 1970s–1980s: UNCTC (UN Centre on Transnational Corporations)
- 1976: OECD Declaration and Guidelines on MNEs (revised in 2000)
- 1977: ILO Tripartite Declaration of Principles Concerning MNE and Social Policy
- 1980: Set of Principles on Restrictive Business Practices approved by the UN General Assembly
- 1985: UN Guidelines for Consumer Protection
- 1999: Sullivan Principles announced as a code of conduct for the promotion of human rights among corporations
- 2000: The UN Global Compact is launched encouraging companies to follow ten principles of social and environmental responsibility
- 2002: Proposals for a UN Corporate Accountability Convention

---

This failure was explained by conflicts of interest between developed and developing countries and the opposition of the United States, in particular, and in 1993 the CTC was restructured to become the Commission on International Investment and Transnational Corporations, housed within the United Nations Conference on Trade and Development.

Guidelines and standards promoted by bodies such as the International Labour Organization (ILO) (The Tripartite Declaration of Principles Concerning Multinational Enterprises (MNEs) and Social Policy) and the OECD (such as the OECD Guidelines on MNEs) are not widely known and therefore rarely used, are entirely voluntary and without sanction, and are outdated, compared even with companies' own codes of conduct (McLaren 2000). Instead, the importance of these agreements may be that they act as benchmarks for other regulatory initiatives and private codes (Jenkins et al. 2002). In addition, as Muchlinski (2001: 24) notes,

> Although the OECD guidelines are non-binding, they do represent a con-
> sensus on what constitutes good corporate behaviour in an increasingly

global economy. Furthermore, they are clear that home countries of TNCs have a moral duty to ensure that the standards contained in the guidelines are maintained worldwide.

This embodies the hope that TNCs, through their operations, globalize responsible environmental conduct.

Whilst innovative and ambitious, national and regional attempts to advance the legal debate about the obligations of TNCs when they invest overseas have also not progressed very far. There have been resolutions before the European Parliament on the creation of a code of conduct for European MNCs operating in developing countries, which sought to set standards that EU companies would have to adopt wherever they operate (Ward 2000), but mandatory approaches have so far been resisted (Davidsson 2002). At national level, there have been attempts to secure similar provisions imposing best practice obligations and a duty of care on corporations (in the UK and Australia, for example) to adopt the same standards throughout their global operations (Australian Senate 2000; CORE 2010). There have also been moves within developing countries to recognize the right of citizens to hold TNCs accountable for personal and environmental injuries committed abroad. The NGO coalition AIDA (the Interamerican Association for Environmental Defense), in Costa Rica, for example, called for a bill 'that would officially recognize the right of Costa Rican citizens to bring suits abroad against foreign corporations for environmental and other damages caused in Costa Rica' (cited in Ward 2000: 23).

What lies behind these initiatives is a particular concern about the perceived imbalance between the rights and responsibilities of TNCs. The history of business regulation reveals an imbalance between the promotion and protection of investor rights over investor responsibilities (Muchlinski 1999): regulation *for* business rather than regulation *of* business (Newell 2001b). The attempt to create a Multilateral Agreement on Investment (MAI) and the WTO's TRIPs agreement are examples of regulation *for* business aimed at facilitating investment opportunities and creating protection for investments. Protection of investor rights can include provisions such as in NAFTA, which permit companies to challenge governments and local authorities about restrictions on their activities (see chapter 4) and which set a precedent for later Free Trade Agreements (FTAs) such as the Central America–Dominican Republic Free Trade Agreement (CAFTA-DR). It also includes the creation of bodies to address investor disputes such as the International Centre for Settlement of Investment Disputes (ICSID) of the

---

Box 5.2   Rebalancing investor rights and responsibilities

- The protection of investors (and the use of law and arbitration) is a means to the end of advancing public welfare and must not be treated as an end it itself.

- Foreign investment can have harmful as well as beneficial impacts on society and it is the responsibility of governments to encourage the beneficial and limit the harmful.

- The rights of states to regulate on behalf of public welfare should not be subordinated to the interests of investors where the right is exercised in good faith and for a legitimate purpose.

- The award of damages in investment arbitration poses a serious threat to democratic choice and the capacity of governments to act in the public interest.

- Private citizens, local communities and civil society organizations (CSOs) should be given rights to participate in decisions which affect their rights and interests including in investor-state disputes or contract renegotiation.

- Investment contracts should be concluded and implemented with public accountability and openness in mind.

Source: *Public Statement on the International Investment Regime*, 9 August 2010

World Bank as well as generic investment treaties of which by 2010 there were 5,900. On average four investment treaties were signed per week in 2009 (UNCTAD 2010). Attempts not only to protect the exit and entry options of TNCs, but also confer them with rights to challenge and reverse the public policies of sovereign governments in the ways noted above, have provoked particular ire. Box 5.2 summarizes key arguments put forward in a public statement by a group of lawyers and academics, including this author, concerned about the current imbalance between rights and responsibilities in the investment regime. These trends provide further evidence of what Gill calls the 'new constitutionalism' which refers to efforts 'to develop a politico-legal framework for the reconstitution of capital on a world scale and thus the intensification of market forms of discipline ... The new constitutionalism seeks to reinforce a process whereby government policies are increasingly accountable to (international) capital and thus to market forces' (1995b: 78–9).

Market-based Regulation and Private Governance

In the absence of effective international public regulation of the environmental responsibilities of corporations, companies have been left with a large degree of discretion regarding how to define and act upon their environmental responsibilities in the different jurisdictions in which they operate simultaneously. In this vacuum we have seen an enormous proliferation in private sector initiatives in sectors ranging from forestry and fisheries to chemicals, cement production and mining. Examples include certification schemes such as Forestry and Marine Stewardship Councils (Murphy and Bendell 1997; Cashore et al. 2004; Gulbrandsen 2010), disclosure projects such as those launched for carbon and water use, or sector-wide initiatives such as the Cement Sustainability Initiative or, going back much further, the Responsible Care programme of the chemical industry established in 1985. Codes of conduct among leading companies are now commonplace in the global North and many of those firms investing overseas are insisting that their suppliers and partners adopt the same principles, as we saw in the case of the retail giant Walmart above. In the energy sector, leading energy firms and large users of energy such as the chemical industry have started to measure their own emissions and set their own targets for emissions reductions. From the company's point of view, this brings benefits such as saving money through reduced use of energy, first-mover advantages that come from developing new technologies and production processes to meet the targets, and the public and employee credibility generated from being seen as an environmentally responsible company. Some global companies such as BP and Shell have also set policy precedents by establishing their own intra-firm emissions trading schemes that pre-empted those set up by states to enable different parts of the company to achieve these targets in the most flexible way possible.

The trend towards the embrace of voluntary measures reflects the preference among firms to set their own standards appropriate to their own circumstances in a way which pre-empts the need for state intervention. The timing of the development of the Responsible Care initiative of the chemical industry, mentioned above, can be understood as an attempt by the industry to demonstrate a willingness and ability to get its own house in order in the face of a rising chorus of demands for far more stringent regulation in the wake of the Bhopal chemical disaster in 1984, which killed at least 20,000 people. Again, whatever their origins, the global ripple effects can be significant. Responsible Care has been adopted in developing countries such as Mexico and Brazil through a process described as 'exporting environmentalism' (Garcia-Johnson 2000).

Private standards also help to reduce transaction costs, as well as afford firms an advantage over smaller producers that may be excluded from markets by their inability to conform with more demanding standards. Environmental management systems such as ISO 14001 or ISO 26000, created by the International Organization for Standardization, discussed in chapter 4, are increasingly popular for this reason. While traditionally such standards have tended only to apply to larger firms that can afford the compliance costs and those seeking access to developed country markets, increasingly SMEs are seeking ISO certification in order to serve as subcontractors for ISO-certified enterprises. It is clear, then, that global market pressures from buyers and consumers increasingly exercise as significant an influence on environmental policy practice in many parts of the world as the international agreements which governments sign up to.

The story of the move towards private governance and self-regulation, as well as offering a way for businesses to define regulation on their own terms in response to environmental pressures, also has to be understood as a product of neo-liberal ideas about the appropriate role of the state that were discussed in chapter 1. State-based 'command-and-control' environmental regulation has been subject to sustained criticism from key actors such as the World Bank on the grounds that it is excessively bureaucratic, inflexible, inefficient and costly, as well as ineffective at delivering the change in behaviour that it intends. Instead, market-based policy tools for incentivizing positive action and deterring polluting activities have been supported and financed. The World Bank (2000) report *Greening Industry: New Roles for Communities, Markets and Governments*, for example, makes a strong case for moving beyond a 'one size fits all' approach to pollution control, advocating pollution rating systems and forms of disclosure as well as more familiar prescriptions for national level economic reforms such as privatization, removal of subsidies and trade liberalization.

Such interventions raise the question of who is served by prevailing modes of regulation. While many of the CSR tools described above undoubtedly have an effect on the behaviour of some companies, especially those seeking to demonstrate renewed commitment to address an issue for which they have been criticized in the past, or that are vulnerable to brand name damage, they are arguably less effective at holding to account the majority of firms around the world not subject to those pressures and that do not report on their activities, CSR or otherwise. Voluntary meas-ures and self-regulation assume both high levels of trust and a responsible company serious about regulating the social and environmental impacts of its activities. This assumption disregards the reasons why many companies choose to operate in locations where labour is cheap and natural resources abundant, where social and environmental impacts are inevitably large, but less regulated than in their home countries (Newell 2005a).

The state plays a complex and problematic role in all of this, simulta-neously cast as rights enforcer and rights violator (Newell and Wheeler 2006). This is so because the state is the duty bearer for the protection of human rights and the implementation of environmental obligations but, as discussed in chapter 2, also increasingly operates as a 'competition state' (Cerny 1995) subject to the disciplines of global capital; a situation that means pressures to create a conducive investment climate often trump the protection of citizens' rights of access to, and control over, natural resources. This, indeed, is the source of many of the conflicts touched upon in the last chapter between indigenous groups and their states over land for oil or mineral extraction. Measures for the regulation of produc-tion which imply a key role for the state may exaggerate either the degree of state capacity that exists, and/or the freedom and willingness that states have to regulate and discipline business actors (Newell 2008f). As my work in India revealed (Newell 2005a), even the state Pollution Control Boards exercise, in reality, only a limited degree of control over the companies whose pollution levels they are charged with monitoring and reporting on in the face of a competition strategy aimed at attracting businesses to a resource abundant area with cheap labour and undemanding environmen-tal regulation. Underlining the importance of state willingness, as well as capacity to act, O'Rourke (2004: 10), based on his work in Vietnam, notes:

> The state, and in particular local environmental agencies, even when they have training and equipment, are rarely autonomous or powerful enough to implement tough regulations on industry. Put simply, it is not just capacity, but incentives within the state which are critical.

In sum, then, the nature of existing forms of national, global and private governance of production has been shaped by a combination of shifting alignments of material drivers and interests, institutional politics, and competition among powerful discourses and counter-discourses about, what in the end, amounts to divergent views about the appropriate role of business in society. At a material level the impetus has been the need for minimal and consistent operating standards (in the case of the ISO, for example), to reduce transaction costs of having to adapt to so many diverse standards across the many markets in which TNCs function (as with OECD and WTO provisions), experienced as barriers to capital accumulation. This has combined with the need to assure consumers that in an economy where sites of production and consumption are increasingly distanced from one another, that the products they buy are produced in responsible and sustainable ways (as with private certification schemes). The institutions and standards considered appropriate to this task reflect these imperatives, emphasizing voluntarism, branding and global reach. They have been enhanced and legitimated by powerful discourses about the positive and essential role of business in delivering sustainable development emanating from businesses themselves, their allies in government and international institutions increasingly keen to forge partnerships with capital (through initiatives such as the Global Compact), as well as a growing industry of environmental service providers, consultants and entrepreneurs for whom there is a strong 'business case' for sustainable development.

Contesting Production

Where public regulation, either national or international, is limited, non-existent or not enforced, as is so often the case, and perhaps especially so in the majority world, and action by industry itself does not go far enough, activists have stepped into the fold developing their own forms of regulation in conflictive and collaborative ways, creating their own mechanisms of governance to incentivize responsible environmental action and penalize polluters. This has been referred to as 'civil regulation': civil society-based regulation of the private sector (Bendell 2000; Newell 2000a; Zadek 2001). It takes as its point of departure and justification for action the lack of effective regulation by states unwilling or unable (or both) to address corporate irresponsibility, or by corporations themselves who may promote acts of corporate responsibility but have few incentives or collective means to confront corporate wrong-doing. These strategies respond to a perceived 'governance deficit', in that the global power of TNCs is not adequately matched by existing regulatory instruments. The limited scope of existing regulation of the environmental impact of companies' activities means that groups have sought to develop their own mechanisms of corporate accountability by forging alliances with consumers, institutional investors and companies themselves.

In considering ways in which civil society groups are contesting prevailing modes of governance, I focus, firstly on civil regulation aimed at holding companies to account for their environmental responsibilities, and, secondly, transnational litigation against companies accused of negligence in one of their overseas operations. Here, it is often the absence or breakdown of effective regulation that makes litigation a last resort strategy for communities blighted by industrial hazards and environmental harm. Both approaches provide interesting insights into the sources and possibilities of non-state regulation in a context of globalization and contribute to our understanding of the prospects of embedding economic activities in social frameworks supportive of sustainable development.

Civil Regulation

Civil regulation describes broad repertoires of protest and engagement that attempt, in very different ways, to exercise social control over global capital (Newell 2000b; 2001a; Bendell and Murphy 2002). Zadek (2001: 56) describes them in the following way:

> Civil regulations . . . are manifestations of essentially political acts that can affect business performance through their influence on market conditions . . . they can best be understood as non-statutory regulatory frameworks governing corporate affairs. They lie between the formal structures of public (statutory) regulation and market signals generated by more conventional individual and collective preferences underpinned by the use and exchange value of goods and services.

The term incorporates a range of 'liberal' strategies of engagement with business that seek to work with and through the market to achieve reform, examples being the negotiation of codes of conduct, shareholder activism and the creation of standards of certification, as well as more critical modes of engagement that aim to contest and control corporate power. These include the organization of consumer boycotts, the creation of 'watchdog' groups that monitor the activities of TNCs, as well as traditional protest strategies of naming and shaming and resistance (Newell 2001b). Examples of liberal strategies include the creation of certification schemes in the forestry and marine sectors or project-specific collaborations between companies such as McDonalds and the environmental NGO Environmental Defense (Murphy and Bendell 1997).

Critical strategies include the activities of groups such as Partizans and BayerWatch which monitor the activities of the minerals giant Rio Tinto and the chemical company Bayer, respectively, sector-based watchdogs such as OilWatch, or generic groups such as CorporateWatch or Multinational Monitor that take a broader cross-sectoral view of TNC activity. Popular boycotts include those organized against Shell around allegations of its complicity in environmental and human rights abuses in Nigeria and against the oil company Exxon for its hostile opposition to action on climate change (Newell 2008e). Not only is it claimed that such strategies provide 'an instrument of accountability for ecological performance' (Mason 2005: 150), a critical dimension of their effectiveness also derives from the construction of mechanisms of *civil redress* (Mason 2005: 150). Loss of market value or consumer confidence, tarnished public reputation and disaffection among shareholders are the tools of persuasion and coercion that serve to 'harden the environmental accountability demands levelled at corporations' (Mason 2005: 151).

While many of the existing forms of private governance discussed above may encourage 'responsible' business to go 'beyond compliance', they provide few checks and balances on the operations of 'irresponsible' business for whom strategies of regulation, sanction and protest continue to be key drivers of change. This is particularly problematic for communities affected by such investment practices that are rarely identified as legitimate stakeholders by business and lack sufficient influence within government policy making to articulate and defend their concerns. In this context, the resort to informal and often confrontational strategies is hardly surprising. Many of the tools and strategies used to hold companies to account to such positive effect in Europe and North America by Northern-based NGOs and unions, for example, are not available to poorer and less well mobilized communities (Garvey and Newell 2005). These include boycotts, where purchasing power and size of market are key; shareholder activism, where access to finance is also key; or accountability tools such as codes of conduct and partnerships over specific issues (Newell 2000a). Codes and partnerships in particular imply a degree of leverage on the part of the communities and a level of equity between business and civil society actors that is often lacking in most parts of the world. There is clearly then an important difference between a well-resourced and globally networked NGO engaging a company in a dialogue about a firm's social and environmental responsibilities, and a poorer community without significant resources or access to global networks, confronting investors from a position of weakness and often dependency.

This is not to suggest that agreements between companies and communities are not possible, as there are cases where this has occurred. The mining company Rio Tinto, for example, cites cases of agreements concluded with aboriginal groups covering socio-economic and environmental issues as well as questions of participation (Rio Tinto 2011). The case studies that adorn the brochures of the World Bank-Care International *Business Partners for Development* initiative also seek to demonstrate the possibility of 'best practice' business–community engagements. And there is evidence of what O'Rourke (2004) calls 'community-driven regulation' (CDR), which draws on the potential complementarities between traditional state strategies of business regulation and the effect of community-based mobilizations for corporate accountability. What results is the co-production of regulation, requiring both 'the energies and actions of average community members and the responses of front-line environmental agencies' (O'Rourke 2004: xvii). It also 'advances a form of accountability politics, raising the question of why the state is not doing its job' (O'Rourke 2004: 221) with regard to both the communities it is meant to serve and the industries it is meant to regulate towards that end.

Lack of material and political resources also often means, however, that groups resort to micro-strategies of resistance or 'weapons of the weak' to coin the title of James Scott's famous work (Scott 1985). Petty sabotage and blockades are among the forms of resistance that the powerless have adopted to express their disapproval of a corporation's activities. Rowell (1996: 266) cites the example of the Penan indigenous peoples of Sarawak, Malaysia: 'Predominantly illiterate and without any kind of political representation, the Penan have used the only option open to them to stop the logging. They have been manning non-violent blockades across the logging roads.' O'Rourke, meanwhile, describes how government officials in Vietnam acknowledged that spontaneous 'gatherings in front of the factory' in protest at chemical pollution of a cooperative fish pond, acted as a 'major pressure' on *Viet Tri Chemicals* to address their grievances. Where channels of dialogue with business are not open and the government unresponsive, direct action can draw attention to issues that would otherwise remain in the shadows.

As important as isolated, or even combined, acts of resistance are in raising awareness, shaming or provoking action, they are clearly not up to the job of effectively regulating business. Whether we chose to acknowledge it or not, then (and many CSR approaches do not), states are implicated in all aspects of the debate about corporate responsibility and accountability (Newell and Frynas 2007). States, though clearly some more than others, are in a position to create a positive enabling environment in which communities can claim and secure rights. Such interventions can take a number of forms from creating and enforcing rights of access to information and disclosure, to guaranteeing due process in consultations around investment decisions, and providing for adequate redress. In cases of extreme and repeated negligence by a company, governments retain the power to revoke its licence to operate. It is the combined inability and/or unwillingness, of states to perform these proactive roles, however, that provides the impetus for the forms of community-mobilizing for corporate accountability described here.

Litigation

For many poorer communities living in areas where the environmental impacts of production are effectively not governed, either by state legislation or by acts of corporate responsibility, it is unsurprising to find an enormous amount of community mobilization (Garvey and Newell 2005). Often this seeks to challenge and operate beyond the law because of the limits of pursuing environmental justice through the law. There are many barriers which prevent poorer groups from using the law to pursue claims of environmental injustice. These include financial disincentives, lack of legal literacy, distrust of legal processes and intimidation (Newell 2001a). Even if a legal case is successful, compensation is often only received by a small number of community members, for example those with a title to the land (which often excludes women, landless peasants and poorer castes), and takes a long time to secure. Perhaps most importantly of all, compensation, by definition, is a reactive strategy, often of little use if livelihood alternatives have been destroyed.

The experience of the environmental justice movement in the US has led critics to question the value of legal over other political strategies that communities can adopt to press for change (Newell and Lekhi 2006). Often bringing a legal case creates expectations of a positive outcome and yet 'lawsuits take place in a forum in which the resources of private corporations and government entities far outweigh community resources' (Cole and Foster 2001: 47). One key lesson Cole and Foster (2011: 47) suggest the groups have learned is that 'while legal action brings much needed attention to environmental justice struggles, legal strategies rarely address what is, in essence, a larger political and structural problem' of exclusion from decision making and or systematic and disproportionate exposure of poorer populations to environmental harm. The same is true of the sorts of global environmental inequalities which the current international legal system is weakly positioned to address.

Nonetheless, in the context of the broader picture of deficits in the global governance of production described above, a number of high-profile cases of transnational environmental litigation (also referred to as foreign direct liability) suggest that holding parent companies to account for the conduct of their subsidiaries, wherever they may operate, provides a potential channel for ensuring that TNCs do not exploit lower environmental standards and poor enforcement regimes at the expense of workers and their environment; and provides a possible vehicle, therefore, for internationalizing standards of protection.

Foreign direct liability refers to two approaches to holding companies legally accountable in their home jurisdiction for negative environmental or health and safety impacts, or complicity in human rights abuses in countries where they operate (Ward 2000: 2). Firstly, appeals have been made using the Alien Tort Claims Act (ATCA) of 1789 in the US, which gives district courts the power to hear civil claims from foreign citizens for injuries caused by action 'in violation of the law of nations or a treaty of the United States' (Shamir 2004). Actions for compensation are based on allegations of corporate complicity in violations of human rights or principles of international environmental law. Examples include litigation against Texaco over environmental damage in Ecuador (Wray 2000; Shamir 2004) and Shell, in relation to alleged human rights abuses in Nigeria (Ward 2000). Key to the successful use of the Alien Tort Claims Act is demonstrating that through a 'symbiotic' relationship with the state, a company is culpable for a violation of international law.[2]

A second type of case has also been brought against parent companies in the UK, Australia and Canada, claiming that they have a responsibility to ensure that home country standards of care apply to subsidiaries, wherever they may be based. A few landmark settlements have been won in this regard, setting important legal precedents. In the Thor case (*Sithole and Others v Thor Chemicals Holdings Ltd*), twenty workers who suffered potentially lethal mercury poisoning in a factory in South Africa won substantial damages (£1.3 million) from the UK parent company because of negligent design, transfer and supervision of an intrinsically hazardous process. In a case brought against Cape plc by workers at their asbestos plant in South Africa for negligence (*Lubbe et al. v Cape plc*), the issue was not that the company had breached British or South African law but that, knowing the harmful effects of asbestos (given the levels accepted in

---

2 The case brought against Unocal for the use of forced labour on their gas pipeline project in Burma, for example, had to demonstrate evidence of clear complicity with the state's use of forced labour.

Britain), the company adopted lower standards in its operations in South Africa (Waldman 2011).

The benefits of bringing such cases include the possibility of generating positive reforms. For example, despite the failings of the case brought against Union Carbide for the Bhopal gas disaster in 1984 (in terms of the amount of compensation that was settled upon, for example), Sripada (1989) argues, the Bhopal incident has prompted further action by governments and corporations. Following the case, TNCs everywhere have been under greater popular and government pressure to disclose information regarding environmental impact and safety and to put in place proper risk assessment and avoidance measures, some of which are covered by the Responsible Care initiative discussed above. Governments, in turn, have also responded by promulgating new environmental legislation or by making existing legislation more stringent. Even if not successful in adequately compensating the victims of corporate negligence, therefore, the act of bringing cases against TNCs can prompt positive reforms.

On the other hand, there are many limitations to using litigation as a strategy for holding companies to account. Legal strategies often reduce complex social problems to questions of monetary compensation. The high levels of legal illiteracy among poorer groups alienates potential users of the law and poorer communities often express distrust and suspicion towards the legal system and the lawyers whom they feel often exploit the plight of the poor for their own ends. In the aftermath of the Bhopal gas leak, US lawyers descended on the slum dwellings of the city, looking for plaintiffs to bring a case against Union Carbide (on the condition that the lawyer received a substantial sum of any award by the Court) (Anderson and Ahmed 1996).

In addition, a key problem in bringing legal suits for negligence on health and environmental grounds, is identifying cause-effect relationships between manifested effects and particular pollutants, as well as deciphering direct from indirect effects. Common law traditions, in particular, establish high requirements for scientific evidence. The technical nature of the industrial processes and the fact that the burden of proof rests on the plaintiff to establish that an environmental standard has been violated, by recourse to independent and reliable technical and scientific data, excludes all but the most wealthy or technically competent from bringing a case. Added to this are concerns about the level of funds required to sponsor such cases and to cover the payment of fees to the defendant in the event that the case is unsuccessful. Intimidation by governments against communities considering bringing cases has also been a key deterrent, especially where governments have often created strong incentives for companies to locate there in the first place. Research on Shell in Nigeria (Frynas 1998, 1999), for example, shows how threats to the personal security of potential plaintiffs have deterred them from bringing cases against the company in seeking compensation for damage to their lands and loss of livelihood earnings.

Community legal actions are also often rejected on the grounds that they do not represent the specific grievances of individuals involved in the case. In Ecuador, for example, unlike the 'class action' system in the US, courts abide strictly by the principle of direct interest in a case. Activist Norman Wray (2000: 6), engaged in a case against Texaco, sums up the situation thus: 'in practice if the trial goes on in Ecuador, the 30 thousand people that constitute this class action suit, have to sue individually . . . This will provoke chaos in the civil court.' India, on the other hand, has an innovative system of public interest litigation in which organizations and individuals not part of the affected class can represent them (Cottrell 1992; Anderson and Ahmed 1996). Nevertheless, in mass tort cases, where large sections of a poor community have been affected by a damaging company investment, issues of who is entitled to speak on behalf of the victims serve to stall or slow the legal process.

The common law legal doctrine of *forum non conveniens* has been the principal means by which transnational cases against companies have been stalled. Whilst the choice of forum is normally the prerogative of the plaintiff, the defendant can invoke the principle to claim that the proposed forum is 'inconvenient', where there is another 'clearly and distinctly more appropriate forum' where justice between the parties will be done. Plaintiffs often argue that, rather than deterring plaintiffs from 'forum-shopping' in order to access higher levels of compensation, this doctrine allows companies to engage in 'reverse forum-shopping' to evade their obligations in their home country. The World Development Movement (1998: 7) argues that:

> such shopping around [by plaintiffs] is not the reason people from developing countries bring cases to Britain or the US. For most of them, it is their only hope of obtaining justice. The choice is not therefore between different levels of compensation, but between justice and no justice at all.

The underdevelopment of the legal personality of corporations means that different components of TNCs are legally accountable only to the laws of the country in which they are operating. This makes it necessary for campaigners involved in transnational litigation to 'pierce the corporate veil' in demonstrating a clear chain of command between the headquarters of a company and its subsidiaries. Difficult in any tort case, the barrier becomes almost unsurpassable when parent companies often claim they are merely stock or shareholders and that they are only connected for book-keeping purposes. Where a plant design or technology has been designed and exported by the parent company for use in a subsidiary country, in the knowledge of the potential dangers associated with its use, the connections are easier to establish (as in the *Thor* case mentioned above). Nevertheless, it is difficult for plaintiffs to identify units within the company that were chiefly responsible for making key decisions. The Indian government made this point to the US Court hearing the Bhopal case: 'Persons harmed by the acts of a multinational corporation are not in a position to isolate which unit of the enterprise caused the harm, yet it is evident that the multinational enterprise that caused the harm is liable for such harm' (Baxi and Paul 1986: v).

As a strategy for addressing the immediate needs of communities affected by damaging investments, litigation is often viewed as a last resort option because of the slowness,[3] complexity and costs of the process and the uncertain nature of the outcomes. For many of the reasons outlined above, pursuing cases against TNCs through foreign courts is not a realistic strategy for communities that are the victim of acts of social or environmental negligence. Working to avoid these problems in the first place, undertaking impact assessments, agreeing standards or negotiating conditions on investments may avoid the need for these cases. Many companies, concerned for their reputation, will respond to such an approach. The problem comes with irresponsible companies, those intent on exploiting lower standards in countries where governments are either unwilling or unable to ensure that adequate safeguards are put in place. This is where a legal approach may be necessary. The suitability of litigation will rest upon the type of change being sought: prevention, exposure, or compensation. The goal will determine the point at which legal remedies stop being useful and informal patterns of soft or civil regulation become important, or perform useful supplementary functions.

The current popularity of *forum non conveniens* as grounds for not hearing cases in foreign courts, the difficulty of using the Alien Tort Claim Act and, in many cases, the impenetrability of the corporate veil, means that companies looking to exploit lower environmental and social standards

---

3 Often up to two years for preliminary appeals, two years substantive trial and two years appellate proceedings.

can often do so without fear of meaningful legal redress. Multi-pronged, multi-level legal and non-legal strategies combining formal and informal mechanisms that reinforce a system of obligations for TNCs are needed to reverse this situation. Achieving a 'deterrent effect' is critical, whereby companies build safeguards into their operations for fear of the penalties they may accrue for acting irresponsibly. This was an issue raised in the Bhopal case, for example, where a call was made for damages 'sufficient to deter' Union Carbide and all TNCs 'involved in similar business activities' from 'wilful, malicious and wanton disregard of the rights and safety of the citizens of India' (Baxi and Dhanda 1990). As well as securing short-term compensation, this surely has to be the aim of litigation; not just making companies liable for their activities wherever they happen to be based, but ensuring that weak systems of governance which expose the poor and their environment to risks that would not be acceptable in richer countries, are not a legitimate basis for comparative advantage.

Interestingly, a combination of the limitations of civil regulation and transnational litigation, as well as their growing popularity, may generate demands from the public and industry themselves for new international and national binding standards. The limited applicability of foreign direct liability in many legal systems and the confusion surrounding many non-state labelling and certification schemes, has heightened the need for broader forms of public regulation. In the legal area, there have been moves, for example, to harmonize jurisdictions and to advance negotiations towards a multilateral convention on civil jurisdiction and judgments under the auspices of the Hague Conference on Private International Law (Muchlinski 2001). Yet corporate actors subject to such actions, or which fear the precedents they might establish, have lobbied hard to check moves aimed at strengthening the accountability of corporations for actions committed in other countries' jurisdictions. Shamir (2004: 636) documents corporate attempts to contain or bar use of the ATCA as part of a suite of strategies 'to stabilize the field around notions of corporate responsibility that are non-enforceable and not binding'. Bodies such as the International Chamber of Commerce (ICC) have demanded an end to the 'misuse' of ATCA by allowing 'foreign companies to be sued in US courts for alleged events in third countries'. The group 'USA-Engage', a coalition of hundreds of TNCs, meanwhile, has sought to discredit the involvement of commercial class action lawyers in the suits by alleging damages being sought by the lawyers are for themselves and not the victims in the case. Part of the smearing of those bringing such cases involves references to 'foreign nationals', 'unaccountable actors' and 'political organizations with unspecified agendas' (Shamir 2004: 652). Other business groups such as the National Foreign Trade Council, the National Association of Manufacturers and the US Chamber of Commerce advocating the elimination of the ATCA have done so by warning against 'American legal imperialism!' (Shamir 2004: 654).

There is an interesting tension that results from competing social forces: between pressures towards deregulation of some forms of social and environmental regulation from those seeking to access global markets with the minimum of costs on the one hand and those, on the other, who assert the need to create more stringent, globally applicable, forms of regulation such as the activists at the World Summit on Sustainable Development 2002 calling for a legally binding UN Corporate Accountability treaty. The World Investment Report for 2010 also observes that 'A dichotomy in investment policy trends is emerging. It is characterized by simultaneous moves to further investment liberalization and promotion on the one hand, and to increased investment regulation in pursuit of public policy objectives on the other' (UNCTAD 2010: xiii).

The appeal of public regulation is its ability to provide the consistency, transparency and enforceability that many civil regulation approaches lack. The history of weak public regulation of the corporate sector suggests, nevertheless, that it is no panacea. More likely is that we will be faced with a dense and interrelated set of regulatory approaches, both formal and informal, existing at multiple levels from the international down to the local level. The challenge is to ensure the combinations of measures adopted are responsive to the needs of those whose bear the highest price for irresponsible and unsustainable investment.

Beyond the realm of formal legal responsibilities, there have been efforts to create alternative arenas of accountability of transnational capital. For example, activists in Latin America have been able to form alliances with groups sympathetic to their plight and keen to expose acts of corporate irresponsibility by Northern-based firms adopting double standards when they operate in developing countries (World Development Movement 1998; Friends of the Earth 2003). The Permanent Peoples' Tribunal launched in Vienna in May 2006 on 'Neo-liberal policies and European TNCs in Latin America and the Caribbean' provided one such opportunity, allowing environmental activists from Uruguay to bring cases against the water companies Suez of France and Aguas de Barcelona and Bilbao from Spain, and Mapuche activists from Patagonia Argentina to provide evidence of alleged illegal sales of their land to foreign investors such as the Italian fashion retailer Benetton (Aborigen Argentino 2005). Their efforts build on a long history which dates back to 1979 of using independent 'peoples' tribunals to hear cases against governments and corporations. In 1996, after the session of Permanent Peoples' Tribunal on Industrial Hazards and Human Rights in Bhopal, 1992, the 'Charter on Industrial Hazards and Human Rights' was also created outlining the respective rights and responsibilities of citizens and corporations alike.

As Shamir notes (2004: 644) 'capitalism has always relied on critiques of the status quo to alert it to any untrammelled development of its current forms and to discover the antidotes required to neutralize opposition to the system'. The challenge for activists is the one Bauman (2002: 15) describes: 'to create and entrench such institutions of effective political action as can match the size and power of the already global economic forces and bring them under political scrutiny and ethical supervision'.

Conclusions

Production is a powerful, if not the central, driving force of social and environmental change. If the current globalization of the world's economy is to be compatible with any meaningful notion of sustainable development, how we produce (and of course consume) has to change profoundly. Change is required in the way we use labour and resources, in the networks of extraction, processing, distribution and transportation that allow goods and products to move around the world in ways which are antithetical to sustainability, and in the rules that govern these complex relationships that privilege market access over social protection and ecological resilience. Basic anomalies such as the limited liability that corporations enjoy, restrictive notions of duty of care and reluctance to impose extra-territorial obligations on firms that impede progress in these areas need to be addressed.

Corporate power has, so far, been effectively brought to bear to check initiatives aimed at increasing the accountability and responsibilities of global corporations in enforceable, tangible and legal ways, even as companies embrace the language of 'corporate citizenship'. The institutions and regulatory frameworks of global governance have managed to secure an emphasis on soft and non-binding notions of partnership and voluntary commitments when it comes to corporate responsibilities, while insisting on the full force of compensation and treaty obligations when it comes to investor accords and tribunals in the area of regulation *for* business. This is explained by the sorts of shifts in power and concepts used to describe them introduced in chapters 1–3 regarding 'disciplinary neo-liberalism', whereby the scope for legitimate state action and progressive democratic politics is circumscribed by global trade and investment accords and the rights of capital over states begin to take the form of a 'new constitutionalism', protected by international law.

This chapter has also told, however, a story of immense change in perceptions about the environmental and social responsibilities of business in society. While it is easy to confuse rhetoric for action, and to interpret the actions of high profile and vocal businesses at the forefront of corporate and social responsibility as evidence of wider change (which in reality is highly dispersed and uneven), it is the case that we have seen shifts in patterns of public regulation, the growth of private regulation and significant forms of contestation about the extent to which and ways in which business, society and ecology interact. With growing levels of market, political and social interaction and integration, norm diffusion, social expectations and supply chain pressures can be expected to globalize pressures for change. This will undoubtedly give rise to new attempts to accommodate and manage such pressures and to engage and co-opt critics to ensure that businesses' ability to accumulate capital is subject to minimal disruption.

There are plenty of grounds to be wary of heralding the greening of business. Corporate irresponsibility continues to be the norm in large parts of the world because of lack of state capacity or complicity, because of weak, non-existent or unenforced regulations and fundamentally because of the lack of incentives and inducements to behave differently. Even firms that have cast themselves as global leaders in corporate environmental responsibility continue to engage in highly polluting and destructive investments such as those in the tar oil sands in Canada, or increase the chances of catastrophic environmental damage by unnecessary risk taking, as with the BP oil spill in the Gulf of Mexico in 2010. Unsustainable development is profitable. Companies that accelerate it continue to be richly rewarded in the global economy we have today. A key challenge remains, therefore, identifying viable accumulation strategies in models of development that are socially just and environmentally sustainable, beyond the sort of niche markets and boutique 'green' products which we already have.

Contesting the structural power of capital to resist progressive change in the form of national regulation, taxation, and international law in the areas of occupational health and safety, environmental protection and accountability which has been used to such effect on so many occasions, remains a formidable challenge. The activism aimed at creating new mechanisms of corporate accountability, exposing double standards and constructing forms of civil regulation has an important role to play and a considerable track record of success to be proud of. Strategic engagement with powerful sectors of capital such as finance, whose power and influence can produce far-reaching reform in the way businesses invest and justify their actions, has also been hugely important (Paterson 1999; Newell and Paterson 2010). But the need for substantive shifts in models (and modes) of production and consumption remains. However compromised they are by their ties to and dependence upon the industries they are charged with regulating, states and international institutions are currently the only bodies and levels of authority we have at our collective disposal that are capable of steering society-wide change on the scale required and with the powers, should they chose to use them, to reward corporate responsibility and sanction corporate irresponsibility.

Chapter 6

Global Finance and the Environment: Gambling on Green

Introduction

Of all the aspects of contemporary globalization that cause most concern and have captured the imagination of commentators, activists and academics alike, global finance, with its volatility, seeming uncontrollability and capacity to destabilize entire economies, emerges as the frontrunner. 'Mad money' (Strange 1998) or 'hot money' are among the phrases used to describe the liberalization of global finance; 'hot' to describe the speed at which finance moves around the world and 'mad' to capture both its capacity to cause damage and the impulses it responds to. Following the instincts of speculators operating with a herd-like mentality, it can cause runs on currencies and dramatic and large-scale capital flight, driven by the pursuit of profitability at seemingly any (social and environmental) cost. As Helleiner (2011: 51) suggests, 'If the global economy is to be made more environmentally sustainable, this powerful "electronic herd" of global money will need to be steered in greener directions.'

The potential for destabilization associated with the contemporary system of 'casino capitalism' (Strange 1986) and the lack of effective global financial governance has generated calls, long before the financial crisis of 2008, for capital controls (Griffiths-Jones and Kimmis 1999) or at the very least, the sequencing of capital account liberalization. In addition to such measures, a growing number of activists and some politicians have demanded a new type of tax, either a Tobin tax, named after James Tobin, the economist who first proposed the idea (Coyle 1999) or a Robin Hood tax. The latter, named after the fictional English legend who notoriously stole from the rich to give to the poor, is a proposal for a tax of about 0.05 per cent on transactions such as stocks, bonds, foreign currency and derivatives that could raise £250 billion a year globally for poverty alleviation or environmental initiatives. Indeed, the pursuit of environmental goals such as tackling climate change, and raising the billions of dollars that will be necessary globally to adequately fund adaptation and mitigation measures

($100 billion a year by 2020 according to the Copenhagen Accord), are increasingly invoked as additional rationales for the adoption of such measures (Robin Hood Tax 2011).

The $1 trillion that changes hands every day in private financial markets, mainly through currency speculation and investments in stocks and bonds, has an obvious, if disputed and difficult to quantify, effect on the global environment and patterns of resource use. The pace of the eclipse of public by private finance is astounding. In 1992 public financial flows were still greater than private financial flows despite successive waves of liberalization in global finance. Yet even by 1996 private flows were more than five times larger (Ganzi et al. 1998). This growth has been driven both by individual and institutional investors in industrialized countries seeking higher returns and diversification by investing abroad, as well as the creation of new investment opportunities by the liberalization of 'emerging market' and 'economies in transition' (to advanced capitalism it is assumed).

Harnessing this acceleration and proliferation of private financial activity to the goal of sustainable development is hindered by several factors. The imperative of accumulating a short-term return creates an incentive structure that often conflicts with the timescales, decision-making processes and priorities required for addressing the long-term challenges of sustainable development. Venture capital is perhaps the most extreme example of this, where profits of up to ten times the original investment are sought within three to seven years on an investment. Private financial investment is clearly driven by the prospect of rapid returns from attractive accumulation sites in the global economy, not by where finance is most needed for sustainable development. Nevertheless, the much feted 'invisible' hand of the market has been held and lined with money to induce investment in sectors and areas of the world where it would not normally invest, through the interventions of governments and multilateral development banks. Yet the global spread of private investment remains uneven. Eighty per cent of private financial flows in the first half of the 1990s were captured by just 12 emerging market economies, none of which was in Africa (World Bank 1997b) and twenty years on BRIC countries (Brazil, Russia, India and China) continue to capture the lion's share of private financial flows to the developing world (UNCTAD 2010).

Alongside heightened interest in private finance, there is renewed interest in the politics of public aid amid the pursuit of the Millennium Development Goals which include the promotion of sustainable development. There has been a wave of debt-relief initiatives, some of which, as we will see below, are harnessed to the goal of sustainable development.

The World Bank and the IMF have also been thrust into the centre of debates about the greening of aid. It comes on the back of years of campaigning to reform the World Bank as a development actor, in particular, amid criticisms of its insensitivity to the needs of local communities hosting the mega-projects it sponsors and the high environmental impact of dams, roads and other infrastructural developments undertaken at its expense (Fox and Brown 1998; Edwards and Gaventa 2001). Such attention to the social and environmental impacts of aid has also extended to the use by states of public finance to support the private sector in the form of loans or export credits for example, which are also explored below.

Finance then, both public and private, is the lubricant of contemporary globalization and bears strongly on the contemporary politics of the environment. The activities and projects funded by the capital of private banks and the financial community and of bilateral and multilateral aid donors, constitute forms of environmental governance in their own right and produce ecological consequences as well as defining the parameters within which other forms of public and private environmental governance are created, or not. They are central, therefore, to our enquiry into the relationship between globalization and the environment. Despite this, as Helleiner (2011: 51) notes, while

> there are many studies of the environmental implications of lending by public international financial institutions such as the World Bank . . . the much larger flows of money associated with private financial markets have largely been neglected within environmental scholarship. This neglect is unfortunate since global financial markets are key drivers of the contemporary global economy.

As with the previous chapters, this chapter is divided as follows. In the first part, I discuss the political ecology of finance in its public and private forms. The second part explores the governance of finance through public and private institutions, while the final section explores the growing number of civil society campaigns that seek to strengthen and reform existing forms of governance as well as construct new forms of social and ecological control over capital flows.

The Political Ecology of Finance

Aid

Given the level of attention directed by activists, academics and policy makers to the relationship between aid and the environment (Hayter 1989;

Rich 1994; Keohane and Levy 1996), it is important to ask how significant aid transfers for the environment are, before also considering the environmental impacts of non-environmental aid. This is not an easy undertaking. In the case of climate change, for example, while many Annex I (developed country) parties have reported on official development assistance transfers, contributions to the Global Environment Facility (GEF) and activities implemented jointly through bilateral and multilateral channels, the UNFCCC (United Nations Framework Convention on Climate Change) Secretariat suggests that it has not been possible to quantify aid flows supportive of the Convention at an aggregate level due to a varying degree of reporting (UNFCCC 1997; Srivastava and Soni 1998). This issue arises in the context of current debates in the wake of the Copenhagen and Cancún summits about fast-start finance and commitments to create the Green Fund that will provide $100 billion a year by 2020 amid claims of double-counting, ambiguous baselines and deliberate misrepresentation of the purposes for which funds are being allocated. Indeed, questions of *additionality* and *conditionality* have a long history in policy debates on environment and development. At the time of the Rio summit on Environment and Development in 1992, developing countries expressed their concern that funds intended to assist them in fulfilling their commitments under the United Nations Conference on Environment and Development (UNCED) treaties would be additional to, rather than derived from, existing aid budgets. In the end the wealthiest countries were only willing to commit $125 billion of the $625 billion estimated to be required to implement the conference's programme of work on sustainable development.

Beyond the realm of aid explicitly labelled 'environmental', the World Bank in particular, has inevitably courted a great deal of attention from environmentalists because of a long history of funding large infrastructural projects (Goldman 2005). Whether it is the Pergau Dam project in Malaysia, the Polonoroeste project in Brazil or the Three Gorges or Narmada dams in China and India respectively, the world's leading multilateral development bank has been a key site in the contest over finance and the environment. The Polonoroeste scheme developed in the early 1980s, for example, sought to move poor settlers from urban areas in the south of Brazil to the northwest region in the Amazon forest. To facilitate this, a major highway was built into Rondônia state, the BR-364. As Clapp and Dauvergne (2005: 199) note: 'Huge swathes of forest were cut down and burned to build the highway and clear new land for the colonists with the aim of growing export crops.' The proportion of deforested area in the state increased from 1.7 per cent in 1978 to 16.1 per cent in 1991. Likewise, the dam proposed for India's Narmada valley served to produce one of the defining moments in India's history of environmental struggle with the mobilization of thousands of activists across the country (Mehta 2006). Such interventions raise profoundly the question of who bears the costs of 'development' and who captures the gains. They suggest that uneven forms of development within the state, along the lines of race, class and gender, can often be exacerbated by flows of external funding which enrich policy elites from the state or private sector and enable and embolden them to enact their own forms of dispossession against groups of their own people with whom they may be in conflict.

Though lessons have clearly been learnt since the early days of ignorance about the potential environmental effects of such large-scale projects, and the World Bank was quick to acknowledge previous errors upon the occasion of its 50th birthday in 1994 (Vidal 1994), activists chose to mark the milestone with the slogan '50 years is enough'. Evidence of organizational change included the creation of an environment department in 1987, the requirement from 1991 of an environmental impact assessment for all projects, and the establishment of an inspection panel in 1993 to improve accountability to project affected communities. Yet the incentive structures that operate within the Bank, discussed further below, and the failure to mainstream environmental concerns across all areas of the Bank's operations, mean it continues to exact a heavy environmental price through its day-to-day functioning. In this sense, it is not so much the spectacular large-scale infrastructural projects that are the only source of concern, even if they continue to bring about large-scale environmental devastation, because they are increasingly controlled by institutions such as the World Commission on Dams or targeted by highly effective environmental movements. The areas of greatest concern perhaps are the non-environmental areas of Bank activity, the core areas of macro-economic policy prescriptions that are more protected from scrutiny and debate, negotiated between state finance ministers and World Bank officials, but which generate the greatest environmental impacts in the long term. The large infrastructural projects, by virtue of their scale and the social and environmental disruption they visibly leave in their wake, attract more day-to-day attention, while the underlying model of export-led resource-intensive growth is not considered open to discussion.

To take one recent example of the failure to mainstream environmental concerns into mainstream lending, despite its rhetoric about being a leading actor on climate change (see below), the World Bank supported the $4.14 billion coal-powered 'Ultra Mega' 4,000 megawatt power plant in Gujarat, India, which will emit more carbon dioxide annually than the whole of Tunisia according to the US Department of Energy (Swan 2008). Moreover, a report by the Washington-based group the World Resources Institute (WRI) found that between 2005 and 2008 less than 30 per cent of the World Bank's lending to the energy sector integrated climate considerations into project decision making. As late as 2007, more than 50 per cent of the Bank's $1.8 billion energy sector portfolio did not include climate change considerations at all (WRI 2008).

Besides these sorts of project lending, the World Bank continues to play a key role in overseeing processes of structural adjustment in the developing world. Prescribing the removal of price controls and subsidies and promoting the privatization of key assets and the liberalization of major sectors, the package of structural adjustment measures required as a condition of World Bank loans inevitably have an impact on the environment as well as on poorer social groups whose access to key resources is affected. By altering price signals, the incentives to exploit particular resources are changed. While from an environmental perspective the removal of subsidies from environmentally damaging activities might be welcomed (as we saw in chapter 4), for example, pressure to adopt export-oriented models of economic growth can often produce negative environmental and social impacts. These result not just from the life cycle of production which involves transportation over long distances to reach consumers in distant export markets, but also packaging and the intensive use of land associated with industrialized forms of agriculture. The production of cotton, flowers and tobacco requires large-scale use of pesticides and fertilizers, with recognized adverse human and environmental side effects. Once again, exposure to those effects is socially differentiated because the work is conducted by informal, often seasonal women workers that are employed in the horticultural sector, for example, or by migrant labour from poorer areas surrounding agricultural zones (Barrientos et al. 1999). These are the social relations that political ecology traditions, highlighted in chapter 2, draw our attention to so usefully.

Price liberalization and currency devaluation, as we saw in the extreme case of the East Asian financial crisis, had the effect of encouraging the intensified production of export crops such as palm oil and rubber, as well as timber (Dauvergne 1999). In countries as diverse as Cameroon, Thailand and the Philippines, increases in tropical timber exports followed the adoption of adjustment reforms (Clapp and Dauvergne 2005). Yet the Bank's own evaluations unsurprisingly suggest that while it is hard to generalize (although in the end they do), in most cases the impact of SAPs on the environment has probably been either neutral or positive (World Bank 2003). One World Bank report noted that '65% of recent SALs (Structural Adjustment Loans) included an explicit environmental section, generally consisting of a statement to the effect that no environmental effects could be expected' (cited in Clapp and Dauvergne 2011: 207). Only through the narrowest possible understanding of the environment as conservation and wildlife could such a statement be made, excluding the possibility that shifts in pricing strongly affect questions of access and incentives to conserve or exploit resources. The separation of economy from resource use here is telling. The IMF, the key ally of the World Bank in the production of Poverty Reduction Strategy Papers (PRSPs) and SAPs, is in many ways a 'silent' environment actor here, one that avoids public debates and scrutiny of its environmental profile, but which nevertheless plays a critical role in global resource governance through its policy prescriptions, ostensibly aimed at providing financial stability to governments facing balance of payments difficulties.

The privatization of natural resource sectors promoted by these international financial institutions and of what are revealingly referred to as 'environmental services' (meaning water, forests and other natural resources) have proved particularly contentious. In 2000 the World Bank declared it would not renew a $25 million loan to Bolivia unless it privatized its water services. The Major Cities Water and Sewerage Rehabilitation Project included a condition to privatize the La Paz and Cochabamba water utilities. Conflicts ensued in the notorious 'water wars' in Cochabamba in which a consortium of private water multinationals including Bechtel was forced to leave Bolivia after drastically increasing the prices of water and attempting to charge poorer communities for collecting rain water (Ceceña 2005).

Beyond project-based lending and structural adjustment conditions, a particular political ecology of aid is also created through the efforts of these institutions to create markets for environmental services such as carbon sequestration through, for example, the World Bank's Forest Carbon Partnership or efforts to create markets for carbon through the Prototype Carbon Fund, further tying poorer peoples' livelihoods to global commodity circuits. Critics have referred to this as 'carbon colonialism' (Bachram 2004), or 'accumulation through de-carbonization' (borrowing from Harvey's idea of accumulation by dispossession discussed in chapter 2) (Bumpus and Liverman 2008) to highlight the way in which external finance can create perverse incentives to remove people, such as forest dwellers, from their land in order to preserve the forests as a carbon sequestration zone. Other studies have also shown how flows of carbon finance, either from MDBs or private finance through instruments such as the Clean Development Mechanism, can prolong the life of polluting industries, often located in areas where poorer people live, by providing a new line of credit for rubbish dumps, for example, that are able to capture and flare methane and thereby earn carbon credits (Lohmann 2006; Newell and Bumpus 2012).

Debt

Given the scale of debt afflicting the developing world and the degree of pressure upon developing countries to pay off those debts through export-led development paths, concern grew in the 1980s that countries would intensify their exploitation of natural resources in order to earn much-needed revenue. In 2001 the total debt stock of the developing world reached $2,442 billion, requiring governments to make regular repayments on the debt and the interest attached to it. The developing world now spends $13 on debt repayment for every $1 it receives in grants. For the poorest countries (approximately sixty), $550 billion has been paid in both principal and interest over the last three decades, on $540 billion of loans, and yet a $523 billion dollar debt burden still remains (Global Issues 2011).

This leads to a situation in which there is a net transfer of resources from the global South to lenders in the North, creating what Susan George famously referred to as the 'debt boomerang' (George 1992). There have been various initiatives aimed at re-scheduling or writing off proportions of countries' debts. In 2005 G8 finance ministers agreed to write off the entire $40 billion debt owed by eighteen highly indebted poor countries (HIPC) to the World Bank, the IMF and the African Development Fund. The annual saving in debt payments amounts to just over $1 billion. Yet the NGO War on Want estimates that $45.7 billion would be required for 62 countries to meet the Millennium Development Goals (War on Want 2005). Finance ministers stated that twenty more countries, with an additional $15 billion debt, would be eligible for debt relief if they met targets on fighting corruption and continue to fulfil structural adjustment conditionalities (to eliminate impediments to investment, privatize industries, liberalize their economies, eliminate subsidies, and reduce budgetary expenditures). The agreement, an extension of the HIPC initiative, came into force in July 2006 and has been called the Multilateral Debt Reduction Initiative (MDRI).

Early concerns that crushing debts would drive countries to over-exploit their natural resources, such as timber, in order to make these payments fed growing interest in the possibility of debt-for-nature swaps whereby a percentage of a country's debt would be written off in exchange for a commitment to conserve a specified natural resource, usually an area of forest cover. Projects along these lines, over thirty-two in total, were adopted in many Central and Latin American countries such as Costa Rica and Bolivia. The reduced prices of commercial debt titles opened up the possibility to create these swaps with countries that were both indebted and endowed with biodiversity. It was Thomas Lovejoy of WWF who is credited with first suggesting the idea in 1984 of linking debt relief with environmental protection based on his concern that financial crises in developing countries were further reducing already meagre environmental budgets. The institutions which then drive the initiative were leading conservation NGOs such as Conservation International, Nature Conservancy and WWF, which would solicit donations for the purchase of a foreign debt title of a developing country at a discount on the face value from a commercial bank. The debt title was then converted into domestic currency, reducing the foreign debt, and freeing up an agreed fraction of the debt title to be used to finance a conservation project. $128 million was raised for environmental projects, while developing countries reduced their stock of foreign debt by $177 million (Jakobeit 1996: 134).

In a second phase of the idea, however, government donors, including most notably Germany, but latterly also Sweden, Canada and the US, got involved in writing off public bilateral debt in exchange for environmental commitments from countries such as Kenya. This allowed significantly greater sums of debt to be written off and therefore the provision of more financial resources for environmental protection. By forgiving $500 million of Kenya's debt, Germany, in one single transaction, quadrupled the face value of all prior debt-for-nature transfers. Ironically, Kenyans used the newly available funds to continue existing projects threatened by cuts from structural adjustment measures! To date, multilateral banks who are in position to multiply the scale of such initiatives, have not shown interest in participating. In the case of the World Bank this derives from a fear of losing their triple 'A' rating critical for securing funds for future lending as well as a concern that writing off debts would undermine their statutory requirement which requires debtors to repay in full and on time.[1]

---

1 Indirect forms of support have been forthcoming, however, for debt-for-nature swaps with the IFC, for example, selling an area of forest in Paraguay to an international NGO in 1990.

The central problem, however, as Jakobeit (1996:127) puts it, is that 'debt-for-nature swaps, although very attractive from a financial point of view, were ultimately limited and short-term and hence had relatively small direct effects on the environmental problems they attempted to address'. They covered small amounts of debt, a narrow range of forest resources, in just a few countries with which a select group of western scientists and NGOs were familiar and were ultimately dependent on the vagaries of the market to generate resources for environmental protection. For example, Costa Rica received one-third of all conservation funds mobilized for fifteen recipient countries, but even here the funds generated were not sufficient to address the root causes of deforestation and rapid loss of biodiversity on a national scale. Moreover, the long-term value of bonds can be driven down by inflation and other factors that reduce significantly levels of funding available for conservation. The 'parks and fences' approach to conservation that many such swaps embodied has also come under fire for excluding indigenous users of forest resources, for example, from access to these areas (Brockington and Igoe 2006). Questions of compliance and enforceability also dogged the debt-for-nature swaps, when long-term guarantees are required in states where political commitments are frequently reversed or ignored. The experience of debt-for-nature swaps yields insights that are highly relevant for emerging proposals for REDD (Reducing Emissions from Deforestation and forest Degradation) and payments for ecosystem services that may encounter many similar problems. Indeed, Cassimon et al. (2011) note how a new wave of debt-for-nature swaps, prompted by interest in forests for carbon sequestration purposes, including a recent swap between the US and Indonesia, show signs of facing many of the problems experienced in earlier projects.

The Governance of Finance

The neo-liberal financial order from the 1970s onwards has been characterized by an unprecedented liberalization of state control over finance (Underhill and Zhang 2003). Pressure on countries to reduce controls on the movement of capital have been orchestrated by the leading public financial institutions on behalf of their main funders, who in turn were looking to globalize their access to key financial centres in the global political economy. At the same time, the increasing reach of global financial actors into the everyday conduct of state financial policy may also serve to diffuse responsibility for the costs of adjustment borne by publics since it allows states to deflect responsibility and escape accountability for painful economic adjustments 'imposed' from outside. Nevertheless, the rise of offshore finance, tax havens and spaces in the global political economy where capital is protected from state regulation, or indeed sovereignty is commercialized, means states are clearly willing partners in the governance and non-governance of global finance (Palan 2003; Palan et al. 2010).

What makes the governance of financial markets difficult to create, let alone enforce, is a prevailing reluctance to expose transactions and dealing to greater transparency. Despite initiatives such as the Basel Accords to improve supervision of the banking sector, one of the key lessons emerging from the East Asian financial crisis of 1997 was the importance of transparency and market regulation amid claims by the IMF that 'crony capitalism' among tightly-knit family investment networks was partly to blame for the crisis, since few people could anticipate how close the system was to economic meltdown. In terms of international mechanisms for promoting transparency and accountability in relation to capital flows, there have been concerted attempts to target taxation, for example. Schemes to encourage firms to 'Publish What you Pay', and targeted specifically at the natural resources sectors (such as the Extractive Industries Transparency Initiative) (see box 6.1), attempt to hold states to account for revenues earned from private sector extraction of their resources who, in turn, are asked to declare how much money they have paid in tax. The ability of private actors to avoid and evade tax payments owed to the state clearly has implications for the resourcing of the state (Brautigam et al. 2008), including its ability to perform key environmental governance functions, though this is rarely the focus of attention.

The Governance of Public Finance

The World Bank

For the reasons noted above, there is increasing pressure to bring about the greening of aid, to align it with broader state environmental policy objectives and ensure that environmental goals are mainstreamed across state foreign policy. This has forced attention to reforms on the part of donors and recipients. The imposition of conditionalities has traditionally provided one, albeit very limited way, of trying to bring about environmental reforms on the part of aid recipients. The effectiveness of conditions is often reduced by the fact that the aid used as an inducement to change often only covers a small percentage of the expenditures required to address a programme of environmental reform in a recipient country. It does even less to compensate for the political costs to be borne by reformers in policy

Box 6.1 The public and private governance of finance: some examples

- **1992**: *UN Environment Programme Finance Initiative*: Now works with 170 financial institutions that support its aim of linking financial performance with the principles of sustainable development.

- **2000**: *Jakarta Declaration for the Reform of Official Export Credit and Investment Guarantee Agencies*.

- **2000**: *Carbon Disclosure Project*: An initiative aimed at raising awareness among investors about the carbon emissions of their investments. Now also hosts the *Water Disclosure Project*, which provides critical water-related data from the world's largest corporations.

- **2002**: *Extractive Industries Transparency Initiative*: Announced at the World Summit on Sustainable Development, this supports improved governance in resource-rich countries through the verification and full publication of company payments and government revenues from oil, gas and mining.

- **2003**: *Equator Principles*: Developed by the International Finance Corporation and private banks, these cover the social and environmental aspects of project financing to developing countries.

- **2006**: *The Principles for Responsible Investment*: A joint initiative between UNEP Finance Initiative and the Global Compact (see chapter 5) which encourages investors who sign up to them to demand reporting on social and environmental issues from their corporate clients.

areas where powerful interests are at play that stand to lose from reform, such as logging (Keohane and Levy 1996; Dauvergne 1997).

In terms of donors themselves, bilateral and multilateral agencies have come under intense pressure to minimize the environmental impact of their lending practices. As the largest development lending agency in the world, the World Bank lends approximately $25 billion a year to developing countries (Clapp and Dauvergne 2011: 201). In response to some of the experiences and criticisms described above, the Bank has evolved a series of mechanisms for screening environmental impacts and consulting with environmental groups in advance of project lending in order to avert some of the large-scale negative environmental impacts associated with previous lending programmes. As far back as 1987, the World Bank has had an environmental department charged with responsibility for addressing the environmental aspects of its work (Piddington 1992), even appointing the ecologist Herman Daly to a prominent position to pacify critics of the organization that interest in green issues amounted to little more than 'green wash'.[2] These reforms are often offset, however, by the fact that environmental objectives are not mainstreamed throughout the organization's work, leading to a classic case of policy incoherence where the pursuit of environmental objectives in one area is undermined by funding for environmentally destructive projects elsewhere. A Friends of the Earth report notes that 'in fiscal year 2000, close to half the lending from the World Bank's private sector divisions was in environmentally harmful sectors such as oil, gas, coal, mining and chemicals and infrastructure projects' (cited in Clapp and Dauvergne 2005: 202). Yet in 2004 World Bank management rejected or weakened many of the recommendations of its own Extractive Industries Review, including on the phase-out of fossil fuel funding (Bretton Woods Project 2011a).

A feature of the way in which the World Bank governs that also merits mention here is the compulsion to spend in large quantities and quickly, which produces time frames and a mentality in conflict with the slower pace required to adequately evaluate longer-term and multi-dimensional environmental problems. Preventing future environmental damage provides fewer short-term and visible results for ambitious bureaucrats within the Bank than, for example, a mega-project that ostensibly delivers electricity to the poor and assigns large amounts of money very rapidly, demonstrating to taxpayers tangible returns on a foreign aid programme.

Besides direct environmental impacts associated with economic prescriptions such as those discussed above, World Bank interventions also have a direct impact on forms of public environmental governance. State-based environmental regulation has been subject to sustained criticism from key development actors such as the World Bank on the grounds that it is excessively inflexible, inefficient, and often ineffective at delivering the change in behaviour that it intends. Increasingly, the preference is for the use of the market as a tool for incentivizing positive action and deterring polluting activities. Examples of pollution charging in China, Colombia and the Philippines are cited to show that pollution from factories has been

---

2 Daly subsequently left the Bank in the early 1990s, citing its obsession with growth at any cost as a key reason (Young 2002: 206).

successfully reduced when steep, regular payments for emissions have been enforced (World Bank 2000). Yet cuts required of environmental programmes in countries such as Thailand, whose budget for pollution control was cut by 80 per cent between 1997 and 1999 under its SAP, clearly undermine environmental progress. Jakobeit (1996) also shows in Costa Rica how IMF/World Bank Structural Adjustment Programmes resulted in disproportionate budget cuts for government agencies responsible for managing protected areas.

The prevalence of a hegemonic discourse about the benefits of market-based approaches to environmental protection also serves to marginalize the promotion of 'green' technologies and policies. The World Bank concedes 'unregulated electricity markets are likely to put renewable energy technologies at a disadvantage in the short-run because they favour the cheapest energy as determined purely by price, but do not capture environmental and social externalities' (cited in Tellam 2000: 33). The 'market-fixated' approach of the Bank prevents direct support for energy efficiency and renewable energy and is apparent in the means the Bank uses to calculate the costs and benefits of projects, which, because they do not use a life-cycle analysis, put energy efficiency technologies that save energy over long time-frames, at a disadvantage (EDF & NRDC 1994). There are currently few incentives or requirements upon Bank task managers to give end-use energy efficiency a high priority in power loans; few loans incorporate demand-side management; and few loans address energy efficiency other than through price increases (Bretton Woods Project 2011b; Strickland and Sturm 1998).

However, as well as being the focus of critiques, demands for environmental action have also presented opportunities for multilateral development banks (MDBs). The World Bank, for example, has sought to carve out for itself a leading role in addressing climate change, most recently through the launch of the Climate Investment Funds (CIFs) which it administers (World Bank 2008a; see table 6.1). In October 2008 it approved its Strategic Framework on Development and Climate Change (World Bank 2008b), the objective of which is to enable the World Bank Group to 'effectively support sustainable development and poverty reduction in the new realm of a changing climate'. As part of the Strategic Framework, two CIFs were approved in July 2008: the Clean Technology Fund (CTF) and the Strategic Climate Fund (SCF). Given the scale and significance of these funds, their governance has been a site of significant contention. In October 2008, seven donor countries (Australia, France, Germany, Japan, Sweden, the UK and the US) and seven *potential* recipient

Table 6.1 World Bank climate finance in brief

Fund	Total amount (US$m)	Period
Carbon Partnership Facility	500 (140 committed)	2008–12
Forest Carbon Partnership Facility	385 (160 committed)	
Climate Investment Funds	6200	2009–12
• Clean Technology Fund	4800	
• Strategic Climate Fund	1400	
– Forest Investment Programme	350	
– Scaling Up Renewable Energy	200	
– Pilot Programme for Climate Resilience	600	

Source: World Bank (2010)

countries (Brazil, China, Egypt, India, Mexico, South Africa and Turkey) were selected as members of the CTF's Trust Fund Committee. The committee will be responsible for approving financing for programmes and projects, deciding on the strategic use of the funds and 'programming priorities'. Although there is a Partnership Forum for the CIFs, which will 'discuss the strategic direction' of the funds and includes representatives from civil society, recipient countries and the UN, it has no formal decision-making power. When the CIFs were first proposed in March 2008, governance issues featured prominently among the concerns of civil society groups and Southern governments, including the limited consultation of developing countries, the lack of clarity over whether money going into the funds would be additional to previously agreed overseas development aid, and whether it would be in the form of grants or loans. In addition, there were worries about the extent to which already existing processes under the UNFCCC would be undermined by the presence of the World Bank in this area (BOND 2008).

Organizational as well as structural and discursive shifts are, therefore, key. To achieve a higher level of policy integration, climate objectives and environmental goals more broadly need to be placed on the same level as Bank business. One report (Porter et al. 1998) found that the World Bank had not

> taken steps to create staff incentives necessary to put global environmental concerns on a par with traditional bank business; that it is has not systematically integrated global environmental objectives into economic and sector work or into the Country Assistance Strategies (CAS) process, and that it has not adequately addressed the impact on the global environment of its financing of fossil fuel power development.

Global Environment Facility (GEF)

If the World Bank is the world's leading financial actor in development, the Global Environment Facility is charged with the responsibility of playing that role in the environmental field. The GEF was set up with a budget of $1.3 billion prior to the Earth Summit as a global fund to oversee the financing of the Rio agreements. In particular, it was charged with overseeing the aid, technology transfer and capacity building required by developing countries in order to meet their obligations under the UNCED agreements. Though poorly defined and even more difficult to quantify, the fund is designed to cover the 'incremental costs' of projects with tangible 'global' benefits. Following this logic, projects were initially focused on the areas of international waters, climate change, biodiversity and ozone depletion, although they now also include land degradation and persistent organic compounds. The GEF has allocated $9.2 billion, supplemented by more than $40 billion in co-financing, for more than 2,700 projects in more than 165 developing countries and countries with economies in transition (GEF 2011). It is meant to act as a catalyst for measures to address global environmental problems rather than as a mechanism to meet all the financing needs of global environmental programmes.

Although the GEF is managed by the World Bank, the UN Development Programme (UNDP) and the UN Environment Programme (UNEP), often in a far from harmonious manner, it is the Bank as trustee of GEF funds that exercises most direct control over the funding and direction of the GEF. This means that no payment can be made by the GEF, even for a project administered by one of the UN agencies, unless the World Bank approves it. According to its critics, this close relationship serves the Bank well by making their loans seem more economic because GEF pays the costs of green components allowing the World Bank to externalize its environmental costs (Young 2002: 15). GEF operates a mixed voting system which combines elements of the Bretton Woods one-dollar-one-vote structure as well as that of the UN's one-country-one-vote structure, and is overseen by the GEF Council which is made up of eighteen recipient country governments, fourteen donor-country participants and five NGOs.

According to Young (2002: 8), the battle to secure the GEF as the preferred institution for overseeing aid and technology transfer for the environment to the developing world has meant that 'Through its effective control of the GEF, the World Bank has been able to bring its economistic vision of development into what was previously UN territory of global environmental protection'. More benignly, World Bank staff describe it as a 'green virus in the Bretton Woods software' (Young 2002: 13). These divergent views of the GEF reflect not just the different ideological positions, but fundamental contests over which institution should set priorities for, and oversee the management of, funds for environmental aid. Many Southern countries, given their experience of bitter relations with the World Bank in the past, were reluctant to see a Bank-controlled GEF emerge as the front-runner. A series of carefully orchestrated moves and diplomatic exchanges, however, served to outmanoeuvre opponents of the GEF, and much work had already been undertaken to ensure the decision about which body would play this role was a *fait accompli* before the UNCED summit got underway. The support of environmental groups in validating this venture was critical. An internal bank memo in 1987 by Bank official David Backmann noted 'Environmental organizations in the industrial countries should feel that this is their idea and they should be the ones to press for it' (Young 2002: 47).

That said, a continual source of criticism in relation to both the Bank and the GEF has been the lack of consultation with civil society actors, such that opportunities for inputs into the decision-making process on projects and priorities for those critical of the environmental benefits of the projects are few are far between. What tends to happen is that more conservative environmental groups are invited into consultations at the expense of more critical groups. For example, while WWF, International Union for the Conservation of Nature (IUCN) and World Resources Institute (WRI) have been part of meetings hosted by GEF, even holding monthly meetings with the US Treasury on GEF-related issues, more critical groups have not been involved. The fact the meetings are held in Washington also immediately excludes those outside the Washington circuits of influence. Many NGOs are highly critical of the GEF's approach to participation in this sense. Clapp and Dauvergne (2005: 209) quote Bruce Rich of the Environmental Defense Fund (EDF):

> The formulation of the GEF was a model of the Bank's preferred way of doing business: Top-down, secretive, with a basic contempt for public participation, access to information, involvement of democratically elected legislatures and informed discussion of alternatives.

That participation is restricted should perhaps be unsurprising. Ultimately, 'the fundamental truth [is] that the Bank is just that: a bank' (Clapp and Dauvergne 2005: 203), which means it lends in order to make money. Though lending at different rates than many commercial banks, it operates according to a commercial rationale in the short term in the sense of repayments, and in a long-term political strategy by making lending conditional on a series of economic and policy changes beneficial to its main sponsors in the financial communities of the industrialized North. Environmentally, lending tends to reflect Northern priorities, often acting as a subsidy to technology providers from those countries (Chatterjee and Finger 1994). Close ties between the GEF and World Bank also mean that the formers' green grants are often used to 'sweeten' the latter's loans. The issue is also not just the limits of banks as vehicles for environmental reform, however, but the limited nature of aid finance in general. As Connolly (1996: 327) concludes, 'Financial transfers alone will save neither the ozone layer nor the Brazilian rain forest. Achieving such objectives will depend on the interest and ability of affected actors to attract and make effective use of other, more substantial financial resources.'

There are issues then of the scale of finance that can be realistically mobilized and the fact that it is dwarfed by flows of unregulated private finance which has enormous potential to undo, bypass and overwhelm positive and incremental gains achieved through use of public monies (Newell 2011b). The political nature of all aid also means that 'donor self-interest will limit the application of environmental aid to a particular set of problems or geographical areas, leaving many important environmental targets untouched' (Connolly 1996: 327). Lending might be based either on what is of commercial interest to firms based in donor countries or responsiveness to those issues that are most pressing to vocal environmental groups in the North, as we have seen with GEF; what Maxwell and Weiner (1993) call 'coalitions of the green and the greedy'. Neither use of finance is governed by which issue is most deserving of attention in terms of the scale, severity or immediacy of the problem, but rather by the fit between political expediency, commercial interest and available resources. We saw this acutely above with the debt-for-nature swaps, where countries with some of the largest rates of tropical deforestation such as Thailand, Cambodia and Indonesia were passed over in favour of Latin American countries where deals could be struck more easily and where leading conservationists already had ties. The symbolism of being seen to do something also deflects public pressure for other more stringent and politically more demanding interventions.

Governing Private Finance

When considering the governance of private finance, the first point to note is that it is highly uneven depending on the type of finance and region in question. There are wide variations in terms of opportunities to influence the behaviour of investors, creditors and underwriters. As Ganzi et al. (1998: 3) put it:

> the threat of being held legally liable for environmental damage has been a critical factor in getting the US commercial banking and insurance sectors to pay attention to environmental issues. However, in countries where environmental standards and judiciary systems are weak, the financial industry faces a different set of incentives.

The Superfund case in the US, for example, where a bank was found liable for the clean-up costs of a site contaminated by a corporate client of the bank (given that it was in a position to influence decisions made by that client), changed the nature of private lending. This has led to widespread reforms not only in the US but in Europe, parts of Asia and Australia aimed at including environmental considerations into loan decisions.[3] In the wake of Superfund legislation,[4] groups such as Credit Suisse, NatWest, HSBC and Deutsche Bank have also voluntarily integrated environmental considerations into their lending practices.

Beyond direct regulation and liability, much emphasis is placed on the importance of mobilizing private transfers in making up for gaps in the funding of responses to global environmental problems given the decline in Overseas Development Assistance (ODA) noted above. Yet private flows are concentrated in more developed middle-income countries of the South and tend to get transferred to those countries which have the capacity to attract capital and not those that most need it. This is a problem in terms of the globally balanced and sustainable financing of environmental responses, but for institutions such as GEF it presents less of a problem given that, although investment is focused primarily on fewer than a dozen countries, these are the countries that are important to the GEF's mandate of maximizing global environmental benefits (Porter et al. 1998).

A key role for the World Bank and other donors, then, is to minimize some of the risks that deter private actors from investing in 'green' projects and sectors. For example the 'Lighting Africa' initiative involves the International Finance Corporation (IFC), 'catalyzing markets for modern lighting' by developing commercial off-grid lighting markets in sub-Saharan Africa (Lighting Africa 2011), while the Scaling up Renewable

---

3 In the US, for example, guidelines produced in 1993 by the Federal Deposit Insurance Corporation require all banks to reserve a senior level position for environmental risk management.
4 Comprehensive Environmental Response, Compensation and Liability Act, 1980.

Energy Programme (see table 6.1), the youngest and least developed of the World Bank's Climate Investment Funds, was launched at the Copenhagen climate summit in 2009 with the aim of catalysing new economic opportunities for private sector investment in renewable energy production in low-income countries. The World Bank also indirectly influences commercial banking activity overseas through its environmental guidelines that have become a default standard from which individual banks may model their own (World Bank 2007). Such tools may also provide potentially important governance mechanisms for the use of public money to support private investments with large environmental impacts such as the construction of dams, roads and power plants. Particularly important here are public sector guarantees from bilateral or multilateral funding sources such as the World Bank's Multilateral Investment Guarantee Agency (MIGA). Since its inception in 1988, MIGA has issued guarantees worth more than $22 billion for more than 600 projects in more than 100 developing countries (MIGA 2011).

Beyond the MDBs, global environmental actors have also sought to work with private finance to exercise some influence over private capital flows. In 1991 UNEP developed a *Statement by Financial Institutions on the Environment and Sustainable Development*, which 200 financial institutions have now signed (as of 2011) committing themselves to 'complying with local, national, and international environmental regulations applicable to our operations and business services [and to] work towards integrating environmental considerations into our operations, asset management, and other business decisions, in all markets' (UNEP 2011a).

The *Equator Principles*, meanwhile, address social and environmental issues in project financing through voluntary standards. In June 2003, ten private banks launched a set of operational principles and standards for managing the environmental and social impacts of loans to large development projects. In terms of the relationship between public and private governance, what is interesting is the way the banks involved chose to base the framework's environmental and social standards on IFC Safeguard Policies, creating, as Wright (2010) puts it 'an unprecedented institutional link between standards developed by and for public financial institutions and the commercial banking practices of private banks'.

Export credits provide another key interface between public and private finance where public money is used to induce private sector investment, often in large-scale projects with widespread environmental consequences. This credit is provided in the form of government-backed loans, investment guarantees and risk insurance. Providing finance at interest rates higher than those of other bilateral and multilateral lenders, the combined total of finance from all export credit agencies (ECAs) is now more than twice the total value of all development assistance, bilateral and multilateral. Official export credit and investment insurance agencies have become the largest source of public international finance, accounting for 24 per cent of all developing country debt, and 56 per cent of the debt owed to official governmental agencies (ECA Watch 2011a). This also amounts to subsidizing nearly 10 per cent of global exports. ECAs allow for an important, though often underused, opportunity to screen investments for their social and environmental impacts. In the UK, for example, no project has ever been denied support from the Export Credit Guarantee Department (ECGD) on environmental grounds. Yet the combined annual emissions of hydrocarbons from two ECGD-supported projects, the Baku-Tbilisi-Ceyhan pipeline and the Bonny Island liquefied natural gas plant in Nigeria, will result in the emission of 660 million tonnes of carbon dioxide, more than the entire annual output from the whole of the UK (WWF 2007). Groups such as Bank Watch and ECA Watch have launched several campaigns exposing the use of public funds to support large projects with damaging social and environmental impacts. As ECA Watch (2011a) put it:

> ECAs are currently the main public financiers of energy projects contributing to climate change. A significant portion of ECA project financing in developing countries is concentrated in sectors that have important implications for climate change . . . fossil-fuelled power generation, oil and gas development, transportation infrastructure, aircraft sales, and energy-intensive manufacturing in developing countries.

What is most significant perhaps from an environmental point of view is the support that ECAs provide to high-risk ventures often associated with resource extraction in environmentally sensitive and socially vulnerable areas of the world. Most ECAs are not subject to social and environmental standards or assessment procedures, and operate in a highly secretive manner, rarely disclosing information about the projects they finance or evaluating the impacts of such projects. There are some exceptions, such as in the US, where environmental assessments are required, especially given their links to aid money from the US Agency for International Development (USAID). The problem then is that more stringent standards by one ECA drive investors to seek support from less demanding ECAs elsewhere, such as happened with the Three Gorges dam project in China (Ganzi et al. 1998).

Contesting Global Finance

This final section of the chapter examines attempts by activists to 'green' global finance and to see it better regulated in line with the imperatives of sustainable development. Their interventions seek to contest and go beyond the limited attempts by public and private financial bodies to screen their investments for negative environmental impacts or use their financial muscle to invest in sustainable technologies and projects. As with other chapters in the book, it explores the contentious politics by which groups both seek to resist environmentally destructive projects supported by powerful financial actors, as well as mobilize for inter-ventions aimed at strengthening existing governance mechanisms or establishing new ones.

Contesting Public Finance

There is now a long history of civil society mobilization around multilat-eral development banks and financial institutions (Fox and Brown 1998; O'Brien et al. 2000; Edwards and Gaventa 2001; Scholte and Schnabel 2002; Park 2011). Here the focus is on highlighting tools, levers and strate-gies employed by environmental activists to pressure and cajole leading financial actors into greening their activities.

Environmental groups have adopted a range of strategies to influence public financial flows for sustainable development, from using mecha-nisms available within multilateral bodies such as the World Bank, to pressuring key lender states. The World Bank inspection panel created in the wake of the controversies discussed above has provided one important entry point for activists. For example, the Chilean Action Group for the BioBio (GABB) filed a complaint with the panel alleging non-compliance with social and environmental standards in the construction of the Pangue Dam on the Biobio River. Following World Bank pressure on the contrac-tor for the project, the Chilean company Endesa re-financed the project with a loan from Dresdner Bank in Germany (Ganzi et al. 1998). The Dresdner Bank, in turn, became a target for activists in Germany who presented a resolution at the bank's shareholders' meeting detailing the political and environmental risks associated with the project and drawing attention to the fact that the bank had failed to abide by its obligations as a signatory of the *UNEP Statement by Financial Institutions on the Environment and Sustainable Development*, referred to above. Although the bank did not withdraw the loan for the dam, it did agree not to finance subsequent dams in Chile planned by Endesa before consulting with GABB and the German group Urgewald.

Other groups have sought to channel their concerns through key country lenders to multilateral institutions such as the World Bank. Indeed, US environmentalists in the 1980s explicitly sought to use their influence in Congress to place conditions on World Bank lending to environmentally sensitive projects. The reliance of the Bank on US capital provided a key point of leverage for environmentalists looking to green the banks' lending activities (O'Brien et al. 2000), often in unholy alliance with right-wing politicians in the US Congress who were sceptical about the utility of funds for multinational organizations. The offensive was successful with the Polonoroeste project being halted in 1985, the first time a project loan was halted on environmental grounds (Edwards and Gaventa 2001). In 1993 the Indian government and the World Bank also decided to discontinue the loan for the Narmada dam project, after significant mobilization and contestation by a range of movements and people facing displacement, opting instead for Indian self-funding in order to avoid the scrutiny of a growing band of international environmental activists.

Given the immense power exercised by export credit agencies, discussed above, it is unsurprising that this source of public finance for private capital has also been the target of significant activism. In April 1998, NGOs from forty-six countries issued to the finance and foreign ministries of the major industrialized OECD countries a 'Call of National and International Non-Governmental Agencies for the Reform of Export Credit and Investment Insurance Agencies'. *The Jakarta Declaration for Reform of Official Export Credit and Investment Insurance Agencies*, as it is known, endorsed by 347 NGOs, called for transparency in ECA decision making, environmental assessment and screening of ECA financial commitments, including participation of affected populations, and social sustainability (equity and human rights concerns) in appraisal of ECA commitments, and for an international agreement in the OECD and/or G8 on common environmental and social standards for ECAs. It demands that the guidelines and standards be coherent with other ongoing international social and environmental commitments and treaties, such as the United Nations Convention on Biological Diversity, and that ECAs must conduct full, transparent accounting for climate change impacts and move to increase investments in sustainable renewable energy (ECA Watch 2011b).

Elsewhere, civil society groups have attempted to hold governments to account for their failure to address the environmental impacts of their support to investors. In August 2005, Greenpeace and Friends of the Earth, together with a series of US cities, alleged that the Export-Import Bank and Overseas Private Investment Corporation illegally provided over \$32 billion in finance and insurance for oil fields, pipelines and power plants for over 10 years without assessing their contribution to global warming or their impact on the US environment. In doing so, the claimants argued that these export credit agencies failed to meet their obligations under the US NEPA (National Environmental Policy Act). On 31 March 2007, the US District Court for the Northern District of California held that the NEPA *does* apply to major federal projects that contribute to climate change. A related example is the case brought by a coalition of German NGOs against their government. In June 2004, GermanWatch and BUND (Friends of the Earth Germany) brought a legal challenge against the German Federal Ministry of Economics and Labour in the Administrative Court of Berlin. They successfully secured an order which forces the German government to disclose the contribution to climate change (in terms of tonnes of CO_2 released) made by projects supported by the German Export Credit Agency Eueler Hermes AG since 1997 (Newell 2008e).

Contesting Private Finance

With respect to private finance, there is a divide among environmental groups between those that are interested in locating and activating levers that exist within the current financial system to engineer positive change, and those that engage in a more full-frontal attack on the basic principles and means by which the financial system operates. This strategic difference separates groups such as BankTrack (2011), engaged in monitoring and exposing acts of environmental negligence enabled by the support of banks, from coalitions of activist investors aiming to work with financial investors to both sensitize them to the importance of environmental risks to their investments, to disclose their investments, and to use their power to disinvest from polluting activities and invest in sustainable projects and sectors of the economy.

Disclosure is key to the success of such strategies. The Greenhouse Gas Protocol, jointly created by the World Resources Institute and the World Business Council for Sustainable Development in 1998, is an example of this. It is a corporate reporting and accounting standard, and now claims to be 'the most widely used international accounting tool for government and business leaders to understand, quantify, and manage greenhouse gas emissions' (GHG Protocol Initiative 2009). Another is the Carbon Disclosure Project, which encourages companies to report their emissions and provides a potentially important risk management tool for the financial community (CDP 2011) (see box 6.1).

Moves by the financial community to shed light on the corporate sector's emissions profile are paralleled by climate activists' attempts to reposition investments in fossil fuels as liabilities rather than assets. A report by the environmental groups PLATFORM and Greenpeace (2008) warns of increasing financial risk for BP and Shell as a result of their investments in the Alberta oil tar sands in Canada. The sector now accounts for 30 per cent of Shell's proven reserves. The report shows that 'tar sands represent not only an enormous threat to the climate, but also to the security of pension fund shareholders of the oil companies' (PLATFORM and Greenpeace 2008). This is because of a number of factors which threaten the long-term profitability of the sector, including: the prospect of low carbon fuel standards, the rising cost of delivering gas to the tar sands, the unreliability of carbon capture and storage (projects to capture carbon dioxide from power station flue gases and put it back in the ground), the extensive clean-up operation, and the potential future litigation from local communities. Andrew Dlugolecki, Director of Andlug Consulting in the UK, and former director of general insurance at insurance giant CGNU, said 'Investors should do all they can to challenge this misguided use of shareholders' money, which will make global warming worse, and instead call for a new approach that is based on the reality of climate change' (PLATFORM 2008). In the same vein, a number of investors in the US put pressure on the Securities and Exchange Commission (SEC) to require companies to disclose their carbon emissions. The principle of disclosure in financial regulation is that investors ought to have available to them the information necessary to make well-informed investment decisions. Companies like Merrill Lynch, who also play a leading role in the CDP, argued that companies ought to be required to disclose their carbon emissions, because such emissions would be materially important to investors.

Shareholder activism, as we saw in chapter 5, offers another avenue for financial investors to exercise their power for reform. The year 2005 saw a record number of shareholder resolutions on global warming. Institutional shareholders have been among those that have filed over thirty global warming resolutions requesting financial risk and disclosure plans to reduce GHG emissions (Butler 2005; CERES 2005). This is three times the number for 2000–1 (Institutional Share Owner 2005). Firms affected include leading players from the automobile sector such as Ford and General Motors, Chevron Texaco, Unocal and Exxon Mobil from the oil sector, Dow Chemicals and market leaders in financial services such as

JP Morgan Chase and Co (CERES 2005). Groups such as CERES (Coalition for Environmentally Responsible Economies) and ICCR (Interfaith Centre for Corporate Responsibility), a coalition of 275 faith-based institutional investors, have used their financial muscle to hold firms to account for their performance on climate change. Approximately one half of the resolutions filed in 2005 were withdrawn by the shareholders after the targeted companies agreed to take actions against global warming that the filers judged to be adequate (Butler 2005).

There are important limits to shareholder activism as a driver of change, however. There is no obligation upon a corporation to implement resolutions that have been passed. In 2005, the coalitions CERES and ICCR organized a resolution at Exxon's Annual General Meeting asking for disclosure of plans to comply with GHG reduction targets in Kyoto jurisdictions. The resolution gained the support of 28 per cent of Exxon shareholders. But the companies' Shareholder Executive Committee authorized Exxon to censor the result, omitting the petition from its report to the SEC. A further commonly acknowledged limitation of shareholder activism is its restriction to countries in the Anglo-Saxon world where finance is particularly dominant. Although there is some evidence of growing interest in socially responsible investment (SRI) in Japan, for example, the global nature of this strategy is limited (Newell 2008e).

Commercial banks collectively represent the world's largest single pool of private capital with assets of tens of trillions of dollars and are often involved in financing large infrastructural projects with significant environmental impacts. Their activities are a key target, therefore, for those seeking to green their investments. The attraction of targeting the investments of key investors is the ripple and spillover effect of this to other investors, and the scale of change that can be achieved by shifting the position of just one powerful financial actor. In response to shareholder pressure, for example, JP Morgan will now assess the financial risks of GHG emissions in loan evaluations. It promises to use carbon disclosure and mitigation in its client review process to assess risks linked with high carbon dioxide emissions. Others may follow suit with growing attention from activist groups such as BankTrack seeking to embarrass banks into action by exposing their role in fuelling (literally) climate change by providing the credit and capital that underwrites large energy intensive projects (BankTrack 2011). The role of banks in project finance renders them particularly vulnerable to project-specific advocacy. As the example of the Dresdner Bank described above shows, banks with a large customer base may also be more sensitive to reputational leverage. Reflecting consumer concern around these issues, banks such as the Cooperative Bank in the UK base their market position on a commitment *not* to invest in what they consider to be socially and environmentally irresponsible activities. The Cooperative Bank has even involved itself in campaigns against other corporations it believes to be behaving irresponsibly, such as Exxon over its hostile stance towards action on climate change (Newell 2008e).

Pension funds have been another target of activists. The advantage of targeting pension funds is that they can afford to employ longer-term time frames given the more stable nature of flows of funds in and out of their portfolios and the fact they are heavily regulated, at least when compared with other sources of private finance considered here. Indeed, the largest pension fund in the US, the California Public Employees Retirement System was persuaded to divest from Maxxam Corporation stock after a successful NGO campaign drawing attention to the companies' involvement in logging old growth redwood forests in northern California. The move was backed up by an effective media campaign targeting the pension funds which ran under the slogan, 'We hear the retirement funds of California State employees are making a real killing' (Ganzi et al. 1998: 47). The fact that pension funds are legally obliged to take into account any information that would materially affect risks and returns on their portfolios presents another, potentially significant, point of leverage.

The insurance industry has also been targeted by activists in relation to its role in providing cover for investments which fuel climate change, generating environmental impacts which the insurance industry then has to pay off for. Climate activists, including most prominently former climate campaigner at Greenpeace Jeremy Leggett, sought to forge alliances with insurance companies to encourage them to shift their lending away from fossil fuels and into renewable energy (Leggett 1996; Paterson 1999). The insurance industry has a particular stake in promoting these changes given that it has suffered in the past and will continue to suffer huge losses from pay-outs following climate-related damage to properties that they have insured. For example, by 1995 leading insurers from all of the world's main insurance centres had spoken of the threat of bankruptcy from unmanageable catastrophe losses. This came on the back of Hurricane Andrew in 1992, which cost the insurance industry $20 billion in pay-outs on weather-related damage (Paterson 1999).

In so far as it can insulate itself from immediate risks, in part merely by withdrawing cover from regions and properties in the front line of the impacts of climate change (Jägers et al. 2005), the insurance industry is unlikely to lead a concerted effort by the financial community to re-orient private investment towards the goals of sustainable development. Indeed, while the underwriting side of the industry is keen to limit its liabilities related to environment-induced claims, the investment side of the industry has not yet shown any leadership with regard to shifting finance towards sustainable energy. Some insurance industries are also clearly more concerned than others, with the majority of signatories to the UNEP *Statement of Environmental Commitment by the Insurance Industry* being based either in Europe or Japan. Reflecting more generally on the potential of institutional investors (mutual funds, pension funds and insurers) to create incentives in the form of price performance for firms to reduce GHG emissions, Harmes (2011) suggests such potential has been considerably overestimated because of the structural constraints faced by most institutional investors.

The protection of environmentally irresponsible investors by export credit agencies or the use of public grants and loans, and the bailouts provided to speculators whose volatile investments and withdrawals exacerbate and heighten conditions of uncertainty and instability, are irrational from an environmental point of view. Where public money is used to support and subsidize private profit-making that passes on costs to the public by externalizing social and environmental costs, there is a basis to make legitimate demands of institutions that, in theory at least, are accountable to the public. Private activities protected or removed from scrutiny are much harder to hold to account. Pension funds and the like, however, can be held to account by public bodies that invest in them, as we saw above. Pressures to make investors accountable for the consequences of how their money is used may also set interesting precedents, as we saw, through compulsory reporting of environmental information alongside data about companies' financial performance. We have to recall, however, that in the final analysis, private financial institutions are primarily accountable to private shareholders and clients rather than to the public. Campaigns targeted at key governments and multilateral institutions can have multiplier effects among both public and private actors, nevertheless. Through their seal of approval, direct support to the business and financial community and advice to borrower countries, multilateral financial institutions are positioned to influence a proportion of global financial flows far greater than those for which they are directly responsible.

In looking at ways to green the private financial community, we should not lose sight of the key role of the financial knowledge brokers in this area that exercise significant influence over investment choices. Investment advisors and credit rating agencies may be particularly important in this respect (Sinclair 2005). We also need to consider a point, emphasized throughout this book, that market actors cannot be seen as unitary or homogeneous actors. As Ganzi et al. (1998: 92) put it, 'A feature common to several financial industry segments is that environmental sensitivity occurs in different degrees in different parts of the same organization.' The underwriting side of the insurance industry has become more concerned about climate change and developed means of dealing with claims related to toxic contamination, while the investment arms of the same companies continue to operate largely unchanged. Untangling issues of responsibility and accountability as a basis for intervening is an increasingly fraught challenge amid consolidation in the sector. Strategically, however, size brings with it profile and, therefore, vulnerability to reputational leverage. Ultimately the financial sector is of such importance to contemporary globalization and efforts to improve its sustainability, not because of its direct ecological footprints, but because of its role in lubricating and financing the productive investments which currently exact such a heavy price from the earth's resources.

Strategic turns towards engaging directly the private and public financial communities are, therefore, understandable and may play a key role in delivering near-term change. They should not perhaps distract from the imperative, however, of working to change state policies which are, at the very least, permissive towards, if not acquiescent in, forms of private destruction of the public commons. Stronger legal frameworks, backed by tough and enforceable sanctions to penalize those transgressing basic environmental norms in their routine conduct, will be preferable to ad hoc systems of self and civil regulation aimed at checking the excesses of the private financial community.

Conclusions

As with other aspects of globalization examined in this book, in the governance of finance we find much greater scrutiny being applied to those aspects of finance that are the most public, the most accountable (in theory) and the least to those which activists have less access to, governments claim they have less control over and yet, at the same time, which (because of their size and reach) have the potential to exact the most significant environmental damage. The reconstitution of public and private authority globally, described in chapters 1–3 of the book, has protected private financial actors from strong levels of public oversight. The environmental consequences of the routine and mundane way in which they conduct their operations only seem to impact upon their decision making when perceptions of risk are altered by access to natural resources or when environmental devastation, often blamed on 'natural disasters', impacts on profits, through pay-outs in the case of the insurance industry, for example.

This presents an enormous challenge for environmentalists. We have seen how some groups have been attempting to form strategic alliances with private financial actors whose vulnerability to environmental damage may lead them to adopt progressive positions on issues such as climate change, as well as evidence of moves to adopt ethical investment policies in some quarters. Important though these moves are, they pale into insignificance when compared with the deliberate un-governance of the majority of global finance which currently has neither the incentive nor obligation to gear its activities towards the construction and maintenance of a sustainable economy and which continues apace funding environmental destruction. Regulation and accountability: a different model of environmental governance for private financial actors is clearly required. But the record of states, alongside multilateral development actors such as the World Bank, which the world's most highly industrialized countries exercise power over and whom they have the right to hold to account, does not offer solid grounds for believing that the governance of finance for sustainable development will be strengthened any time soon.

As with previous chapters, the actors, events and trends analysed in this chapter highlight, and are usefully understood, in relation to themes highlighted in chapters 1–3. This includes the ways in which the rights of private financial actors to create profits are fiercely protected and regulated, while the social and environmental consequences of their accumulation strategies are not: privatizing the benefits and socializing the costs. This is true even in financial terms as we currently observe in the current crisis whereby reckless speculation results in state bailouts, followed by handsome bonuses of public money awarded to the heads of banks who brought about the crisis: all of which results in a series of cuts to public budgets and welfare programmes to make up for the losses incurred by the bailout! The question of who bears the costs of crisis, who makes the sacrifices in terms of austerity and for whom the state is willing to intervene when push comes to shove reveal clear class preferences.

The discussion has also highlighted the important role of global governance institutions such as the World Bank and IMF in creating the enabling conditions for investment opportunities for transnational capital. Whether it be the water privatizations, pressures to liberalize the economy or the promotion of payments for ecosystem services, discursive and organizational power is wielded by these institutions on behalf of those states which exercise most power in the institutions which govern the global economy. But we have also seen many instances and sites of resistance by communities expected to host mega-projects such as dams, or who find their key services subject to privatization that have won some key battles, and by aligning on occasion with other transnational movements have been able to coordinate pressure on public and private banks, credit rating agencies and governments to effect real change. Even in the relatively closed and unaccountable world of finance, social forces have scored some victories in the struggle for a different type of order.

Chapter 7

Conclusions: Ecologizing Globalization/ Globalizing Ecology

Introduction

> By 2050, humanity could devour an estimated 140 billion tons of minerals, ores, fossil fuels and biomass per year, three times its current appetite, unless the economic growth rate is decoupled from the rate of natural resource consumption. Developed countries' citizens consume an average of 16 tons of those four key resources per capita (ranging up to 40 or more tons per person in some developed countries). By comparison, the average person in India today consumes four tons per year. With the growth of both population and prosperity, especially in developing countries, the prospect of much higher resource consumption levels is far beyond what is likely sustainable if realized at all given finite world resources (UNEP 2011b).

The opening pages of this book contained a passage from the *Global Environmental Outlook* report at the turn of the century which spelled out the dark and worsening predicament that we face. The challenge it laid down was clear: 'The processes of globalization that are so strongly influencing social evolution need to be directed towards resolving rather than aggravating the serious imbalances that divide the world today' (UNEP 1999: xx). More than ten years on at the time of Rio +20, as the above quotation from UNEP in 2011 makes alarmingly clear, there is little evidence that we have begun to forge the sorts of collective responses necessary to construct a sustainable economy.

The consequences of our failure to steer the global economy onto a more sustainable footing are now known to us to an unprecedented degree, therefore, but the challenge is not a new one. Writing almost 70 years ago, the political economist Karl Polanyi was attuned to the repercussions of global market forces being allowed to reign without serious social or ecological restraint. With hindsight and foresight he wrote in 1944 that:

> To allow the market mechanism to be sole director of the fate of human
> beings and their natural environment . . . would result in the demolition
> of society . . . Nature would be reduced to its elements, neighbourhoods
> and landscapes defiled, rivers polluted, military safety jeopardized, the
> power to produce food and raw materials destroyed . . . [T]he commod-
> ity fiction disregarded the fact that leaving the fate of soil and people to
> the market would be tantamount to annihilating them (1980 [1944]: 73).

This final chapter pulls together some of the themes that have run through
the discussion of the patterns and politics of trade, production and finance
and their relationship to the environment, and to suggest ways in which
actually existing globalization is being challenged, re-cast and potentially
ultimately transformed by a range of social forces that seek either to
reverse or control its destructive tendencies or demand the transformation of the very economic system upon which it rests. This returns us,
therefore, to the questions posed in the introduction about the extent to
which the relationship between globalization and the environment is being
effectively governed and on whose behalf and, more profoundly, whether
the particular form of globalized capitalism that defines the era in which
we live is capable of addressing the sorts of ecological and social problems
generated by its everyday existence.

Our discussion of the political ecology, governance (and un-
governance) and contestation of trade, production and finance, has
suggested several reasons why, despite unprecedented economic wealth,
technological progress and scientific understanding of the nature and
gravity of our collective predicament, we continue to organize the global
economy in ways which are literally compromising our ability to sustain
ourselves on this planet.

First, and perhaps most benignly, change takes time. There is an inevitable and understandable gap between recognition of a problem and the
time it takes to mobilize a political response. Institutional inertia, the challenges of coordinating responses between 190 states and the inevitability
of competing problem definitions conspire to impede consensus and action
on responses to environmental threats. The history of trade regulation, the
slow evolution from the GATT to the more institutionalized form of the
WTO, or the history of international business regulation where, despite
decades of mobilization around the need for legally binding obligations on
TNCs, we still have a weak and ineffectual system of regulation, suggest
that institutional innovation takes time and that mere evidence of problems is no guarantee of a speedy response. The example of the global trade
regime also suggests that projects to strengthen international institutions

occur most rapidly when they have the backing of powerful states that stand to gain from them, most notably in this case the US. When we compare this with on-going calls from other states for a more robust global environmental architecture, perhaps in the form of a World Environment Organization, to provide an institutional counterweight to global economic institutions that have been ignored and marginalized (Biermann 2001; Newell 2001c; von Moltke 2001; Whalley and Zissimos 2001), it is clear that change is an awful lot easier when supported by (or at least not resisted by) the world's most powerful states.

Second, change is fiercely resisted by those who benefit from the existing way of doing things, from what we might call business as usual. Businesses threaten to relocate in the face of pollution charges, taxes or moves to strengthen their accountability to citizens. They resist the incorporation of minimal environmental standards in trade agreements. Banks mobilize against Tobin taxes aimed at taming volatile and destructive short-term and speculative financial flows. We have seen consistently throughout the book that the governance of globalization, such as it exists, is much stronger, more effective, more wide-reaching and more aggressively enforced when it takes the form of regulation *for* business rather than regulation *of* business. That regulation is cast by and for those that wield most power in the global economy is unsurprising and well explained by the sort of political economy framework presented in chapters 2 and 3, but it does present key strategic challenges for those interested in profound change.

Third, those responses that have emerged to a variety of environmental issues often exacerbate the very problems they were set up to address. Because they have been created in a context of advanced neo-liberalism, they have been developed in such a way as to enhance, deepen or at least be non-threatening to the growth imperatives of capitalism and rather aim to generate new accumulation opportunities. This means moving problems around: relocating polluting industries to poorer parts of the world. It means creating new industries to clean up the mess created by other sectors: managing the waste generated by global circuits of production, for example. Or it can take the form of selling services to other capitalists so that they may continue with business as usual; whether it is public relations companies offering brand and image management services to corporations in the midst of controversies about their operations, or the provision of solutions that displace the need for action (carbon offsets being a clear example of this). The recent increase in interest in global geo-engineering solutions to the problem of climate change (Victor et al. 2009) reveals both the desperate lack of progress of international efforts to control emissions and a widespread reluctance to compromise accelerated pollution-intensive industrial development, whatever its ecological and social consequences.

In terms of policy responses, many traditional tools of environmental regulation, standards, subsidies and trade measures or bans have been replaced by a stronger emphasis on voluntary measures and market-based mechanisms, although the state retains a key, yet often understated, role in creating and supervising markets: establishing rules and allocating property rights. Payments for ecosystem services are preferred to laws to protect access to water or forests. It becomes logical (as well as profitable) to address climate change not by reducing greenhouse gases at source in those countries that generate most of them, but to pay other countries that contribute far less to the problem to reduce their own emissions on the basis that it is cheaper to do. Economic (il)logic trumps eco-logic.

Fourth, while we have seen substantial and, in some cases, genuine shifts in the discourses about environmental change and the creation of new institutional arrangements (as well as the strengthening of existing ones), which have made important contributions to containing negative environmental change, materially the global economy remains firmly on collision course with the goal of a sustainable economy. We see this clearly in the case of climate change. There is an emerging consensus that warming should be restricted to 2 or even 1.5° compared with pre-industrial levels, since to allow for further warming is to accept that large parts of the planet become uninhabitable – a position that it is morally impossible to accept. Yet data from UNEP (2011b), the IEA (2011) and other bodies show clearly the policies and mechanisms currently in place do not even come close to meeting these targets, and financial and resource flows continue to move in the opposite direction. This of course relates strongly to the message that comes out loudly from the UNEP reports: incremental gains are being offset and reversed by the exponential increase in resources in a growth-oriented economy.

Capitalism and Growth

Given this, there is increasing and inevitable attention to the question of capitalism's ability to reconcile its growth needs with the need to sustain and enrich life on a finite planet. Whether it is the development of indices of 'happiness' or ideas about de-growth or 'prosperity without growth' (Jackson 2011), a growing body of critical and mainstream opinion recognizes that business as usual is not an option (Porritt 2007). The extent to which business has to be done differently continues to divide: whether more meaningful accounting and disclosure, along the lines of the Carbon and Water Disclosure Projects, discussed in chapters 5 and 6, combined with strong incentives for shifts in investment patterns, is sufficient. Or whether the time has come to pose more fundamental questions about for whom and what growth is for: recovering the idea that growth is a means to an end and not an end in itself. Corporations are given charters to serve a public purpose through wealth creation. If their activities result in a depletion of wealth or fail to serve a meaningful notion of the public interest, the legitimacy of their operations should be called into question (Korten 1995). It is clear that creating more business, accumulating more capital, has become an end in itself devoid of any prior sense of what public purpose it might serve, what benefits it brings to the population at large, or even the extent to which it may be undermining the health, well-being and productivity of other people and economic sectors. We have seen how within institutions of environment governance (the climate and forest regimes being prime examples), the creation of markets and means to support them have become ends in themselves without critical attention to the extent to which they provide solutions to the problems they were set up to address.

Speth (2008), in his book on capitalism and the environment *The Bridge at the Edge of the World*, argues that it is important not only to hold corporations to account for their actions, but also to re-focus our obsession with GDP growth in order to concentrate on ways to promote healthy, sustainable growth such as universal access to quality health care and education, to rely less on materialism as a measure of success and happiness and to change the market to one that works with the environment, not against it. Yet it is not clear that such changes, central and far-reaching as they undoubtedly are, will address the central problem he identifies: the fact that the relentless drive to grow and consume is incompatible with sustaining the environment as well as securing social well-being.

Economists suggest that the key challenge is to internalize externalities through taxation or better regulation. Lord Stern famously referred to climate change as the world's greatest market failure (Stern 2006). Yet the same point applies about incremental gains: the scale and depth of behavioural shifts achieved by taxation and regulation alone is swamped by overall increases in a global economy driven by the growth imperative. The problem is systemic, but not necessarily just about capitalism. Although the scale of capital flows and intensity of resource use overseen by the financial and corporate actors explored in this book suggest the peculiar ecological significance of capitalism in general, and its contemporary globalized form in particular, it is worth recalling that many parts of the world are either non-capitalist or exist beyond the reach of market institutions. The problems with capitalism are, in many ways, the problems with industrialism in general, including socialist centrally planned models of industrialization (Porritt 1989); it is just that capitalist economies are more dominant and powerful. Is there something then about the combination of wage labour and property rights intrinsic to capitalism that makes this economic system particularly problematic? Certainly attempts to privatize and commodify resources, justified in the name of incentivizing conservation and efficiency, have resulted in the exclusion of poorer people from access to water and forests, for example (Goldman 1998; Martínez-Alier 2002). Capital continues its restless search to isolate and commodify nature's functions in ways which can serve as viable accumulation strategies. Putting a price on avoided consequences as carbon markets do, or on the carbon absorption function of trees in order to trade credits, or seeking to commodify innovations in seed use and management overseen by communities the world over for generations before the advent of intellectual property rights, suggest we have yet to reach the limits of capital's imagination and thirst to make money from nature.

Or is the problem the spatial politics of accumulation strategies that create an ability to maintain a distance between sites of production and consumption which separates people from the consequences of their consumer choices and of the social and environmental costs they exact, so that rubbish and waste and primitive working conditions are kept from view? Or, is it rather the basic contradictions that result when growth runs up against the natural (and social) limits to growth (Meadows et al. 1972)? Although early predictions of the timing of resource exhaustion were overly pessimistic, and failed to take into account the role of technology innovation in reducing the intensity of resource depletion, many of the core assumptions and claims underpinning the notion of limits to growth still hold true. We see this with the current debate about peak oil. New discoveries of oil deposits in ever more remote locations (such as the arctic, now ironically made more accessible by melting ice sheets), or from places where it is difficult to extract (tar sands in Alberta), or technologies which use those fuels in more efficient ways, undoubtedly buy time. But they do nothing to alter the basic reality that the era of oil, one day or another, sooner or later, will come to an end. This has vast consequences for the tenability of the project of globalization based as it is on the abundant supply of fossil fuels to move goods over longer distances and to provide cheap energy to an ever expanding industry.

Optimists point to India and China and to a lesser extent the US and EU for evidence of 'carbon capitalism'; examples of the embrace of innovative low carbon technologies and the use of markets to bring down emissions (Lovins and Cohen 2011). Showing that efforts are being made by state and corporate actors to address climate change alongside other key objectives such as ensuring energy security, reducing risk or maximizing positive public relations is one thing. It is quite another to claim that we have achieved what Mat Paterson and I call 'climate capitalism' (Newell and Paterson 2010): a situation in which capital's growth alignments are met through low carbon forms of development. This is because of the still small percentage of economic flows currently constituted by clean energy which continue to be overwhelmed by fossil fuel use and because of the sorts of contradictions highlighted by Jevons nearly 150 years ago whereby efficiency savings have the ironic and unfortunate effect of encouraging further energy use with the money saved (Jevons 1865; Sorrell 2010).

Re-embedding Globalization

> The crisis consists precisely in the fact that the old is dying and the new cannot be born; in this interregnum a great variety of morbid symptoms appear (Gramsci 1971).

Despite the claims reviewed in chapter 1 about the inevitability and irreversibility of globalization, it is important to recall the enormous changes that have taken place in the history of the world economy to guard against the notion that because things are the way they are now, they will always be thus. Change and transformation are the only things that are guaranteed. That change results from capital's restless need to secure and intensify ways of making money in a crowded world with a depleting resource base. This requires new production processes and changes in technology that have dramatically changed the world before and will no doubt do so again. Optimism about the ability to orchestrate a new industrial revolution along cleaner, greener lines can be interpreted in this vein. New innovations and technologies, in turn, will generate fresh calls for governance and regulation of the problems that ensue and the tussle between deregulation and re-regulation will continue to unfold. The question will be in what direction and on whose terms.

Civil society will be key to how this happens. Civil society is as much a part of globalization as business or the World Trade Organization. While many groups position themselves in opposition to globalization, their modes of organization, use of global media and ability to re-brand themselves for the purposes of alliance building or appealing to public audiences are intrinsically a manifestation of early twenty-first-century glo-balized politics. Nevertheless, for the majority of civil society organizations working tirelessly in locales the world over on a bewildering array of social, economic and political issues, connections to the so-called anti-globaliza-tion movement are tenuous at best and in most cases non-existent. Theirs is not a new politics. It is a very traditional politics defined by age-old strat-egies of local protest and mobilization, not centred on global economic events or political summits, but targeting everyday forms of injustice, often in regions far removed from the epicentre of global economic activ-ity. Much such activism is captured by Martínez-Alier's (2002) notion of the 'environmentalism of the poor'. This is not to say that connections are not being increasingly and effectively forged between local conflicts and global processes overseen by the managers of the global economy. One of the achievements of the 'anti-globalization' movement has been an ability to identify connections and patterns of causation between local events and broader structural changes in the global economy. By these means, the Movement of the Landless (MST) in Brazil, farmers' protests against genetically modified crops in India and protests over the privatization of water in Bolivia are seen to share something in common: an opposition to the commodification of life, a questioning of the logic of 'market über alles', of the principle of profit over people.

One of the challenges for (global) civil society is to engage with or confront the institutions and actors that are driving the ideology of glo-balization, as well as providing the resources and institutional backing to realize it in practice: transnational companies, the banking and financial community and the key global economic institutions – the World Bank, IMF and WTO. Through their day-to-day operations and investment deci-sions, they fashion the world according to the key elements and versions of the Washington consensus, whose key tenets endure despite repeated criticism and attempts to accommodate critiques at the margins. They form part of a 'transnational managerial class' (Cox 1996; Sklair 2002b) that shares a common though evolving world view about how the global economy should be ordered. It would be naïve to suggest that there are not oppositional elements within each of these actors and institutions that do not see the world in these terms, or that the programmes and prescrip-tions of these institutions operate in harmony. But the mandates of the organizations, the methods of coordination among them, the mutually enforcing nature of the narratives they construct (and enact) about what count as legitimate forms of state economic policy, the incentive structures that operate within them, their recruitment policies and the social and educational backgrounds of the people they hire, help to reinforce a sense of shared interests and common threats.

As Susan George points out in polemical terms, this transnational elite bears a disproportionate responsibility for many of the interrelated problems that have been discussed in this book. In her book *Whose Crisis, Whose Future?*, she claims:

> Whether it's growing poverty and inequality or shrinking access to food and water, the collapse of global financial markets or the dire effects of climate change, every aspect of this crisis can be traced to a transnational neoliberal elite that has steadily eroded our rights and stripped us of power (George 2010).

It is also the case that from the World Bank to Shell International, strenuous efforts have been made to engage critics, understand the nature of the opposition and in some cases even employ its spokespeople, as in the case of the World Bank's appointment some years ago of the radical environmental critic Herman Daly (see chapter 6). It is testimony to the perceived and actual influence of prominent global movements, including the labour, environmental and women's movements, that the key global economic institutions have each sought to develop mechanisms for consulting with their critics within civil society (O'Brien et al. 2000; Scholte 2011). They increasingly see such engagements as important to shoring up their legitimacy as well as providing opportunities to capitalize on the expertise and networks that many NGOs have at their disposal. From questioning their rightful place in the politics of global governance, emphasis has shifted to identifying and refining mechanisms for improving the contribution of civil society organizations in exchange for commitments from groups to improve their own accountability and transparency as part of a 'new deal' for global governance (Edwards 2000).

It is increasingly recognized, however, that it is ultimately states that provide the resources and lend their legitimacy to global institutions, whose policies they are then expected to enforce. Many NGOs and trades unions have recognized this from the outset, despite the popularity among anti-globalization activists of targeting high-profile global institutions that suit more readily caricatures of global leviathans. What is also being acknowledged is that within the state, some elements of government are more globalized than others, as we saw in chapter 1. The internationalization of the state has meant that ministries of trade and finance have assumed a key role in adjusting their economies to the requirements of global market integration, often in the face of opposition from other government departments sensitive to political constituencies that will suffer the displacement of neo-liberal adjustment in sectors such as agriculture, labour and environment. Problematic for activists campaigning on these issues, therefore, is the entrenched marginalization of those parts of the state with which they have traditionally allied themselves. This is the broad canvass that characterizes the contemporary political arena upon which those elements of civil society that are engaged with global politics have to operate.

Renewed efforts are nevertheless required to democratize global decision making around trade, production and finance. The consequences of decisions taken in bodies such as the WTO and IMF are too important to be left to an elite made up of state officials, representatives from the financial and corporate sector and a narrow sub-set of global civil society. This is not about getting more people into those institutions, but drawing powers of decision making away from them to arenas where fuller democratic scrutiny is possible: national parliaments and regional assemblies, for example. Raising peoples' awareness of what is at stake places large demands on economic literacy campaigns and strategies that seek to connect disparate global communities that are played off against one another by regional and global trade accords and investment treaties. Securing greater procedural justice, including of course reforming the mandates of key institutions and ensuring greater equity and balance among them, offers one route to altering the nature of distributional justice and the skewed outcomes that characterize contemporary globalization. The forms of contestation documented throughout the book highlight clearly the myriad ways in which the social and environmental consequences of the exercise of unequal power in the global political economy are being resisted.

The Global Politics of a Just Transition

We have seen, then, throughout the book how civil society is actively engaged in contesting, producing and, in some cases, re-defining the many different constitutive elements of the phenomena we have come to call globalization. From struggles to create new rules or to contest those rules that exist, to strategies of resistance to the cultural symbols of globalization, the environmental movement is now a key actor in the unfolding drama of globalization. We have seen how in opposing those forms of globalization that generate social injustice and environmental degradation, activists have made effective use of media, advertising and the internet;

the very tools that globalizers use to expand their power and market reach. We have also seen how some activists have sought to work with and against corporations, with and against global economic institutions, pursuing different agendas of change, but recognizing political power increasingly resides with these actors as well as with the state actors that have traditionally been the target of their lobbying, and that continue to be ultimately accountable for decisions made by these institutions.

The future direction of the movement is difficult to predict given that it is so strongly defined by the historical and material context in which it is operating and at the same time trying to define. It should be clear, however, that despite the many gains that civil society actors have made in contesting current forms of globalization and in seeking to move towards an alternative, some of the most powerful actors in the global economy benefit enormously from the status quo. They can draw on extensive financial resources and channels of political influence to counter opposition to a global order which they helped to design and from which they profit. This occurs through numerous means including through social networks, direct lobbying, funding of political parties and civil society organizations and control of the media. Change will, therefore, be hard fought and not achieved in any substantive sense, in the short term. It requires continued efforts to construct new alliances across regions, movements and issues and to work on multiple fronts to meet the challenges of globalization in the multitude of arenas and practices through which it manifests and advances itself.

One of the key insights that flows from both the empirical analysis in chapters 4, 5 and 6 as well as the theoretical frameworks set out in chapters 1–3 is the imperative of forming broad-based coalitions for change, as well as pursuing strategic collaborations with actors that are particularly powerful under conditions of globalization. The experience of activism around globalization and specific aspects of it, whether the negotiation of regional and global trade accords or new investment rules, as well as efforts to contest the effects of such policies by environmental justice movements, suggests the value of links across environmental, labour, gender and indigenous peoples' movements (Obach 2004). Tensions and trade-offs will always characterize efforts to construct multi-movement coalitions (Icaza et al. 2010), where different priorities, ideologies and protest cultures compete and combine with very distinct social bases and levels of public representation and membership. But pursuing struggles not solely as environmental campaigns, but identifying, naming and contesting the multiple forms of social injustice and exclusion they imply, is critical to mobilizing the sorts of movements necessary to counter the use and abuse of existing power as well as to advocate for alternatives.

Moves towards a lower impact economy, one that is welfare-oriented rather than purely profit-oriented, will mean not only working with and against the power of wealthy corporate and financial actors, but also, if broader alliances are to be effectively constructed, recognizing the impact on working-class communities of transitions away from a carbon and resource-intensive economy which employs many millions of people in mining, the oil and auto industries, for example, for whom alternative forms of employment will have to be found. So far it has been relatively easy for large industry organizations to count on the support of trades unions in opposing environmental measures on the grounds of the threat they pose to jobs in conventional sectors. The green new deal rhetoric and calls for 'just, green jobs' – the strategic use of public money to stimulate the economy in sectors which will form the basis of a low carbon transition – seek to forge new links between unions and environmental movements, but further work is clearly required to consolidate and build common ground (Obach 2004).

There have been moves in this direction. Aside from calls for 'just transitions' in international arenas: mechanisms to ensure a fair transition for workers that might suffer socio-economic impacts of climate mitigation measures, there have been movements mobilizing around this idea, going beyond a focus on 'transition towns' which have been initiated in the UK, for example, which aims to prepare for a world after oil (Bulkeley and Newell 2010), to emphasize the social justice elements of such a transformation. For example, the Just Transition Alliance is a coalition of environmental justice and labour organizations which brings together frontline workers and community members who live alongside polluting industries. It focuses on contaminated sites that should be cleaned up, and on the transition to clean production and sustainable economies. For example, on issues such as 'clean coal', the Just Transition Alliance voices objections based on local as well as global impacts, including local air pollution, working conditions and the detrimental environmental impacts of mining on local landscapes and water use. In Los Angeles, meanwhile, a grassroots coalition of community-based organizations, trades unions and environmental groups (the LA Apollo Alliance) campaigned to ensure that programmes by the city council to improve energy efficiency and the use of renewable energy also brought economic benefits to disadvantaged people living in the city. This included retrofit of public buildings in low-income communities, jobs for poorer people and supporting businesses owned by local minorities and women (Bird and Lawton 2009; Evans 2010; JTA 2011).

Important though they are, such campaigns, experiments and victories also need to form linkages and coordinate their work with other movements and activists if broader change is to occur, in order to be able to demonstrate that other modes of production and another world is possible. Success stories and powerful narratives about the necessity and desirability of a 'just transition' are essential, but so too will be contesting, engaging and seeking to transform those actors with the control over the material resources required to deliver larger changes in the structures and practices of the global economy.

Theory for Change

Understanding the complex and mutually constitutive relationship between economy, ecology and society in order to both make future interventions more effective, as well as to be able to articulate connections between seemingly discrete issues, requires us to bring to bear a range of theoretical resources. We need to explain why, in the face of evidence of social inequality and environmental devastation, change is often not forthcoming. This means understanding power: the power to change and the power to resist change. We saw in chapter 3 how reducing environmental politics to the question of international cooperation and creation of international law, while useful, provides only a limited understanding of the deeper and structural reasons why, despite the flurry of institutional activity at the global level over the last forty years, environmental degradation continues and accelerates apace. Powerful states such as the US and China have resisted calls to reduce their contribution to global problems such as climate change, while the EU and Japan, despite occasional claims to the contrary, have not been able to fill the leadership gap. In any case, a narrow focus on relations between states gives only a partial account of the drivers and barriers to change. States maintain only partial control over the processes of production, the technology and the capital which are currently insinuated both in producing environmental harm as well as potentially providing the means of reducing it, and have to negotiate and accommodate with those private actors that do have such control.

We have also seen how efforts to address environmental problems reflect and embody the political-economic context in which they emerge. In a neo-liberal world the preference is for voluntary, private and market-based responses to environmental challenges over 'top down' so-called 'command-and-control' measures. The need to locate solutions which are compatible with the requirements of capitalism as it is currently constituted significantly constricts the scope for politically acceptable and effective policy interventions. We have seen how understanding the links between environmental governance and capitalism (and industrialism more broadly) is vital to understanding the potential and limits to meaningful efforts to advance sustainability.

In terms of future efforts to employ theory towards this central aim of understanding the opportunities for change within and beyond a global economy organized along capitalist lines, a number of lines of enquiry might be useful. It has been suggested here that various strands of historical materialism, when combined with political ecology, might be usefully applied and adapted to understand the dynamics described in this book. This is because, as we saw in chapter 2, capitalism develops through nature–society relations. Capitalism does not just have ecological consequences; it is also an ecological regime in its own right. As Smith (2006: 21–2) claims 'the production of nature mutates from an incidental and fragmented reality to a systemic condition of social existence, from a local oddity into a global ambition'. That is, 'the universal production of nature was written into the DNA of capitalist ambition from the start: neoliberal globalization is only its latest incarnation' (Smith 2007: 6). Insights such as these are important to situating the attempts at governing the environment in a context of globalization that have been described in this book as one site within a broader system of social, economic and ecological relations. It underlines the importance of connecting particular (political) ecologies to the circuits of capital and political power which produce them, without losing sight of what makes ecologies and social relations different in particular locales. This includes their ability to negotiate globalization on different terms, to resist commodification and privatization of resources in some instances and, in others, to suggest alternative ways of constructing nature–society relations which go beyond the imperatives of capital accumulation.

Ultimately as Marx challenged us to consider, 'The philosophers have only interpreted the world, in various ways; the point is to change it' (Marx 1969 [1845]). There remains a key challenge to distil, articulate and communicate evidence about the everyday effects of the current global economy; to engage multiple publics in discussion about its implications and to deliberate on the trade-offs that flow from efforts to address poverty, sustainability and well-being simultaneously. Doing this in an integrated global economy, where one set of decisions increasingly has impacts elsewhere, tests to the limit the sorts of democratic institutions we currently have. But efforts to democratize decision making around the future of the planet must go alongside efforts to challenge the current orientation of the global economy in order to subject globalization to a greater degree of popular control such that we may at least have a greater chance of generating and sharing wealth in a way which reduces poverty and minimizes environmental degradation.

References

Aborigen Argentino (2005) Familia Mapuche enfrenta al grupo Benetton por tierra que le pertenece. Available at: www.aborigenargentino.com.ar (accessed 23 December 2007).

Acción Ecológica (2004) Acción Ecológica, www.accionecologica.org/alca.htm (accessed 5 October 2004).

Adams, W. and J. Hutton (2007) People, parks and poverty: political ecology and biodiversity conservation. *Conservation and Society* 5(2): 147–183.

Adkin, L. (2000) Democracy, ecology, political economy: reflections on starting points. In F. Gale and M. M'Gonigle (eds.) *Nature, Production and Power: Towards an Ecological Political Economy*. Cheltenham: Edward Elgar, 59–83.

Altvater, E. (1997) *Grenzen der Globalisierung: Ökonomie, Ökologie und Politik in der Weltgesellschaft*. Münster: Westfälisches Dampfboot.

Altvater, E. (2006) The social and natural environment of fossil capitalism. In L. Panitch and C. Leys (eds.) *Coming to Terms with Nature: Socialist Register 2007*. London: Merlin Press, 37–60.

Amoore, L. (2000) International political economy and the contested firm. *New Political Economy* 5(2): 183–204.

Anderson, M. and A. Ahmed (1996) Assessing environmental damage under Indian law. *RECIEL* 5(4): 335–341.

Andrée, P. (2005) The genetic engineering revolution in agriculture and food: strategies of the 'Biotech Bloc'. In D. Levy and P. Newell (eds.) *The Business of Global Environmental Governance*. Cambridge, MA: MIT Press, 135–166.

Angel, D., T. Hamilton and M. Huber (2007) Global environmental standards for industry. *Annual Review of Environment and Resources* 32(1): 295–316.

Arts, B. (1998) *The Political Influence of Global NGOs: Case Studies on the Climate Change and Biodiversity Conventions*. Utrecht: International Books.

Arts, B. (2005) Non-state actors in global environmental governance: new arrangements beyond the state. In M. Koenig-Archibugi and M. Zürn (eds.) *New Modes of Governance in the Global System: Exploring Publicness, Delegation and Inclusiveness*. Basingstoke: Palgrave, 177–201.

Audley, J. (1997) *Green Politics and Global Trade: NAFTA and the Future of Environmental Politics*. Washington, DC: Georgetown University Press.

Australian Senate (2000) Corporate Code of Conduct Bill: A bill for an act to impose standards on the conduct of Australian corporations which under-take business initiatives in other countries and for related purposes, drafted by Senator Bourne.

Bachram, H. (2004) Climate fraud and carbon colonialism: the new trade in greenhouse gases. *Capitalism, Nature, Socialism* 15(4): 1–16.

Bailey, I., A. Gouldson and P. Newell (2011) Ecological modernisation and the governance of carbon: a critical analysis. *Antipode* 43(3): 682–703.

Bakker, K. (2005) Neoliberalizing nature? Market environmentalism in water supply in England and Wales. *Annals of the Association of American Geographers* 95(3): 542–565.

Bakker, K. (2010) *Privatising Water: Governance Failure and the World's Urban Water Crisis*. Ithaca: Cornell University Press.

BankTrack (2011) About BankTrack. Available at: www.banktrack.org/show/pages/about_banktrack (accessed 3 July 2011).

Barkin, S. (2008) Trade and environment institutions. In K. Gallagher (ed.) *Handbook on Trade and the Environment*. Cheltenham: Edward Elgar, 318–326.

Barrientos, S., A. Bee, A. Matear and I. Vogel (1999) *Women and Agribusiness: Working Miracles in the Chilean Fruit Export Sector*. Basingstoke: Palgrave.

Bartels, L. (2004) The separating of powers in the WTO: how to avoid judicial activism. *International Comparative Law Quarterly* 53: 861–895.

Bauman, Z. (2002) *Society under Siege*. Cambridge: Polity Press.

Baxi, U. and A. Dhanda (1990) *Valiant Victims and Lethal Litigation*. New Delhi: Indian Law Institute.

Baxi, U. and T. Paul (1986) *Mass Disasters and Multinational Liability*. Bombay: N.M. Tripathi Press.

Bebbington, A. (2003) Global networks and local developments: agendas for development geography. *Tijdschrift voor Economische en Sociale Geografie* 94(3): 297–309.

Bendell, J. (ed.) (2000) *Terms of Endearment: Business, NGOs and Sustainable Development*. Sheffield: Greenleaf Publishing.

Bendell, J. and D. Murphy (2002) Towards civil regulation: NGOs and the politics of corporate environmentalism. In P. Utting (ed.) *The Greening of Business in Developing Countries*. London: Zed Books, 245–267.

Benton, B. (2000) An ecological historical materialism. In F. Gale and M. M'Gonigle (eds.) *Nature, Production and Power: Towards an Ecological Political Economy*. Cheltenham: Edward Elgar, 83–105.

Bernstein, S. (2001) *The Compromise of Liberal Environmentalism*. New York: Columbia University Press.

Betsill, M. and E. Corell (2001) NGO influence in international environmental negotiations: a framework for analysis. *Global Environmental Politics* 1(4): 65–85.

Bhagwati, J. (1993) The case for free trade. *Scientific American* 269(5): 18–23.

Biermann, F. (2001) The emerging debate on the need for a World Environment Organisation: A commentary. *Global Environmental Politics* 1(1): 45–56.

Bird, J. and K. Lawton (2009) *The Future's Green: Jobs and the UK Low-carbon Transition*. London: IPPR.

Blaikie, P. (1985) *The Political Economy of Soil Erosion in Developing Countries*. London: Longman.

Blaikie, P. and H. Brookfield (1987) *Land Degradation and Society*. London: Methuen.

BOND (Development and Environment Group (DEG) of British Overseas NGOs for International Development) (2008) Letter from UK NGOs to Douglas Alexander, Secretary of State for International Development, 11 March. Available at: www.ifiwatchnet.org/sites/ifiwatchnet.org/files/Letter%20to%20ministers%20Feb%2008%20-%20Douglas%20Alexander.pdf (accessed 12 November 2008).

Borras, J., R. Hall, I. Scoones, B. White and W. Wolford (2011) Towards a better understanding of land grabbing. *The Journal of Peasant Studies* 38(2): 209–217.

Boyce, J.K. (2008) Globalization and the environment: convergence or divergence? In K. Gallagher (ed.) *Handbook on Trade and the Environment*. Cheltenham: Edward Elgar, 97–116.

Brack, D. (1996) *International Trade and the Montreal Protocol*. London: RIIA/Earthscan.

Brack, D. (1997) Trade and environment: an update of the issues. RIIA Briefing Paper 35. February.

Braithwaite, J. and P. Drahos (2000) *Global Business Regulation*. Cambridge: Cambridge University Press.

Brand, U., C. Görg, J. Hirsch and M. Wissen (2008) *Conflicts in Environmental Regulation and the Internationalization of the State*. London: Routledge.

Brautigam, D., O.H. Fjeldstad and M. Moore (2008) *Taxation and State-Building in Developing Countries: Capacity and Consent*. Cambridge: Cambridge University Press.

Breslin, S. (2003) Reforming China's embedded socialist compromise: China and the WTO. *Global Change, Peace and Security* 15(3): 213–229.

Bretton Woods Project (2011a) Environment. Available at: www.brettonwoodsproject.org/item.shtml?x=537807 (accessed 7 July 2011).

Bretton Woods Project (2011b) Energy for the poor: World Bank urged to make a clean break. Available at: www.brettonwoodsproject.org/art-567934 (accessed 8 September 2011).

Brockington, D. and J. Igoe (2006) Eviction for conservation: a global overview. *Conservation and Society* 4(3): 424–470.

Brunnengräber, A. (2006) The political economy of the Kyoto Protocol. In L. Panitch and C. Leys (eds.) *Coming to Terms with Nature: Socialist Register 2007*. London: The Merlin Press, 213–231.

Bryant, R. (1999) A political ecology for developing countries. *Zeitschrift für Wirtschaftsgeographie* 43(3–4): 148–157.

Bryant, R. and S. Bailey (1997) *Third World Political Ecology*. London: Routledge.

Buck, D. (2006) The ecological question: can capitalism prevail? In L. Panitch and C. Leys (eds.) *Coming to Terms with Nature: Socialist Register 2007*. London: The Merlin Press, 60–72.

Budds, J. (2004) Power, nature and neoliberalism: the political ecology of water in Chile. *Singapore Journal of Tropical Geography* 25(3): 322–342.

Bulkeley, H. (2005) Reconfiguring environmental governance: Towards a politics of scales and networks. *Political Geography* 24: 875–902.

Bulkeley, H. and P. Newell (2010) *Governing Climate Change*. London: Routledge.

Bullard, R.D. (2005) *The Quest for Environmental Justice: Human Rights and the Politics of Pollution*. Berkeley, CA: University of California Press.

Bumpus, A. and D. Liverman (2008) Accumulation by de-carbonization and the governance of carbon offsets. *Economic Geography* 84(2): 127–155.

Burkett, P. and J. Bellamy Foster (2006) Metabolism, energy and entropy in Marx's critique of political economy: beyond the Podolinsky myth. *Theory and Society* 35(1): 109–156.

Butler, T. (2005) Corporate America, activists and circumventing Washington: a new approach to environmental lobbying. Available at: http://news.mongabay.com/2005/0427-tina_butler.html (accessed 18 February 2008).

Carmin, J. and J. Agyeman (eds.) (2011) *Environmental Justice Beyond Borders: Local Perspectives on Global Inequities*. Cambridge, MA: MIT Press.

Cashore, B., G. Auld and D. Newsom (2004) *Governing Through Markets: Forest Certification and the Emergence of Non-State Authority*. New Haven, CT: Yale University Press.

Cassimon, D., M. Prowse and D. Essers (2011) The pitfalls and potential of debt-for-nature swaps: a US-Indonesian case study. *Global Environmental Change* 21(1): 93–102.

Castree, N. (2000) Marxism and the production of nature. *Capital and Class* (72) 5–36.

Castree, N. (2003) Commodifying what nature? *Progress in Human Geography* 27(3): 273–297.

Castree, N. (2008) Neoliberalising nature: the logics of deregulation and reregulation. *Environment and Planning A* 40(1): 131–152.

Castree, N. and B. Braun (2001) *Social Nature: Theory Practice and Politics*. Oxford: Blackwell.

CDP (Carbon Disclosure Project) (2011) www.cdproject.net/en-US/Pages/HomePage.aspx (accessed 8 September 2011).

Ceceña, A.E. (2005) *La Guerra por El Agua y por La Vida*. Buenos Aires: Ediciones Madres de la Plaza de Mayo.

CERES (2005) www.ceres.org/investorprograms/shareholder_action.php (accessed 4 July 2005).

Cerny, P. (1995) Globalization and the changing logic of collective action. *International Organization* (49)4: 595–625.

Charnovitz, S. (2008) An introduction to the trade and environment debate. In K. Gallagher (ed.) *Handbook on Trade and the Environment.* Cheltenham: Edward Elgar, 237–246.

Chatterjee, P. and M. Finger (1994) *The Earth Brokers: Power, Politics and World Development.* London: Routledge.

CIEL (Centre for International Environmental Law) (2006) *EC-Biotech: overview and analysis of the panel's interim report.* Available at: www.ciel.org/ Publications/EC_Biotech_Mar06.pdf (accessed 6 November 2007).

Clapp, J. (1998) The privatisation of global environmental governance: ISO 14001 and the developing world. *Global Governance* 4(3): 295–316.

Clapp, J. (2001) *Toxic Exports: The Transfer of Hazardous Wastes from Rich to Poor Countries.* Ithaca, NY: Cornell University Press.

Clapp, J. (2005) The privatisation of global environmental governance: ISO1400 and the developing world. In D. Levy and P. Newell (eds.) *The Business of Global Environmental Governance.* Cambridge, MA: MIT Press, 223–249.

Clapp, J. (2006) International political economy and the environment. In M. Betsill, K. Hochstetler and D. Stevis (eds.) *International Environmental Politics.* Basingstoke: Palgrave, 142–172.

Clapp, J. and P. Dauvergne (2005) *Paths to a Green World: The Political Economy of the Global Environment,* 1st edn. Cambridge, MA: MIT Press.

Clapp, J. and P. Dauvergne (2011) *Paths to a Green World: The Political Economy of the Global Environment,* 2nd edn. Cambridge, MA: MIT Press.

Clark, B. and J.B. Foster (2009) Ecological imperialism and the global metabolic rift: unequal exchange and the guano/nitrates trade. *International Journal of Comparative Sociology* 50(3–4): 311–334.

Clark, B. and R. York (2005) Carbon metabolism: global capitalism, climate change and the biospheric rift. *Theory and Society* 34(4): 391–428.

Clausen, R. and B. Clark (2005) The metabolic rift and marine ecology: an analysis of the oceanic crisis within capitalist production. *Organization & Environment* 18(4): 422–444.

The Climate Group (2006) About the Climate Group. Available at: www.the-climategroup.org/about-us/ (accessed 27 February 2006).

Cole, L. and S. Foster (2001) *From the Ground Up: Environmental Racism and the Rise of the Environmental Justice Movement.* New York: New York University Press.

Collinson, H. (ed.) (1996) *Green Guerrillas: Environmental Conflicts and Initiatives in Latin America and the Caribbean.* London: Latin American Bureau.

Conca, K. (2000a) The WTO and the undermining of global environmental governance. *Review of International Political Economy* 7(3): 484–494.

Conca, K. (2000b) Beyond the statist frame: environmental politics in a global economy. In F. Gale and M. M'Gonigle (eds.) *Nature, Production and Power: Towards an Ecological Political Economy*. Cheltenham: Edward Elgar, 141–159.

Conca, K. (2005) Old states in new bottles? The hybridization of authority in global environmental governance. In J. Barry and R. Eckersley (eds.) *The State and the Global Ecological Crisis*. Cambridge, MA: MIT Press, 181–207.

Connolly, B. (1996) Increments for the Earth: the politics of environmental aid. In R. Keohane and M. Levy (eds.) *Institutions for Environmental Aid*. Cambridge, MA: MIT Press, 327–365.

Copeland, B. (2008) The pollution haven hypothesis. In K. Gallagher (ed.) *Handbook on Trade and the Environment*. Cheltenham: Edward Elgar, 60–71.

CORE (The Corporate Responsibility Coalition) (2010) *Protecting Rights, Repairing Harm: How State-based Non-judicial Mechanisms Can Help Fill Gaps in Existing Frameworks for the Protection of Human Rights of People Affected by Corporate Activities*. London: CORE Coalition. Available at: http://corporate-responsibility.org/wp/wp-content/uploads/2010/11/core_SRS Gsubmission.pdf (accessed 15 August 2011).

Cosbey, A. (2008) *Border Carbon Adjustment*. Winnipeg: International Institute for Sustainable Development.

Cottrell, J. (1992) Courts and accountability: public interest litigation in the Indian high courts. *Third World Legal Studies* 11: 199–213.

Cox, R. (1981) Social forces, states and world orders: beyond International Relations theory. *Millennium* 10(2): 126–155.

Cox, R. (1987) *Production, Power and World Order*. New York: Columbia University Press.

Cox, R. (1994) Global restructuring: Making sense of the changing international political economy. In R. Stubbs and G. Underhill (eds.) *Political Economy and the Changing Global Order*. Basingstoke: Macmillan, 45–60.

Cox, R. (ed.) (1996) *Business, State and International Relations*. New York: New York University Press.

Coyle, D. (1999) *Governing the Global Economy*. London: Polity.

Crenson, M. (1971) *The Un-Politics of Air Pollution*. Baltimore, MD: Johns Hopkins University Press.

Cromwell, D. (2001) *Private Planet: Corporate Plunder and the Fight Back*. Chipping Norton: Jon Carpenter.

Curtis, M. (2001) *Trade for Life: Making Trade Work for Poor People*. London: Christian Aid.

Cutler, C. (2002) Historical materialism, globalization and law. In M. Rupert and H. Smith (eds.) *Historical Materialism and Globalization*. London: Routledge, 230–256.

Daly, H. (1993) The perils of free trade. *Scientific American* 269(5): 24–29.

Dauvergne, P. (1997) *Shadows in the Forest: Japan and the Political Economy of Deforestation in South East Asia*. Cambridge, MA: MIT Press.

Dauvergne, P. (1999) The environmental implications of Asia's 1997 financial crisis. *IDS Bulletin* 30(3): 31–42.

Dauvergne, P. (2008) *The Shadows of Consumption: Consequences for the Global Environment*. Cambridge, MA: MIT Press.

Dauvergne, P. and J. Lister (2010) The power of big box retail: Bringing commodity chains back into IR. *Millennium* 39(1): 145–160.

Davidsson, P.A. (2002) Legal enforcement of CSR within the EU. *Columbia Journal of European Law* 8(3): 529–556.

Derber, C. (2010) *Greed to Green: Solving Climate Change and Re-Making the Economy*. London: Paradigm Publishers.

Dobson, A. (1990) *Green Political Thought*. London: Routledge.

Douthwaite, R. (1996) *Short Circuit: Strengthening Local Economies for Security in an Unstable World*. Totnes, Devon: Green Books.

Duffy, R. (2005) The politics of global environmental governance: the powers and limitations of transfrontier conservation areas in Central Americas. *Review of International Studies* 31: 307–323.

ECA Watch (Export Credit Agency Watch) (2011a) www.eca-watch.org/ (accessed 6 September 2011).

ECA Watch (2011b) Jakarta Declaration for Reform of Official Export Credit and Investment Insurance Agencies. Available at: www.eca-watch.org/ goals/jakartadec.html (accessed 27 January 2012).

EDF and NRDC (Environmental Defense Fund and Natural Resources Defense Council) (1994) *Power Failure: a Review of the World Bank's Implementation of its New Energy Policy*. Washington, DC: EDF & NRDC.

Edwards, M. (2000) *NGOs Rights and Responsibilities: A New Deal for Global Governance*. London: The Foreign Policy Centre.

Edwards, M. and J. Gaventa (eds.) (2001) *Global Citizen Action*. Boulder, CO: Lynne Rienner.

Ellis, K. and M. Warner (2007) Is the time ripe for a 'good for development' product label? *ODI Opinion 88*. London: Overseas Development Institute.

Evans, G. (2010) *A Just Transition to Sustainability in a Climate Change Hot-Spot: From Carbon Valley to a Future Beyond Coal*. Saarbrücken: VDM.

Evans, G., J. Goodman and N. Lansbury (2002) *Moving Mountains: Communities Confront Mining and Globalization*. London: Zed Books.

Evans, P. (1995) *Bringing the State Back In*. Cambridge: Cambridge University Press.

Fairhead, J. and M. Leach (1998) *Reframing Deforestation: Global Analysis and Local Realities: Studies in West Africa*. New York: Routledge.

Falkner, R. (2003) Private environmental governance and International Relations: exploring the links. *Global Environmental Politics* 3(2): 72–88.

Falkner, R. (2008) *Business Power and Conflict in International Politics*. Basingstoke: Palgrave.

Finger, M. and L. Tamiotti (1999) New global regulatory mechanisms and the environment: the emerging linkage between the WTO and the ISO. *IDS Bulletin* 30(3): 8–15.

Ford, L. (2005) Challenging the global environmental governance of toxics: social movement agency and global civil society. In D. Levy and P. Newell (eds.) *The Business of Global Environmental Governance*, 305–329.

Forsyth, T. (2003) *Critical Political Ecology: The Politics of Environmental Science*. London: Routledge.

Foster, J.B. (1999) Marx's theory of metabolic rift: classical foundation for environmental sociology. *American Journal of Sociology* 105(2): 366–405.

Foster, J.B. and B. Clark (2009) The paradox of wealth: capitalism and ecological destruction. *Monthly Review* 61(6). Available at: http://monthlyreview. org/2009/11/01/the-paradox-of-wealth-capitalism-and-ecological-destruc tion (accessed 15 August 2011).

Foster, J.B., B. Clark and R. York (2010) *The Ecological Rift: Capitalism's War with the Earth*. New York: Monthly Review Press.

Fox, J. and D. Brown (eds.) (1998) *The Struggle for Accountability: The World Bank, NGOs and Grassroots Movements*. Cambridge, MA: MIT Press.

Freese, B. (2003) *Coal: A Human History*. London: Basic Books.

French, H. (1993) Costly trade-offs: reconciling trade and environment. Worldwatch Paper 113, March. Washington, DC: Worldwatch Institute.

Friends of the Earth (2003) *UKplc in Latin America*. Friends of the Earth Briefing, September. London: Friends of the Earth.

Friends of the Earth International (2006) Looking behind the US spin: WTO ruling does not prevent countries from restricting or banning GMOs. Friends of the Earth International Briefing Paper. Available at: www.foei. org/en/media/archive/2006/WTO_briefing.pdf/view   (accessed   15 August 2011).

Frynas, G. (1998) Political instability and business: focus on Shell in Nigeria. *Third World Quarterly* 19(3): 457–478.

Frynas, G. (1999) Legal change in Africa: evidence from oil-related litigation in Nigeria. *Journal of African Law* 43: 121–150.

Frynas, G. (2000) Shell in Nigeria: a further contribution. *Third World Quarterly* 21(1): 157–164.

Fukuyama, F. (1993) *The End of History and the Last Man*. New York: Avon Books.

Gale, F. (1998) Cave! Hic dragones: a neo-Gramscian deconstruction and reconstruction of international regime theory. *Review of International Political Economy* 5(2): 252–283.

Gale, F. and M. M'Gonigle (eds.) (2000) *Nature, Production and Power: Towards an Ecological Political Economy*. Cheltenham: Edward Elgar.

Gallagher, K. (ed.) (2005) *Putting Development First: The Importance of Policy Space in the WTO and International Financial Institutions*. London: Zed Books.

Gallagher, K. and L. Zarsky (2007) *The Enclave Economy: Foreign Investment and Sustainable Development in Mexico's Silicon Valley*. Cambridge, MA: MIT Press.

Ganzi, J., F. Seymour and S. Buffett with N. Dubash (1998) *Leverage for the Environment: A Guide to the Private Financial Services Industry*. Washington, DC: World Resources Institute.

Garcia-Johnson, R. (2000) *Exporting Environmentalism: US Chemical Corporations in Mexico and Brazil*. Cambridge, MA: MIT Press.

Garvey, N. and P. Newell (2005) Corporate accountability to the poor? Assessing the effectiveness of community-based strategies. *Development in Practice* 15 (3–4): 389–405.

GEF (Global Environment Facility) (2011) About GEF. Available at: www.thegef.org/gef/whatisgef (accessed 27 January 2011).

George, S. (1992) *The Debt Boomerang*. London: Pluto Press.

George, S. (2010) *Whose Crisis, Whose Future?* Cambridge: Polity.

GHG Protocol Initiative (2009) About the Greenhouse Gas Protocol. Available at: www.ghgprotocol.org/about-ghgp (accessed 13 April 2009).

Giddens, A. (1990) *Consequences of Modernity*. Cambridge: Polity Press.

Gill, S. (1995a) Globalization, market civilisation and disciplinary neoliberalism. *Millennium: Journal of International Studies* 24(3): 399–423.

Gill, S. (1995b) Theorising the interregnum: the double movement and global politics in the 1990s. In B. Hettne (ed.) *International Political Economy*. London: Zed Books, 65–99.

Gill, S. (2002) Constitutionalizing inequality and the clash of globalizations. *International Studies Review* 4(2): 47–65.

Gill, S. and D. Law (1988) *The Global Political Economy*. Hemel Hempstead: Harvester Wheatsheaf.

Gill, S. and D. Law (1989) Global hegemony and the structural power of capital. *International Studies Quarterly* 33: 475–499.

Global Issues (2011) Third World Debt Undermines Development. Available at: www.globalissues.org/issue/28/third-world-debt-undermines-development (accessed 29 June 2011).

Glover, D. (1999) Defending communities: local exchange trading systems from an environmental perspective. *IDS Bulletin* 30(3): 75–81.

Goldman, M. (ed.) (1998) *Privatising Nature: Political Struggles for the Global Commons*. London: Pluto Press.

Goldman, M. (2005) *Imperial Nature: The World Bank and Struggles for Social Justice in an Age of Globalization*. New Haven, CT: Yale University Press.

Görg, C. and U. Brand (2006) Contested regimes in the international political economy: global regulation of genetic resources and the internationalisation of the state. *Global Environmental Politics* 6(4): 101–123.

Graham, E. (2000) *Fighting the Wrong Enemy: Anti-global Activists and Multinational Enterprises*. Washington, DC: Institute for International Economics.

Gramsci, A. (1971) *Selections from the Prison Notebooks*, edited and translated by Q. Hoare and G. Nowell Smith. New York: International Publishers.

Grant, W., D. Matthews and P. Newell (2000) *The Effectiveness of EU Environmental Policy*. Basingstoke: Palgrave.

Grieco, J. (1988) Anarchy and the limits of cooperation: a realist critique of the newest liberal institutionalism. *International Organisation* 42: 485–507.

Griffiths-Jones, S. with J. Kimmis (1999) Stabilising capital flows to developing countries: the role of regulation. In S. Piccottio and R. Mayne (eds.) *Regulating International Business: Beyond Liberalisation*. Basingstoke: Palgrave Macmillan, 161–182.

Gulbrandsen, L.H. (2010) *Transnational Environmental Governance: The Emergence and Effects of the Certification of Forests and Fisheries*. Cheltenham: Edward Elgar.

Haas, P. (1990a) Obtaining international environmental protection through epistemic consensus. *Millennium: Journal of International Studies* 19(3): 347–363.

Haas, P. (1990b) *Saving the Mediterranean: The Politics of International Environmental Cooperation*. New York: Columbia University Press.

Haas, P., R. Keohane and M. Levy (1993) *Institutions for the Earth: Sources of Effective Environmental Protection*. Cambridge, MA: MIT Press.

Hajer, M. (1995) *The Politics of Environmental Discourse: Ecological Modernisation and the Policy Process*. Oxford: Oxford University Press.

Harmes, A. (2011) The limits of carbon disclosure: theorising the business case for investor environmentalism. *Global Environmental Politics* 11(2): 98–119.

Harvey, D. (1981) The spatial fix: Hegel, von Thünen and Marx. *Antipode* 13(3): 1–12.

Harvey, D. (2003) *The New Imperialism*. Oxford: Oxford University Press.

Harvey, D. (2005) *A Brief History of Neoliberalism*. Oxford: Oxford University Press.

Harvey, D. (2010) *Enigma of Capital and the Crises of Capitalism*. London: Profile Books.

Haynes, J. (1999) Power, politics and environmental movements in the third world. In C. Rootes (ed.) *Environmental Movements: Local, National and Global*. London: Frank Cass, 222–242.

Hayter, T. (1989) *Exploited Earth: Britain's Aid and the Environment*. London: Earthscan.

Held, D. and M. Koenig-Archibugi (2005) (eds.) *Global Governance and Public Accountability*. Oxford: Blackwell Publishing.

Held, D., A. McGrew, D. Goldblatt and J. Perraton (1999) *Global Transformations: Politics, Economics and Culture*. Stanford, CA: Stanford University Press.

Helleiner, E. (1996) International political economy and the Greens. *New Political Economy* 1(1): 59–77.

Helleiner, E. (2011) The greening of global financial markets? *Global Environmental Politics* 11(2): 51–53.

Heynen, H., H. Perkins and P. Roy (2006) The political ecology of uneven urban green space. *Urban Affairs Review* 42(1): 3–25.

Hildyard (1993) Foxes in charge of the chickens. In W. Sachs (ed.) *Global Ecology: A New Arena of Political Conflict*. London: Zed Books, 22–35.

Hines, C. (1997) Big stick politics. *The Guardian*, 8 October, 4–5.

Hirst, P., G. Thompson and S. Bromley (2009) *Globalization in Question*, 3rd edn. Cambridge: Polity Press.

Hogenboom, B. (1998) *Mexico and the NAFTA Environment Debate*. Utrecht: International Books.

Holliday, C., S. Schmidheiny and P. Watts (2002) *Walking the Talk: The Business Case for Sustainable Development*. Sheffield: Greenleaf Publishing.

Hoogvelt, A. (1997) *Globalization and the Postcolonial World*. Basingstoke: Macmillan.

Houtart, F. (2009) *Agro-fuels: Big Profits, Ruined Lives and Ecological Destruction*. London: Pluto Press.

Huber, M. (2008) Energizing historical materialism: fossil fuels, space and the capitalist mode of production. *Geoforum* 40: 105–115.

Hurrell, A. and B. Kingsbury (eds.) (1992) *The International Politics of the Environment: Actors and Institutions*. Oxford: Clarendon Press.

Hutter, C., H. Keller, L. Ribbe and R. Wohlers (1995) *The Eco-Twisters: Dossier on the European Environment*. London: Green Print.

Icaza, R., P. Newell and M. Saguier (2010) Citizenship and trade governance in the Americas. In J. Gaventa and R. Tandon (eds.) *Globalizing Citizens: New Dynamics of Inclusion and Exclusion*. London: Zed Books, 163–185.

ICC (1995) Statement by the International Chamber of Commerce at Conference of the Parties 1, 29 March, Berlin.

Icke, D. (1990) *It Doesn't Have to be Like This: Green Politics Explained*. London: Green Print.

ICTSD (International Centre for Trade and Sustainable Development) (2011a) Climate change takes centre stage at WTO environment committee. *Bridges Trade BioRes* 11(13), 11 July.

ICTSD (2011b) China to end challenged subsidies in wind power case. *Bridges Trade BioRes* 11(11), 13 June.

IEA (International Energy Agency) (2010) *World Energy Outlook 2010*. Paris: International Energy Agency.

IEA (2011) Prospect of limiting global increase in temperature is getting bleaker, 30 May 2011. Available at: www.iea.org/index_info.asp?id=1959 (accessed 1 June 2011).

Institutional Share Owner (2005) www.ishareowner.com/news/article. cgi?sfArticleId=1717 (accessed 12 November 2007).

Jackson, J. (1998) *The World Trade Organisation: Constitution and Jurisprudence*. London: Pinter and RIIA.

Jackson, T. (2011) *Prosperity without Growth: Economics for a Finite Planet*. London: Earthscan.

Jacobs, M. (1997) Sustainability and markets: on the neoclassical model of environmental economics. *New Political Economy* 2(3): 365–385.

Jägers, S.V., M. Paterson and J. Stripple (2005) Privatising governance, practicing triage: securitization of insurance risks and the politics of global warming. In D. Levy and P. Newell (eds.) *The Business of Global Environmental Governance*. Cambridge, MA: MIT Press, 249–275.

Jakobeit, C. (1996) Non-state actors leading the way: debt-for-nature swaps. In R. Keohane and M. Levy (eds.) *Institutions for Environmental Aid*. Cambridge, MA: MIT Press, 127–167.

Jenkins, R., Pearson, R. and G. Seyfang (eds.) (2002) *Corporate Responsibility and Labour Rights: Codes of Conduct in the Global Economy*. London: Earthscan.

Jevons, W.S. (1865) The coal question: can Britain survive? In A.W. Flux (ed.) *The Coal Question: An Inquiry Concerning the Progress of the Nation and the Probable Exhaustion of Our Coal Mines* (1905), 3rd edn. New York: Augustus M. Kelley.

Jones, A. (2006) *Dictionary of Globalization*. Cambridge: Polity.

Jornal do Brasil (2002) Dez milhões contra a ALCA, 18 September.

JTA (Just Transition Alliance) (2011) About the Just Transition Alliance. Available at: www.jtalliance.org/docs/aboutjta.html (accessed 2 March 2011).

Kaldor, M., T. Lynn Karl and Y. Said (eds.) (2007) *Oil Wars*. London: Pluto Press.

Kanie, N. and P. Haas (eds.) (2004) *Emerging Forces in Environmental Governance*. Hong Kong: United Nations University Press.

Kaplinsky, R. (2001) Is globalization all it's cracked up to be? *Review of International Political Economy* 8(1): 45–65.

Karliner, J. (1997) *The Corporate Planet: Ecology and Politics in the Age of Globalization*. San Francisco, CA: Sierra Club Books.

Keeley, J. (1990) Toward a Foucauldian analysis of international regimes. *International Organisation* 44(1): 83–105.

Keohane, R. and M. Levy (eds.) (1996) *Institutions for Environmental Aid*. Cambridge, MA: MIT Press.

Keohane, R. and J. Nye (1972) *Transnational Relations and World Politics*. Cambridge, MA: Harvard University Press.

Khor, M. (1995) Address to the International Forum on Globalization. New York City, November.

Kneen, B. (2002) *Invisible Giant: Cargill and its Transnational Strategies*. London: Pluto Press.

Koenig-Archibugi, M. (2005) Transnational corporations and public accountability. In D. Held and M. Koenig-Archibugi (eds.) *Global Governance and Public Accountability*. Oxford: Blackwell Publishing, 110–135.

Koenig-Archibugi, M. (2006) Institutional diversity in global governance. In M. Koenig-Archibugi and M. Zürn (eds.), *New Modes of Governance in the Global System: Exploring Publicness, Delegation and Inclusiveness*. Basingstoke: Palgrave, pp. 1–31.

Korten (1995) *When Corporations Rule the World*. West Hartford, CT: Kumarian Press.

Kovel, J. (2002) *The Enemy of Nature: The End of Capitalism or The End of the World*. London: Zed Books.

Krasner, S. (1983) Structural causes and regime consequences: regimes as intervening variables. In S. Krasner (ed.) *International Regimes*. Ithaca, NY: Cornell University Press, 1–23.

Krueger, J. (1999) *International Trade and the Basel Convention*. London: Earthscan/RIIA.

Krut, R. and H. Gleckman (1998) *ISO 14001: A Missed Opportunity for Sustainable Global Industrial Development*. London: Earthscan.

Kütting, G. (2005) *Globalization and the Environment: Greening Global Political Economy*. Albany, NY: State University of New York Press.

Laferrière, E. and P. Stoett (1999) *International Relations Theory and Ecological Thought: Towards a Synthesis*. London: Routledge.

Lang, T. and C. Hines (1993) *The New Protectionism: Protecting the Future Against Free Trade*. London: Earthscan.

Lee, J. (1994) Process and product: making the link between trade and the environment. *International Environmental Affairs* 6(4): 320–341.

Leftwich, A. (1994) Governance, the state and the politics of development. *Development and Change* 25(2): 363–386.

Leggett, J. (1996) *Climate Change and the Financial Sector*. Munich: Gerling Akademie Verlag.

Leonard, H.J. (1998) *Pollution and the Struggle for the World Product*. Cambridge: Cambridge University Press.

LeQuesne, C. (1996) *Reforming World Trade: The Social and Environmental Priorities*. Oxford: Oxfam Publishing.

Levy, D. (1997) Business and international environmental treaties: ozone depletion and climate change. *California Management Review* 39(3): 54–71.

Levy, D. and P. Newell (2002) Business strategy and international environmental governance: toward a neo-Gramscian synthesis. *Global Environmental Politics* 3(4): 84–101.

Levy, D. and P. Newell (eds.) (2005) *The Business of Global Environmental Governance*. Cambridge, MA: MIT Press.

Lewis, N. (1996) Introduction. In V.I Lenin, *Imperialism: the Highest Stage of Capitalism*. London: Pluto Press.

Lieberman, S. and T. Gray (2008) The WTO's report on the EU's moratorium on biotech products: the wisdom of the US challenge to the EU in the WTO. *Global Environmental Politics* 8(1): 33–52.

Lighting Africa (2011) Lighting Africa: catalysing markets for modern lighting. Available at: www.lightingafrica.org (accessed 7 July 2011).

Lipschultz, R. with J. Rowe (2005) *Globalization, Governmentality and Global Politics: Regulation for the Rest of Us?* New York: Routledge.

Litfin, K. (1995) *Ozone Discourses: Science and Politics in Global Environmental Cooperation*. New York: Columbia University Press.

Loeppky, R. (2005) History, technology and the capitalist state: the comparative political economy of biotechnology and genomics. *Review of International Political Economy* 12(2): 264–286.

Lohmann, L. (2006) *Carbon Trading: a Critical Conversation on Climate Change, Privatisation and Power*. Dorset: The Corner House.

Lovins, L.H. and B. Cohen (2011) *Climate Capitalism: Capitalism in the Age of Climate Change*. New York: Hill & Wang.

Lukes, S. (1974) *Power: A Radical View*. London: Macmillan.

McCarthy, J. (2002) First World political ecology: lessons from the Wise Use Movement. *Environmental and Planning A* 34(7): 1281–1302.

MacLaren (2000) *The OECD's revised Guidelines for Multinational Enterprises: A step towards corporate accountability?* London: Friends of the Earth.

Madeley, J. (2000) *Hungry for Trade: How the Poor Pay for Free Trade*. London: Zed Books.

Magdoff, F. and J. Bellamy Foster (2010) What every environmentalist needs to know about capitalism. *Monthly Review* 61(10): 37–60.

Mann, G. (2009) Should political ecology be Marxist? A case for Gramsci's Historical Materialism. *Geoforum* 40: 335–344.

Mansfield, B. (2004) Neoliberalism in the oceans: 'rationalization', property rights, and the commons question. *Geoforum* 35(3): 313–326.

Mansfield, B. (2007) Articulation between neoliberal and state-oriented environmental regulation: fisheries privatization and endangered species protection. *Environment and Planning A* 39(8): 1926–1942.

Martínez-Alier, J. (2002) *The Environmentalism of the Poor: a Study of Ecological Conflicts and Valuation*. Cheltenham: Edward Elgar.

Martínez-Alier, J. (2007) Marxism, social metabolism and international trade. In A. Hornburg, J.R. McNeill and J. Martínez-Alier (eds.) *Rethinking Environmental History: World Systems History and Global Environmental Change*. Lanham, MD: Altamira, 221–239.

Marx, K. (1969 [1845]) *Theses On Feuerbach. Marx/Engels Selected Works, Volume One*. Moscow: Progress Publishers.

Marx, K. (1974) *Capital*. London: Lawrence and Wishart.

174   *References*

-page

Marx, K. (1975) *The German Ideology*. London: Lawrence and Wishart.

Marx, K. (1981) *Capital*, Volume 3. Harmondsworth: Penguin.

Marx, K. and F. Engels (1998) [1848]. *The Communist Manifesto*. London: Verso.

Mason, M. (2005) *The New Accountability: Environmental Responsibility Across Borders*. London: Earthscan.

Maxwell, J. and S. Weiner (1993) Green consciousness or dollar diplomacy: the British response to ozone depletion. *International Environmental Affairs* 5: 19–41.

Meadows, D., D. Meadows, J. Randers and W. Behrens (1972) *The Limits to Growth*. London: Pan Books.

Mehta, L. (2006) *The Politics and Poetics of Water*. Delhi: Orient Longman.

MIGA (Multilateral Investment Guarantee Agency) (2011) About MIGA: Overview. Available at: www.miga.org/about/index_sv.cfm?stid=1736 (accessed 8 July 2011).

Mittelmann, J.H. (2000) *The Globalization Syndrome: Transformation and Resistance*. Princeton, NJ: Princeton University Press.

Mol, A. (2003) *Globalization and Environmental Reform: The Ecological Modernization of the Global Economy*. Cambridge, MA: MIT Press.

Moore, J.W. (2011a) Transcending the metabolic rift: a theory of crises in the capitalist world ecology. *The Journal of Peasant Studies* 38(1): 1–46.

Moore, J.W. (2011b) Ecology, capital, and the nature of our times: accumulation and crisis in the capitalist world ecology. *Journal of World-Systems Research* 17(1): 108–147.

Morici, P. (2002) *Reconciling Trade and the Environment in the WTO*. Washington, DC: Economic Strategy Institute.

Morton, A. (2007) *Unravelling Gramsci: Hegemony and the Passive Revolution in the Global Political Economy*. London: Pluto Press.

Muchlinski, P. (1999) A brief history of business regulation. In S. Picciotto and R. Mayne (eds.) *Regulating International Business: Beyond Liberalization*. Basingstoke: Macmillan, 47–60.

Muchlinski, P. (2001) Corporations in international litigation: problems of jurisdiction and the UK asbestos case. *International and Comparative Law Quarterly* 50(1): 1–25.

Murphy, D. and J. Bendell (1997) *In the Company of Partners*. Bristol: Policy Press.

Murphy, J. and L. Levidow (2006) *Governing the Transatlantic Conflict over Agricultural Biotechnology: Contending Coalitions, Trade Liberalization and Standard Setting*. London: Routledge.

NEF (New Economics Foundation) (2003) *Collision Course: Free Trade's Free Ride on the Global Climate*. London: New Economics Foundation.

Neumayer, E. (2001a) Do countries fail to raise environmental standards? An evaluation of policy options addressing 'regulatory chill'. *International Journal of Sustainable Development* 4(3): 231–244.

Neumayer, E. (2001b) Pollution havens: an analysis of policy options for dealing with an elusive phenomenon. *Journal of Environment Development* 10(2): 147–177.

Newell, P. (1999) Globalization and the environment: exploring the connections. *IDS Bulletin* 30(3): 1–7.

Newell, P. (2000a) *Climate for Change: Non-State Actors and the Global Politics of the Greenhouse*. Cambridge: Cambridge University Press.

Newell, P. (2000b) Environmental NGOs and globalization: the governance of TNCs. In R. Cohen and S. Rai (eds.) *Global Social Movements*. London: Athlone Press, 117–134.

Newell, P. (2001a) Access to environmental justice? Litigation against TNCs in the South. *IDS Bulletin* 32(1): 83–93.

Newell, P. (2001b) Managing multinationals: the governance of investment for the environment. *Journal of International Development* 13(7): 907–919.

Newell, P. (2001c) New environmental architectures and the search for effectiveness. *Global Environmental Politics* 1(1): 35–45.

Newell, P. (2003) Globalization and the governance of biotechnology. *Global Environmental Politics* 3(2): 56–72.

Newell, P. (2004) Globalization and the environmental movement: Cooperation, confrontation and resistance. *Noveaux Mondes*, July, Geneva.

Newell, P. (2005a) Citizenship, accountability and community: the limits of the CSR agenda. *International Affairs* 81(3): 541–557.

Newell, P. (2005b) Race, class and the global politics of environmental inequality. *Global Environmental Politics* 5(3): 70–94.

Newell, P. (2005c) Towards a political economy of global environmental governance. In P. Dauvergne (ed.) *Handbook of International Environmental Politics*. Cheltenham: Edward Elgar, 187–202.

Newell, P. (2006) Environmental justice movements: taking stock, moving forward. *Environmental Politics* 15(4): 656–660.

Newell, P. (2007a) Trade and environmental justice in Latin America. *New Political Economy* 12(2): 237–259.

Newell, P. (2007b) Corporate power and bounded autonomy in the global politics of biotechnology. In R. Falkner (ed.) *The International Politics of Genetically Modified Food*. Basingstoke: Palgrave, 67–85.

Newell, P. (2008a) The marketisation of global environmental governance: manifestations and implications. In J. Parks, K. Conca and M. Finger (eds.) *The Crisis of Global Environmental Governance: Towards a New Political Economy of Sustainability*. London: Routledge, 77–96.

Newell, P. (2008b) Lost in translation? Domesticating global policy on GMOs: comparing India and China. *Global Society* 22(1): 117–138.

Newell, P. (2008c) The political economy of global environmental governance. *Review of International Studies* 34(3): 507–529.

Newell, P. (2008d) Civil society participation in trade policy-making in Latin

America: the case of the environmental movement. In K. Gallagher (ed.) *Handbook on Trade and the Environment*. Cheltenham: Edward Elgar, 171–183.

Newell, P. (2008e) Civil society, corporate accountability and the politics of climate change. *Global Environmental Politics* 8(3): 124–155.

Newell, P. (2008f) CSR and the limits of capital. *Development and Change* 39(6): 1063–1078.

Newell, P. (2008g) Trade and biotechnology in Latin America: Democratization, contestation and the politics of mobilization. *Journal of Agrarian Change* 8(2–3), 345–376.

Newell, P. (2011a) The elephant in the room: capitalism and global environmental change. *Global Environmental Change* 21(1): 4–6.

Newell, P. (2011b) The governance of energy finance: the public, the private and the hybrid. *Global Policy* 2(3): 1–12.

Newell, P. (2012) The political ecology of globalization. In P. Dauvergne (ed.) *Handbook of Global Environmental Politics*. Cheltenham: Edward Elgar.

Newell, P. and A. Bumpus (2012) The global political ecology of the CDM. *Global Environmental Politics* 12(4).

Newell, P. and G. Frynas (2007) Beyond CSR? Business, poverty and social justice. *Third World Quarterly* 28(4): 669–681.

Newell, P. and R. Lekhi (2006) Environmental injustice, law and accountability. In P. Newell and J. Wheeler (eds.) *Rights, Resources and the Politics of Accountability*. London: Zed Books, 186–204.

Newell, P. and R. MacKenzie (2000) The 2000 Cartagena Protocol on Biosafety: Legal and political dimensions. *Global Environmental Change* 10(3): 313–317.

Newell, P. and M. Paterson (1998) Climate for business: global warming, the State and capital. *Review of International Political Economy* 5(4): 679–704.

Newell, P. and M. Paterson (2010) *Climate Capitalism: Global Warming and the Transformation of the Global Economy*. Cambridge: Cambridge University Press.

Newell, P. and J. Wheeler (eds.) (2006) *Rights, Resources and the Politics of Accountability*. London: Zed Books.

Newell, P., J. Phillips and D. Mulvaney (2011) *Pursuing Clean Energy Equitably*. Human Development Research Paper 2011/03. New York: UNDP.

North, P. (2007) *Money and Liberation: The Micro-Politics of Alternative Currency Movements*. Minneapolis, MN: University of Minnesota Press.

O'Brien, R., A.M. Goetz, J.A. Scholte and M. Williams (2000) *Contesting Global Governance*. Cambridge: Cambridge University Press.

O'Connor, M. (ed.) (1994) *Is Capitalism Sustainable? Political Economy and the Politics of Ecology*. New York: Guilford Press.

O'Connor, M. (1998) *Natural Causes: Essays in Ecological Marxism*. London: Guildford Press.

O'Rourke, D. (2004) *Community-Driven Regulation: Balancing Environment and Development in Vietnam*. Cambridge, MA: MIT Press.

Obach, B. (2004) *Labor and the Environmental Movement: The Quest for Common Ground*. Cambridge, MA: MIT Press.

Ohmae, K. (2004) The end of the nation state. In F. Lechner and J. Boli (eds.) *The Globalization Reader*. Malden, MA: Blackwell Publishers, 214–218.

Okanta, I. and O. Douglas (2001) *Where Vultures Feast: Shell, Human Rights and Oil in the Niger Delta*. New York: Sierra Club.

Okereke, C. (2010) *Global Justice and Neoliberal Environmental Governance: Sustainable Development, Ethics and International Co-operation*. London: Routledge.

Oosthoek, J. and B. Gills (eds.) (2008) *The Globalization of Environmental Crisis*. London: Routledge.

Palan, R. (2003) *The Offshore World: Sovereign Markets, Virtual Places, and Nomad Millionaires*. Ithaca, NY: Cornell University Press.

Palan, R., R. Murphy and C. Chavagneux (2010) *Tax Havens: How Globalization Really Works*. Ithaca, NY: Cornell University Press.

Palermo, V. and C. Reboratti (eds.) (2007) *Del Otro Lado del Río: Ambientalismo y política entre Uruguayos y Argentinos*. Buenos Aires: Edhasa.

Park, S. (2011) *The World Bank Group and Environmentalists: Changing International Organisation Identities*. Manchester: Manchester University Press.

Paterson, M. (1999) Global finance and environmental politics: the insurance industry and climate change. *IDS Bulletin* 30(3): 25–30.

Paterson, M. (2000) Car culture and global environmental politics. *Review of International Studies* 26(2): 253–271.

Paterson, M. (2001a) Risky business: insurance companies in global warming politics. *Global Environmental Politics* 1(3): 18–42.

Paterson, M. (2001b) *Understanding Global Environmental Politics: Domination, Accumulation, Resistance*. Basingstoke: Palgrave.

Paterson, M., D. Humphreys and L. Pettiford (2003) Conceptualizing global environmental governance: from interstate regimes to counter-hegemonic struggles. *Global Environmental Politics* 3(2): 1–10.

Pattberg, P. (2007) *Private Institutions and Global Governance: The New Politics of Environmental Sustainability*. Cheltenham: Edward Elgar.

Paulson, S., L. Gezon and M. Watts (2003) Locating the political in political ecology: an introduction. *Human Organisation* 62(3): 205–217.

Payne, A. (2005) *The Global Politics of Unequal Development*. Basingstoke: Palgrave.

Peet, R. and M. Watts (eds.) (2004) *Liberation Ecologies: Environment, Development, Social Movements*, 2nd edn. London: Routledge.

Peet, R., P. Robbins and M. Watts (eds.) (2011) *Global Political Ecology*. London: Routledge.

Pellow, D. and L.S-H. Park (2002) *The Silicon Valley of Dreams: Environmental Injustice, Immigrant Workers, and the High-Tech Global Economy*. New York: New York University Press.

Peluso, N. (1992) The political ecology of extraction and extractive reserves in East Kalimantan, Indonesia. *Development and Change* 23(4): 49–74.

Petras, J. and H. Veltmeyer (2001) *Globalization Unmasked: Imperialism in the 21st Century*. Delhi: Madhyam Books.

Piddington, K. (1992) The role of the World Bank. In A. Hurrell and B. Kingsbury (eds.) *The International Politics of the Environment*. Oxford: Clarendon Press, 212–228.

PLATFORM (2008) Oil giants 'underestimating investor risk' on tar sands. Available at: www.carbonweb.org/showitem.asp?article=352&parent=39 (accessed 1 September 2011).

PLATFORM and Greenpeace (2008) *BP and Shell: Rising Risks in Tar Sands Investments*. Available at: www.greenpeace.org.uk/files/pdfs/climate/RisingRisks.pdf (accessed 7 July 2011).

Polanyi, K. (1980) [1944] *The Great Transformation*. Boston, MA: Beacon Press.

Ponting, C. (2007) *A New History of the World: The Environment and the Collapse of Great Civilisations*. London: Vintage.

Porritt, J. (1989) *Seeing Green: The Politics of Ecology Explained*. Oxford: Basil Blackwell.

Porritt, J. (2007) *Capitalism as if the World Matters*, 2nd edn. London: Earthscan.

Porter, G., R. Clémençon, W. Ofosu-Amaah and M. Phillips (1998) *Study of GEF's Overall Performance*. Washington, DC: Global Environment Facility.

Prahalad, C. (2005) *The Fortune at the Bottom of the Pyramid*. Upper Saddle River, NJ: Wharton School Publishing.

Prakash, A. (2000) *Greening the Firm: The Politics of Corporate Environmentalism*. Cambridge: Cambridge University Press.

Prakash, A. and M. Potoski (2006) Racing to the bottom? Trade, environmental governance and ISO 14001. *American Journal of Political Science* 50(2): 350–364.

Pritchard, B. (2005) How the rule of the market rules the law: the political economy of WTO dispute settlement as evidenced in the US-Lamb-meat decision. *Review of International Political Economy* 12(5): 776–803.

Public Statement on the International Investment Regime (2010) 9 August. Available at: www.tppdigest.org/images/stories/publicstatement.pdf (accessed 12 September 2010).

Raustiala, K. (1997) The domestic politics of global biodiversity protection in the United Kingdom and United States. In M. Schreurs and E. Economy (eds.) *The Internationalisation of Environmental Protection*. Cambridge: Cambridge University Press, 42–74.

Raustiala, K. and D.G. Victor (2004) The regime complex for plant genetic resources. *International Organisation* (58): 277–309.

Rees, J. (2001) Imperialism: globalization, the State and war. *International Socialism* 93.

Rich, B. (1994) *Mortgaging the Earth: The World Bank, Environmental Imperialism and the Crisis of Development*. London: Earthscan.

Rio Tinto (2011) Communities. Available at: www.riotinto.com/our approach/17215_communities.asp (accessed 8 September 2011).

Risse-Kappen, T. (1995) *Bringing Transnational Relations Back In*. Cambridge: Cambridge University Press.

Ritzer, G. (1993) *The McDonaldization of Society*. Thousand Oaks, CA: Pine Forge Press.

Robbins, P. (2000) The practical politics of knowing: state environmental knowledge and local political economy. *Economic Geography* 76(2): 126–144.

Robbins, P. (2004) *Political Ecology: A Critical Introduction*. Oxford: Blackwell.

Roberts, J.T. and B.C. Parks (2008) Fuelling injustice: globalization, ecologically unequal exchange and climate change. In J. Ooshthoek and B. Gills (eds.) *The Globalization of Environmental Crises*. London: Routledge, 169–187.

Roberts, J.T. and N.D. Thannos (2003) *Trouble in Paradise: Globalization and Environmental Crisis in Latin America*. London: Routledge.

Roberts, J.T., P. Grimes and J. Manale (2003) Social roots of global environmental change: a world-systems analysis of carbon dioxide emissions. *Journal of World-Systems Research* 9(2): 277–315.

Robin Hood Tax (2011) About the Robin Hood Tax. Available at: http://robin hoodtax.org/ (accessed 26 January 2011).

Robinson, W. (2004) *A Theory of Global Capitalism: Production, Class and State in a Transnational World*. Baltimore, MD: Johns Hopkins University Press.

Rocheleau, D. and D. Edmunds (1997) Women, men and trees: gender, power and property in forest and agrarian landscapes. *World Development* 25(8): 1351–1371.

Rocheleau, D., B. Thomas-Slayter and E. Wangari (1996) *Feminist Political Ecology: Global Issues and Local Experiences*. London: Routledge.

Rosenburg, J. (2000) *The Follies of Globalization Theory*. London: Verso.

Rowell, A. (1996) *Green Backlash: Global Subversion of the Environmental Movement*. London: Routledge.

Rupert, M. (1995) *Producing Hegemony: The Politics of Mass Production and American Global Power*. Cambridge: Cambridge University Press.

Rupert, M. and H. Smith (eds.) (2002) *Historical Materialism and Globalization*. London: Routledge.

Sachs, W. (ed.) (1993) *Global Ecology: A New Arena of Political Conflict*. London: Zed Books.

Sáez, R. (2000) The case of a renewable natural resource: timber extraction and trade. In D. Tussie (ed.) *The Environment and International Trade Negotiations: Developing Country Stakes*. Basingstoke: Macmillan, 13–33.

Sandler, B. (1994) Grow or die: Marxist theories of capitalism and the environment. *Rethinking Marxism* 7(2): 38–57.

Saurin, J. (1996) International relations, social ecology and the globalization of environmental change. In J. Vogler and M. Imber (eds.) *The Environment in International Relations.* London: Routledge, 77–99.

Saurin, J. (2001) Global environmental crisis as 'disaster triumphant': the private capture of public goods. *Environmental Politics* 10(4): 63–84.

Schatan, C. (2000) Lessons from the Mexican environmental experience: first results from NAFTA. In D. Tussie (ed.) *The Environment and International Trade Negotiations: Developing Country Stakes.* Basingstoke: Macmillan, 167–187.

Schattschneider, E. (1960) *The Semi-Sovereign People: A Realist's View of Democracy in America.* New York: Holt, Rinehart and Winston.

Schmidheiny, S. (1992) *Changing Course.* Cambridge, MA: MIT Press.

Scholte, J.A. (2000) *Globalization: A Critical Introduction.* Basingstoke: Palgrave.

Scholte, J.A. (ed.) (2011) *Building Global Democracy? Civil Society and Accountable Global Governance.* Cambridge: Cambridge University Press.

Scholte, J.A. and A. Schnabel (eds.) (2002) *Civil Society and Global Finance.* London: Routledge.

Schroeder, R.A. (1999) *Shady Practices: Agro-forestry and Gender Politics in the Gambia.* Berkeley, CA: University of California Press.

Scott, J. (1985) *Weapons of the Weak: Everyday Forms of Peasant Resistance.* New Haven, CT: Yale University Press.

Sell, S.K. (1999) Multinational corporations as agents of change: the globalization of intellectual property rights. In C. Cutler, V. Haufler and T. Porter (eds.) *Private Authority and International Affairs.* Albany, NY: State University of New York Press, 169–198.

Sell, S.K. (2003) *Private Power, Public Law: the Globalization of Intellectual Property Rights.* Cambridge: Cambridge University Press.

Selwyn, B. (2012) Beyond firm-centrism: re-integrating labour and capitalism into global commodity chain analysis. *Journal of Economic Geography* 12(1): 205–226.

Shamir, R. (2004) Between self-regulation and the Alien Tort Claims Act: on the contested concept of corporate social responsibility. *Law & Society Review* 38(4): 635–664.

Shiva, V. (1998) *Staying Alive: Women, Ecology and Development.* London: Zed Books.

Sinclair, T. (2005) *The New Masters of Capital.* Ithaca, NY: Cornell University Press.

Sklair, L. (2002a) The transnational capitalist class and global politics: deconstructing the corporate-state connection. *International Political Science Review* 23(2): 159–174.

Sklair, L. (2002b) *Globalization: Capitalism and its Alternatives*. Oxford: Oxford University Press.

Smith, N. (2006) Nature as accumulation strategy. In L. Panitch and C. Leys (eds.) *Coming to Terms with Nature*. Socialist Register 2007. Monmouth: The Merlin Press, pp. 16–37.

Smith, J. (2010) *Biofuels and the Globalization of Risk: The Biggest Change in North-South Relationships Since Colonialism?* London: Zed Books.

Sornarajah, M. (2006) A law for need or a law for greed? Restoring the Lost Law in the international law of foreign investment. *International Environmental Agreements: Politics Law and Economics* 6(4): 329–357.

Sorrell, S. (2010) Energy, Growth and Sustainability: Five Propositions. SPRU Working Paper 185. Brighton: University of Sussex Science and Technology Policy Research Unit.

Speth, G.J. (ed.) (2003) *Worlds Apart: Globalization and Environment*. Washington, DC: Island Press.

Speth, G.J. (2008) *The Bridge at the Edge of the World: Capitalism, the Environment and Crossing from Crisis to Sustainability*. New Haven, CT: Yale University Press.

Sripada, S. (1989) The multinational corporation and environmental issues. *Journal of the Indian Law Institute* 31(4): 534–552.

Srivastava, L. and P. Soni (1998) Financing options for protecting the climate. In W. Gupta and S.K. Kumar (eds.) *Climate Change: Post-Kyoto Perspectives from the South*. Delhi: Tata Energy and Resources Institute, 95–126.

Stern, N. (2006) *The Stern Review on the Economics of Climate Change*. London: HM Treasury.

Stevis, D. and V. Assetto (eds.) (2001) *The International Political Economy of the Environment: Critical Perspectives*. Boulder, CO: Lynne Rienner.

Storper, M. and R. Walker (1989) *The Capitalist Imperative: Territory, Technology and Industrial Growth*. Cambridge, MA: Blackwell.

Stott, P. and S. Sullivan (2000) *Political Ecology: Science, Myth and Power*. Oxford: Oxford University Press.

Strange, S. (1983) Cave! Hic dragones: A critique of regime analysis. *International Organization* 36(2): 488–90.

Strange, S. (1986) *Casino Capitalism*. Oxford: Basil Blackwell.

Strange, S. (1994) Rethinking structural change in the international political economy: states, firms and diplomacy. In R. Stubbs and G. Underhill (eds.) *Political Economy and the Changing Global Order*. Basingstoke: Macmillan, 103–116.

Strange, S. (1996) *The Retreat of the State*. Cambridge: Cambridge University Press.

Strange, S. (1998) *Mad Money: When Markets Outgrow Governments*. Ann Arbor, MI: University of Michigan Press.

Strickland, C. and R. Sturm (1998) Energy efficiency in World Bank power sector policy and lending. *Energy Policy* 26(11): 873–883.

Swan, C. (2008) Zoellick fossil fuel campaign belied by World Bank's Tata loan. Bloomberg.com, 13 August.

Swyngedouw, E. (2004) *Social Power and the Urbanisation of Water: Flows of Power*. Oxford: Oxford University Press.

Swyngedouw, E. and A. Merrifield (1996) *The Urbanization of Injustice*. London: Lawrence and Wishart.

Swyngedouw, E., N. Heynen and M. Kaika (eds.) (2006) *In the Nature of Cities*. London: Routledge.

Tellam, I. (ed.) (2000) *Fuel for Change: World Bank Energy Policy – Rhetoric and Reality*. London: Zed Books.

Third World Network (2006) WTO dispute panel on GMOs issues final report. TWN Biosafety Email Information Service, 17 May.

Thomas, C. (1996) Unsustainable development? *New Political Economy* 1(3): 404–407.

Trainer, T. (1996) *Towards a Sustainable Economy: the Need for Fundamental Change*. Oxford: Jon Carpenter.

UNCTAD (United Nations Conference on Trade and Development) (2010) *World Investment Report: Investing in a Low Carbon Economy*. Geneva: UNCTAD.

Underhill, G. and X. Zhang (eds.) (2003) *International Financial Governance Under Stress: Global Structures Versus National Imperatives*. Cambridge: Cambridge University Press.

UNEP (1999) *Global Environment Outlook 2000*. London: Earthscan.

UNEP (2011a) UNEP Statement by Financial Institutions on the Environment and Sustainable Development. Available at: www.unepfi.org/statements/fi/index.html (accessed 27 January 2011).

UNEP (2011b) *Decoupling Natural Resource Use and Environmental Impacts from Economic Growth*. Nairobi: United Nations Environment Programme.

UNFCCC Secretariat (United Nations Framework Convention on Climate Change) (1997) *Trends of financial flows and terms and conditions employed by multilateral lending institutions*. First Technical Paper on Terms of Transfer of Technology and Know-how 25/7/97. FCCC/TP/1997/1. Geneva: UNFCCC Secretariat.

Utting, P. (2002) *The Greening of Business in Developing Countries*. London: Zed Books.

van Bergeijk, P. (1991) International trade and the environmental challenge. *Journal of World Trade* 25(5): 105–115.

van der Pijl, K. (1998) *Transnational Classes and International Relations*. London: Routledge.

Victor, D., M. Granger Morgan, J. Apt, J. Steinbruner and K. Ricke (2009) The geo-engineering option: a last resort against global warming? *Foreign Affairs* 88(2): 64–76.

Vidal, J. (1994) The bank that likes to say sorry. *The Guardian*, 22 July.

Vlachou, A. (1993) The contradictory interaction of capitalism and nature. *Capitalism, Nature, Socialism* 4(1): 102–108.

Vlachou, A. (2004) Capitalism and ecological sustainability: the shaping of environmental policies. *Review of International Political Economy* 11(5): 926–952.

Vogel, D. (1997) *Trading Up: Consumer and Environmental Regulation in the Global Economy*, 2nd edn. Cambridge, MA: Harvard University Press.

Vogler, J. (1995) *The Global Commons: A Regime Analysis*. Chichester: John Wiley & Sons.

Vogler, J. (2005) In defense of international environmental cooperation. In J. Barry and R. Eckersley (eds.) *The State and the Global Ecological Crisis*. Cambridge, MA: MIT Press, 229–255.

von Moltke, K. (2001) The organisation of the impossible. *Global Environmental Politics* 1(1): 23–29.

Wade, R. (2003) What strategies are viable for developing countries today? The WTO and the shrinking of development space. In J. Timmons Roberts and A. Bellone Hite (eds.) (2007) *The Globalization and Development Reader*. Oxford: Wiley-Blackwell.

Waldman, L. (2011) *The Politics of Asbestos: Understandings of Risk, Disease and Protest*. London: Earthscan.

Wallerstein, I. (1979) *The Capitalist World Economy: Essays by Immanuel Wallerstein*. Cambridge: Cambridge University Press.

Walmart (2011) Climate and Energy. Available at: http://walmartstores.com/Sustainability/7673.aspx (accessed 26 January 2011).

War on Want (2005) G8: Massive shortfall exposed in Gleneagles deal. Available at: www.waronwant.org/news/press-releases/10287-g8-massive-shortfall-exposed-in-gleneagles-deal (accessed 2 July 2011).

Ward, H. (1996) Game theory and the politics of global warming: the state of play and beyond. *Political Studies* 44(5): 850–871.

Ward, H. (2000) Foreign direct liability: exploring the issues. Workshop background paper. London: Chatham House.

WCED (World Commission on Environment and Development) (1987) *Our Common Future: Report of the Brundtland Commission on Environment and Development*. Oxford: Oxford University Press.

Weiss, L. (1998) *The Myth of the Powerless State*. Cambridge: Polity Press.

Whalley, J. (1996) Trade and environment beyond Singapore. NBER Working Paper 5768. Cambridge, MA: National Bureau of Economic Research.

Whalley, J. and B. Zissimos (2001) What could a World Environment Organisation do? *Global Environmental Politics*. 1(1): 29–35.

Wilkinson, R. (2002) The contours of courtship: the WTO and civil society. In

R. Wilkinson (ed.) *Global Governance: Critical Perspectives*. London: Routledge, 193–212.

Williams, M. (1994) International trade and the environment: issues, perspectives and challenges. *Environmental Politics* 2(4): 80–97.

Williams, M. (1996) International political economy and global environmental change. In J. Vogler and M.F. Imber (eds.) *The Environment and International Relations*. London: Routledge, 41–58.

Williams, M. (2001a) In search of global standards: the political economy of trade and the environment. In D. Stevis and V. Assetto (eds.) *The International Political Economy of the Environment: Critical Perspectives*. Boulder, CO: Lynne Rienner, 39–63.

Williams, M. (2001b) Trade and the environment in the world trading system: a decade of stalemate? *Global Environmental Politics* 1(4): 1–10.

Wilson, C. and P. Wilson (2006) *Make Poverty Business: Increase Profits and Reduce Risks by Engaging with the Poor*. Sheffield: Greenleaf Publishing.

Wise, T., H. Salazar and L. Carlsen (2003) *Confronting Globalization: Economic Integration and Popular Resistance in Mexico*. Bloomfield, CT: Kumarian Press.

Wolf, M. (2004) *Why Globalization Works: The Case for the Global Market Economy*. New Haven, CT: Yale University Press.

World Bank (1992) *World Development Report 1992: Development and the Environment*. New York: Oxford University Press.

World Bank (1997a) *World Development Report 1997: the State in a Changing World*. New York: Oxford University Press.

World Bank (1997b) *Private Capital Flows to Developing Countries: The Road to Financial Integration*. Washington, DC: World Bank.

World Bank (2000) *Greening Industry: New Roles for Communities, Markets and Governments*. New York: Oxford University Press.

World Bank (2003) *Dynamic Development in a Sustainable World: Transformation in the Quality of Life, Growth, and Institutions*. World Development Report. New York: Oxford University Press.

World Bank (2007) *World Bank Environmental Guidelines on Project Finance*. Available at: www-esd.worldbank.org/pph/ (accessed 6 June 2008).

World Bank (2008a) *Climate Investment Funds*. Washington, DC: World Bank (www.worldbank.org/cifs).

World Bank (2008b) *Development and Climate Change: A Strategic Framework for the World Bank Group*. Report to the Development Committee. Washington, DC: World Bank.

World Bank (2010) *Development and Climate Change*. World Development Report. Washington, DC: World Bank.

World Bank (2011) *The Changing Wealth of Nations: Measuring Sustainable Development in the New Millennium*. Washington, DC: World Bank

World Development Movement (1998) Law unto themselves: Holding

Multinationals to Account. Discussion Paper, September. London: WDM.

World Development Movement (2002) *Out of Service: The Development Dangers of the General Agreement on Trade in Services*. London: World Development Movement.

Wray, N. (2000) Texaco document. Centre for Social and Economic Rights. Quito: Ecuador.

Wright, C. (2010) International project finance and risk insurance in Asian energy markets. Draft paper prepared for the Global Energy Governance Workshop, National University of Singapore, May.

WRI (World Resources Institute) (2008) *Correcting the World's Greatest Market Failure: Climate Change and Multilateral Development Banks*. Washington, DC: WRI (www.wri.org/publication/correcting-the-worlds-greatest-market-failure).

WTO (World Trade Organisation) (1996) *Guidelines for Arrangements on Relations with NGOs*. Document WT/L/162, 18 July.

WWF (1991) *The General Agreement on Tariffs and Trade, Environmental Protection and Sustainable Development*, WWF Discussion Paper, November.

WWF (1999) *Foreign Direct Investment and Environment: From Pollution Havens to Sustainable Development*. WWF-UK report for OECD conference, Paris, 20–21 September.

WWF (2007) WWF files court proceedings against government department over Sakhalin II oil-and-gas project, 15 August. Available at: www.thecornerhouse.org.uk/resource/wwf-files-court-proceedings-against-government-department (accessed 7 September 2011).

Young, A. (2005) Picking the wrong fight: why attacks on the WTO pose the real threat to national environmental and public health protection. *Global Environmental Politics* 5(4): 48–72.

Young, O. (1998) *Global Governance: Learning Lessons from the Environmental Experience*. Cambridge, MA: MIT Press.

Young, O. (2010) *Institutional Dynamics: Emergent Patterns in International Environmental Governance*. Cambridge, MA: MIT Press.

Young, Z. (2002) *A New Green Order? The World Bank and the Politics of the Global Environment Facility*. London: Pluto Press.

Zadek, S. (2001) *The Civil Corporation: The New Economy of Corporate Citizenship*. London: Earthscan.

Zarsky, L. (2006) From regulatory chill to deepfreeze? *International Environmental Agreements: Politics Law and Economics* 6(4): 395–399.

Zimmerer, K. and T. Bassett (2003) *Political Ecology: An Integrative Approach to Geography and Environment-Development Studies*. London: Guilford Press.

Index